THE SOLDIER'S TWO BODIES

THE SOLDIER'S TWO BODIES

Military Sacrifice and Popular Sovereignty in Revolutionary War Veteran Narratives

JAMES M. GREENE

Louisiana State University Press
Baton Rouge

Published with the assistance of a subsidy from Indiana State University.

Published by Louisiana State University Press

Manufactured in the United States of America
First printing

DESIGNER: Michelle A. Neustrom
TYPEFACE: Adobe Caslon Pro
PRINTER AND BINDER: Sheridan Books, Inc.

LIBRARY OF CONGRESS CATALOGING-IN-PUBLICATION DATA

Names: Greene, James M., 1980– author.
Title: The soldier's two bodies : military sacrifice and popular sovereignty in Revolutionary War veteran narratives / James Greene.
Other titles: Military sacrifice and popular sovereignty in Revolutionary War veteran narratives
Description: Baton Rouge : Louisiana State University Press, [2019] | Includes index.
Identifiers: LCCN 2019018886 | ISBN 978-0-8071-7164-6 (cloth) | ISBN 978-0-8071-7271-1 (epub) | ISBN 978-0-8071-7270-4 (pdf)
Subjects: LCSH: Veterans' writings, American—History and criticism. | United States—History—Revolution, 1775–1783—Veterans. | United States—History—Revolution, 1775–1783—Personal narratives. | Soldiers in literature. | Sovereignty in literature. | American literature—18th century—History and criticism. | American literature—19th century—History and criticism. | 2019018886
Classification: LCC PS153.V48 G74 2019 | DDC 810.9/358733—dc23
LC record available at https://lccn.loc.gov/2019018886

The paper in this book meets the guidelines for permanence and durability of the Committee on Production Guidelines for Book Longevity of the Council on Library Resources. ♾

CONTENTS

ACKNOWLEDGMENTS

WRITING THIS BOOK has involved countless hours of isolation, but completing it has only been possible thanks to the support of countless friends and colleagues.

I would like to thank my editor, James Long, and the rest of the staff at Louisiana State University Press for their interest in this project and support throughout the publication process.

I have been fortunate to present aspects of this research at numerous conferences over the years, and I appreciate all those who offered suggestions or comments at these events. In particular, I would like to thank Robert Levine and the seminar group he organized on *Israel Potter* at the 2017 meeting of the International Melville Society for their responses to parts of the fifth chapter. I would also like to thank Dennis Moore for inviting me to participate in one of his famous colloquies at the American Society for Eighteenth Century Studies, in 2016, where I was able to share ideas from the second chapter.

Over the course of writing this book, I have been fortunate to be a part of two supportive and collegial English departments. I am grateful to Robert Perrin and my colleagues at Indiana State University for helping me transition smoothly to a new job while I completed this book's final revisions.

I owe an extensive debt to Celia Patterson and my former colleagues at Pittsburg State University for their unwavering support of me as a junior scholar. Conversations with Jamie McDaniel, Sandra Cox, and Casie Hermansson helped me navigate the path from book proposal to book contract. These three friends are also indefatigable researchers, and their examples remain good motivation for me.

For fear of leaving someone out, I will offer a general thanks to all the friends who encouraged me while writing this book. That said, I need to acknowledge Laura Covert-Miller for hours spent writing together, Miles Grier for reading an early version of the third chapter, and Jessica Queener for listening to me complain throughout the whole process.

Much of what I know about being a writer can be traced to two people: John Ernest and Dana Nelson. They have been exceptional role models as scholars with a deep belief in literature's power to change society.

Much of what I know about being a professional academic can be traced to two people: Laura Brady and Tim Sweet. They remain the best mentors I could imagine.

Much of what I know about being a human can be traced to two people: James and Glenda Greene. Their love and support remains the greatest gift I have ever received.

Finally, this book would never have happened if my three closest friends from high school, Chuck Abbott (USAF), Jeremiah Anderson (USMC), and Brian Napier (USMC) had not chosen to serve their country. I hope this book acknowledges the depth of the sacrifice they and all other veterans have made.

THE SOLDIER'S TWO BODIES

Introduction

IMAGINE THIS SCENE at a football game; it could be at the high school, college, or even NFL level. A local family is introduced on the field during the pregame coin toss. It's Military Appreciation Night, and the Smiths—Mrs. Smith and her two preteen children—are being honored while their husband and father—Sergeant Smith—is deployed overseas. The crowd stands and claps the steady, smooth applause of appreciation that American football fans use for the game's calmer moments, such as an injured player's first tentative steps toward the sideline. Mrs. Smith and her children stand between the captains of the two opposing teams at the center of the field, on the fifty-yard line.

The referee, in his black-and-white-striped shirt, leans down to give instructions to the youngest Smith, who will actually toss the coin in the air. The referee reaches into his pocket for the coin, but his pocket is empty. He briefly pantomimes a man searching his pockets before turning from the Smiths to call over one of the other officials from where they have lined up a few feet away. This man strides toward the referee with a coin in his outstretched hand. As he gets closer, he removes his pinstriped official's cap and the Smith family suddenly rushes to embrace him. They have just recognized that this is no line judge but Sergeant Smith, returned home from his deployment weeks earlier than expected!

The crowd explodes into the more boisterous applause it usually saves for touchdowns, as the public address announcer explains the surprising scene. Cameras sweep around the tearful Smiths, capturing every moment of the emotional reunion. Depending on the level of the game, the reunion might be a feel-good story on the local news or it might be part of a highlight reel for the game, shown that night on *SportsCenter.* It also might end up on YouTube, either as its own clip or as part of a compilation of videos with titles like "Heartwarming Military Reunions" or "Year's Best Surprise Military Reunions." As this video afterlife suggests, the reunion has become as much a public performance as a family's personal moment.

Although I have invented the foregoing scene, a quick internet search will easily locate dozens like it. Reunions at sporting events might be the most immediately public version of this practice, but a review of the videos posted online shows that they can take place in a range of settings, from private homes to churches to schools.[1] Not all surprise reunions feature the kind of elaborate orchestration I have described in my hypothetical example, and, obviously, most reunions between deployed service members and their family members are not filmed for public consumption. But the appeal of public reunions to news programmers and sports teams is easy to understand. They invite viewers to share vicariously in a family's joy at the safe return of a loved one. They also provide an opportunity to display support for one of the most highly regarded institutions in contemporary American life. In 2017, 72 percent of Americans expressed confidence in the military, compared with only 40 percent for the Supreme Court, 32 percent for the presidency, and 12 percent for Congress.[2] Programming that celebrates the homecoming of American soldiers thus seems to provide a relatively uncontroversial appeal to audiences that are often deeply divided on political issues.[3]

These reunions celebrate the humanity of soldiers and their families, while acknowledging the danger and reality of war. The emotional appeal for an audience comes from the combination of those ideas. The audience witnesses the personal sacrifice being made by the soldier and remembers the larger sacrifice all soldiers make on behalf of the nation. Yet, in the context of the open-ended conflicts that make up the post-9/11 "War on Terror," these reunions create a false sense of closure. The audience enjoys the individual homecoming of a soldier but not the mass homecoming that would mark the turn from wartime to peacetime. In many cases, the soldiers honored in these reunions will actually be redeployed and returned to danger, sometimes within just a few weeks of the reunion.

Publicizing individual homecomings, then, effectively presents them as periodic reminders to be patriotic. Noncombatants can honor the soldier through a sympathetic affect (whether that be cheers or tears), but they are not required to take any concrete actions to support the soldier. Nor are they encouraged to view war as a rupture from ordinary life. Rather, the war *is* ordinary life. Just as some Americans work overnight shifts or face long commutes, some Americans spend months deployed in a foreign country in a conflict zone. Events like these military reunions sustain the contemporary fantasy that a nation can "support the troops" while also pursuing a war with no end in sight.

Public reunions put human faces to the sacrifices made by soldiers. They remind civilians of the physical and emotional toll taken on those who defend the nation. At the same time, such efforts objectify soldiers and veterans as symbols in a history of national triumph. Service members and their families become props in a drama that depicts war as an inevitability and imagines liberty as a prize to be won. Celebrating the humanity of soldiers, in fact, makes them more effective as symbols of this patriotic nationalism because it emphasizes the hardships they have faced on behalf of the nation. Their service is upheld, within nationalist discourse, as what created and sustains the nation as a sovereign body. "Freedom isn't free," we're told as Americans; we owe our rights and liberties as citizens to the soldiers who fought for them. This rhetoric connects military sacrifice to the fundamental concept of American popular sovereignty by suggesting that self-government emanates from a people's willingness to fight for it.

The public surprise reunion bears many hallmarks of our twenty-first-century media culture—the omnipresence of cameras, the arranged drama of reality television, and the performance of our private lives encouraged by social media. At its base, though, this practice reflects an aporia in our conceptions of the American soldier that has existed from the nation's very beginning. American soldiers simultaneously appear as vulnerable humans and as idealized heroes—as individual bodies subject to death and injury and as parts of an immortal military body that defends the nation. Veterans can be imagined as both sovereign and subject, as the agents of sovereign violence and also its victims. How, then, do we acknowledge the contributions of veterans without also reinforcing the nationalism that objectifies them? How do we separate the human being from the heroic myth, when representations of the soldier as a unique individual are so easily appropriated within nationalist discourse as testaments to patriotism? Can we honor the service of veterans while also seeking new ways to imagine sovereignty, apart from war and sacrifice?

In this book, I trace the history of that double view to representations of the nation's first soldiers, veterans of the Revolutionary War. In the years after the war, its soldiers were lionized for their role in the struggle for independence. Revolutionary veterans received commendation across early national culture, from parades and civic tributes, to painting and fine art, to popular ballads and songs, to statuary and public memorials, to appearances in drama, history, and fiction. In just those written spaces, we might think of examples as diverse as plays like Royall Tyler's *The Contrast,* or biographies of Revolutionary heroes from writers like Mason Locke Weems or Jared Sparks, or popular historical romances like James Fenimore Cooper's *The Spy* and William Gilmore Simms's *The Partisan.* As historians such as David Waldstreicher and Sarah Purcell have shown, honoring and memorializing these soldiers helped give shape to US nationalism.[4]

The development of a national mythology around the Revolutionary army likely came as a surprise to many of its soldiers, however. Veterans of the war told stories of being underfed, underclothed, and underpaid during their service, and overlooked in the years after. Such stories offered a contrast to heroic myths of selfless Minutemen by recalling the on-the-ground experience of battle and camp life. The many accounts provided in response to the pension act Congress approved in 1832 exemplify this contrast. While the first federal pension act of 1818 was limited to the indigent, the 1832 act was open to all Revolutionary War veterans, regardless of financial need, provided they could prove their service by describing facts such as their commanding officers and engagements in which they participated.[5] Hundreds of veterans came forward, far surpassing the expectations of Congress.[6]

In recalling their service, to local officials, veterans stressed their commitment to the cause of independence and lamented that their country did not show the same commitment to their welfare. Veteran Sylvanus Wood typifies this attitude in the closing statement of his pension testimony: "I am worth nothing but what has been drawn from my fingers' ends. If I am favored ever with anything for service done in the army, I need it now as well as my fellow soldiers who have done no more than I have. I think I have been neglected."[7] Wood's blunt statement asserts his specific, individual, needs against a vision of the army as a patriotic collective. Heroic tributes and memorials to that collective offered Wood little recompense for his individual service.

Similar sentiments can also be found in one of the most famous firsthand accounts from a Revolutionary soldier, Joseph Plumb Martin's 1830 personal narrative. Martin directly criticizes his countrymen for their failure to support the army. His text often refers to the hunger he experienced during his service, and he notes that soldiers regularly had to make due with inadequate provisions. Martin recalls the frustration he and his comrades felt, "starving in detail for an ungrateful people who did not care what became of us [the army], so they could enjoy themselves while we were keeping a cruel enemy from them."[8] Unlike the veterans who gave statements to apply for a pension, however, Martin shared his criticism with a wide reading audience. His text represents a prominent example of a genre that persisted throughout the decades after 1783, the commercially printed Revolutionary War veteran narrative. Like contemporary surprise military reunions, these early national texts presented to the public the soldier in both his human and his heroic capacities.

Revolutionary veteran narratives were published from diverse motives, but they shared an underlying drive to win recognition for the veteran as a specific individual, not just as a member of an abstract military body. At the same time, these narratives present membership in the army that founded the nation as their primary claim to public attention. Veterans were cast as both peripheral and central to the nation, simultaneously. These narratives helped inaugurate a mode of military representation in the United States in which efforts to acknowledge the experience of specific soldiers also always appropriate those individuals within a nationalist vision of sovereignty. The perpetual tension between the individual and the collective within these narratives makes them an invaluable resource for understanding the complex presence of the soldier in US culture, particularly in relation to beliefs about the origin of American sovereignty in revolutionary violence.

Revolutionary veteran narratives took various forms, from short pamphlets describing one battle or incident to book-length narratives of the entire conflict to complete autobiographies of the writer. Some texts were published versions of the writer's actual war journal, and some were transcribed or ghostwritten versions prepared by an amanuensis, but most were retrospective, first-person, accounts written by the veteran himself. Scott Casper has described these veteran stories as true "narratives," since they generally offer distinct episodes and not an overall biography, though some veteran narratives did include a detailed account of events after 1783.[9]

Many veterans wrote to earn through book sales the financial support they felt their government had neglected to provide both during the war and in the years after. Like the pension applications made by many veterans, such examples traded on the implied sense of debt owed to the Revolutionary soldier by subsequent generations of Americans. Buying a copy of the veteran's narrative became a literal repayment for his service.

Revolutionary veterans were far from unique in selling their stories to an audience. Many ordinary Americans who had experienced a hardship—captives, beggars, fugitive slaves, condemned criminals, and so forth—sought to monetize their suffering by retelling it in print form during the early national era.[10] And not all veterans wrote for economic recompense; many wrote simply to record their experiences for posterity.[11] Yet, even within such examples, the Revolutionary War stands as the central event that makes the life of the protagonist worthy of public attention.

These narratives not only make the Revolutionary War the defining moment in the life of their protagonists but also portray the conflict as the defining moment that brought the nation into being. The genre pays little attention to political negotiations, however. In the stories it tells, the military unit outshines the committee of correspondence. Military sacrifice appears as the source of American sovereignty. The genre thus anticipates Carl Schmitt's influential conception of sovereignty based in the state of exception. The early twentieth-century German jurist and legal philosopher's dictum that the sovereign is "he who decides on the exception" has gained increased significance in a post-9/11 era, when questions over the authority to define and suspend the rule of law in moments of national emergency have risen to the fore of political theory. Schmitt defines the concept of exception as "principally unlimited authority, which means the suspension of the entire existing order" and comments that in "such a situation it is clear that the state remains, whereas law recedes."[12] The veteran narrative implies that the transformation of British royal sovereignty to American popular sovereignty occurred through the medium of thousands of ordinary Americans joining together in force. The veteran narrative as a genre posits a sovereign body politic that preexists the declaration of a new American legal order.

While the Declaration of Independence describes the North American colonies as having become "free and independent states," suggesting an alliance between multiple sovereign governments, veteran narratives offer a view of the war as the work of a continental nation embodied through its soldiers. For instance, David Perry's 1822 narrative laments the divisions within the United States during the War of 1812, warning that such divisiveness "threatened the destruction of those liberties, which I had some small share in establishing."[13] For this veteran, the War of 1812 and the partisan political debates surrounding it represented a decline from an idealized Revolutionary unity.[14] The genre imagines that union as the moment when a collective acted with the purpose that Schmitt attributes to a unitary sovereign.

Remembering the war in this way supported the kind of nationalist sentiment and centralized authority that would become a key plank of the Federalist Party. At the same time, the vision of popular sovereignty in the veteran narrative can offer a locus for "the people" that might conflict with Federalist constitutionalism. Where the Constitution locates sovereignty in the performative utterance of the preamble's "We the People," the veteran narrative suggests that the people consisted of the actual bodies that assembled on battlefields and at sea against the British.

As Perry's concern over 1812 indicates, that moment of Revolutionary unity was quickly lost. But that quality of loss and the appeal to an earlier age of heroes are the qualities that make the Revolutionary army such an effective symbol of popular sovereignty. The veteran narrative imagines the Revolutionary War as a time when the American people asserted sovereignty by collectively rejecting British rule and forcefully defending their own claim to self-government. It posits an ideal memory that subsequent generations of Americans must uphold. It frames the war as the moment when the people could be remembered as acting together in a physical, not just a representative, sense.

Legal scholar David C. Williams asserts that the framers of the Constitution imagined popular political violence as a legitimate *revolution* only when it emerged from the unified will of the body of the people to replace a corrupt government.[15] The phrase the "body of the people" signified the all-encompassing population of the body politic, united by a shared culture, in distinction to self-interested factions within the society, no matter how large or powerful. Political violence taken without the mandate of the body of the people appeared under these terms as an illegitimate *rebellion* against a freely elected government.

This idealized memory of unity attempts to address the problem of self-authorization inherent in popular sovereignty. This problem asks how a sovereign people can exist without the laws that classify a group of individuals as a specific body politic. Put simply, it's a political version of *Which came first, the chicken or the egg?* How could the American people declare themselves independent while they were still subjects of the British crown? On what basis could they claim that authority? European monarchy had sought the transcendent authority of a Christian God as the basis for the royal sovereignty of a hereditary monarch, but how could this authority be shared by a collective body?

Without recourse to transcendental justifications, American popular sovereignty appears as a tautology, wherein the people are both the source and the subjects of their own authority. This condition has drawn the attention of observers of US politics since the nation's earliest days. In *Democracy in America,* Alexis de Tocqueville famously described how, in American politics, the people "are the cause and the aim of all things; everything comes from them, and everything is absorbed in them."[16] Schmitt cites this claim from Tocqueville to argue for the persistence of a notion of divine authority in the transition from monarchal sovereignty to popular sovereignty. Rather than viewing sovereignty as emanating from the divinity to a monarch, Schmitt states that Americans imagined their popular will as the immanent source of their political authority.[17]

As Jennifer Greiman notes, for Schmitt, this notion was more of a lingering afterglow from divine justifications of sovereignty than a completely new understanding of the idea.[18] As this glow faded, Schmitt maintains, popular sovereignty lost the unifying force that emerged from the personal, decision-making capacity of an individual sovereign. Where a monarch could be imagined to bring forth the state like God brought forth the world, the will of the people lacked the focus of a singular intent. Schmitt writes that although "absolute monarchy made the decision and thereby created the unity of the state . . . the unity that a people represents does not possess this decisionist character."[19]

The veteran narrative, and the larger cultural view of US soldiers it exemplifies, seeks to retain this link between the decision and the unity of the people by invoking war as the source of American sovereignty. War makes popular will sovereign will. Very few soldiers can express that will through governance, but they can take part in it through fighting and/or suffering.

The veteran's account of personal suffering gives sovereignty its popular aspect because it suggests that the individual sacrifice of bodily autonomy was an independent choice made for the greater good and that self-government requires such individuals willing to put their lives in danger. By choosing to serve, the veteran participated in the sovereign decision. With its focus on the soldier as the source of sovereignty, the veteran narrative makes a republican revision of the doctrine of the king's two bodies, the European legal and religious tradition that cast the monarch as both a living person and an immortal embodiment of the political community.[20] The veteran narrative adapts to an American context the Christian story of sacrificial unity that provided a basis for European monarchy. Michael Rogin writes that, where Christ created a new kingdom through the sacrifice of his mortal body, the European monarch named the nation through the representative role of his physical presence; the veteran narrative combines the sacrificial and the representative modes, such that the Revolutionary soldier can be imagined to have brought the nation into being through the sacrifices of his military service and to represent those sacrifices in the years after the war as a veteran.[21]

Yet, while the king's royal body empowered his mortal body with transcendent authority, the soldier's military and civilian bodies exist in an uneasy tension with each other. Describing this tension, Elizabeth Samet has asserted that "the same patriotism and passion for liberty prompting the citizen to volunteer in the first place may ultimately unfit him for military service."[22] Samet asks whether the independence of the citizen can coexist with the discipline of the soldier—a question that goes to the heart of the representational challenge raised by the veteran narrative.

The citizen-soldier's two bodies sometimes appear incompatible, yet they always appear inextricable. Representations of veterans cannot resolve the tension between these two bodies within the cultural script that links popular sovereignty to Revolutionary force. The veteran narrative as a genre is uniquely equipped to display these two sides in their constant tension because it recounts both the veteran's submission to authority and his passion for liberty. The veteran accepts whatever suffering may come his way, on behalf of his country. For example, John Joseph Henry addresses his 1812 narrative to his children and states, as part of his conclusion, his hope that "they will always be ready and active, to rally round the standard of Freedom, the principles of which we derived from our forefathers, whose blood freely flowed in its defense." In language common to almost any US military tribute, Henry's narrative links the liberty enjoyed by American citizens to the sacrifices made by American soldiers. It also notes the chronic pain Henry experienced for the rest of his life as a result of injuries sustained during the failed invasion of Canada in 1775, furthering the sense of obligation between soldiers and civilians.[23] Similarly, Nathaniel Segar wrote of how his service in youth left him disabled in old age, in his 1825 narrative. Segar's response to his debility could summarize the underlying sentiment throughout many examples of the form: "I hope the results of my toils and sufferings will be acknowledged by my country, and prove a lasting blessing to it, and be handed down unsullied to the latest posterity."[24]

Veterans appear as a heroic class who fought on behalf of the nation and as specific individuals who suffered from that fight. The narratives of Revolutionary War veterans keep those aspects constantly before an audience. The more the genre demands recognition for the hardships of an individual veteran, the more support it gives to the view of sovereignty as the product of violence and decision, which appropriates the veteran as a patriotic symbol. This paradox often occurs through representations of individual veterans as disinterested patriots who rise above their more selfish peers. Alexander Graydon, for instance, directly admonishes those who engage in what he calls "the scramble," the competition for place and prestige among men during and after the war. He writes that "at no period in my recollection, was the worship of Mammon more widely spread, more sordid and disgusting" than in the early 1780s.[25] William Wallace, a young lieutenant in the artillery service during the war, was captured and then was offered a commission at a higher rank in the British Army, with a promise of half-pay for life should he accept. He declined this offer, out of loyalty to the American cause, and thus expressed in his narrative no little frustration at receiving as compensation nothing but a depreciated note from Congress for five years' pay.[26] Wounded veterans like Nathaniel Segar or his fellow New Englander Lemuel Roberts present themselves as left behind by the nation for which they fought and bled.[27] Their narratives contrast the vigor the veteran possessed as a young man with his frailty as an older man—the implication being that, had the veteran not shared his strength with the military, it would have remained his personal possession to use for his own advancement.

All of these examples seek to challenge readers to live up to the virtuous standard set by Revolutionary soldiers. But, in doing so, they reinforce the tension between the military body and the individual civilian body. The self-denial of the veteran during the war, and any hardships he has suffered after it, make him a greater example of the ideal of Revolutionary military sovereignty.

Maintaining the belief that sovereignty emerges from a people's willingness to claim it through force requires that neither side of the veteran's identity—the disciplined soldier or the suffering human—gains greater resonance. This double nature makes efforts to critique the appropriation of the veteran into a symbol of nationalism much more difficult. Efforts to criticize the dehumanizing treatment of soldiers or their neglect by the nation actually help support the image of patriotic suffering that undergirds the link between sovereignty and violence. In the chapters to come, I will focus on how the Revolutionary veteran narrative has served as a cultural text that vividly documents that link, and the paradoxical vision of soldiers it entails. The examples I have chosen include the best-known examples of the genre (Ethan Allen, Israel Potter, Joseph Plumb Martin, and Deborah Sampson), along with a few more obscure texts.

The first chapter compares two figures associated with revolutionary violence in the early United States, Ethan Allen of Vermont and Daniel Shays of Massachusetts. Both men appeared as the leaders of aggressive frontier populist movements that asserted local sovereignty over the authority of distant governments, and both would frame their actions as part of the broader Revolutionary cause. Yet Allen succeeded in presenting himself as a Revolutionary hero, whereas Shays was cast in infamy. The chapter explores Allen's 1779 narrative as the primary cause of this distinction. Contrasting the reputations of Allen and

Shays demonstrates how the figure of the Revolutionary soldier came to be understood as a source of US sovereignty.

Allen begins his narrative with his assault on Fort Ticonderoga, an assault made under an unclear sense of authority, as both Allen and Benedict Arnold claim to have been commissioned to lead this attack. Allen famously resolved this uncertainty by demanding the fort's surrender "in the name of the great Jehovah, and the Continental Congress." Allen's unsanctioned claim to lead the venture suggests the unpredictability inherent in a broad notion of sovereignty that potentially enables all citizens to act with legitimate force. At the same time, his decision to present himself as a representative not of an individual colony but of a national body indicates a potential solution to this instability by connecting military loyalty to national, rather than local, interests.

Allen's acceptance into US cultural nationalism stems from his willingness to express his claims to sovereignty in a written form, which matched the preferred modes of federalist republicanism, in contrast to the unwritten, unrepresented claims to sovereignty made by Daniel Shays. Allen's vision of the Revolutionary soldier resembles federalist notions of representative governance—both emphasize individuals in their capacity to stand for the larger body politic. On the other hand, despite his claims to be a mere spokesmen for his neighbors, Daniel Shays would be judged within this frame of elite representatives and was therefore seen as a demagogic threat to the nation.

The second chapter examines how the figure of the Revolutionary soldier expanded into an ideal of a national army that would bind Americans to a continental vision of sovereignty. It analyzes two narratives collected by Hugh Henry Brackenridge: the accounts of John Knight and John Slover, who were both taken captive after William Crawford's failed expedition against Indian settlements in the upper Ohio Valley in May 1782. Brackenridge transcribed, edited, and published these narratives, and he portrays Knight and Slover, along with their doomed commanding officer, Crawford, as examples of patriotic American virtue. As Brackenridge transforms these men into national military heroes, he also relocates military authority into the hands of a centralized government. Brackenridge criticizes the drive to self-defense that encouraged frontier conflict, and he seeks to disperse this drive in a broader vision of a sovereign people. To emphasize Brackenridge's concern about populist violence, I close this chapter by reading the accounts of Knight and Slover in relation to Brackenridge's subsequent response to the Whiskey Rebellion, *Incidents of the Insurrection in the Western Part of Pennsylvania in the Year 1794*.

Crawford's expedition had been an attempt by William Irvine, commander of the Western Department of the Continental Army, to reassert order in a region riven by clashes between British-allied Indians and American settlers—conflict that had reached a boiling point earlier that year with a local militia's massacre of ninety-six Christian Indians living in the Moravian settlement of Gnadenhutten. I argue that the Crawford expedition narratives should be viewed not only as a patriotic, anti-British/anti-Indian text but also as a rebuke to the militia that perpetrated the Gnadenhutten massacre. The figure of the patriotic Revolutionary soldier invoked in the narratives of Knight and Slover attempted to encourage respect for the protection offered by a professional army that would subsume the use of force by smaller local militias. In his later record of the Whiskey Rebellion, Brackenridge expressed anxiety that violence or the threat of violence provides the most ready opportunity to establish not only a cohesive sense of group identity but also a feeling of empowered participation within a body politic endowed with popular sovereignty. Reading this anxiety, we can more clearly recognize Brackenridge's effort to imagine Knight, Slover, and Crawford as part of a continental military culture that would replace direct involvement in popular violence.

In the third chapter, I turn to two of the best-known examples of the postwar veteran narrative, Joseph Plumb Martin's 1830 autobiographical account and *The Female Review,* Herman Mann's 1797 account of Deborah Sampson. As narratives published years after the war, both texts add an additional layer of difference to the divide between the military body and the civilian body by juxtaposing the older veteran relating his/her story with the younger soldier who has faced the dangers of combat.

Martin's narrative exemplifies a common refrain of the genre as it criticizes the lack of social and political recognition Martin and his comrades received in the nation their service helped establish. Martin asks to be acknowledged as a participant within a moment of collective sovereignty; his narrative asserts that sacrifices by soldiers like him created the rupture with British authority that brought the United States into being. However, such an appeal relies on a claim to the kind of exceptional status that supports the vertical model of sovereignty that veterans like Martin critique. Martin asserts the individuality of his human body, but that assertion is intertwined with a discourse of military nationalism that elides such individuality.

In contrast, Sampson's narrative cannot claim recognition within sovereignty for its protagonist, given her explicit exclusion from the body politic as a woman. *The Female Review* instead imagines sovereign power as a consciously constructed performance, unbound from the claims of particular human bodies. Rather than insisting on recognition for her individual body, *The Female Review* imagines Deborah Sampson as a series of personas—an adventurous girl, a skilled fighting man, a virtuous republican wife—that bear only a tenuous relationship to the actual Massachusetts woman who enlisted in the Continental Army. Read together, Sampson and Martin indicate how the assertion of the civilian body within their narratives effectively supports the appropriation of the military body within popular sovereignty.

The last two chapters turn toward later antebellum narratives that function less as personal accounts of the war than as fables of national origins. In the fourth chapter, I examine how the divide between the soldier's two bodies created a space where white supremacist thought could become tied to Revolutionary history, through the analysis of two narratives of soldiers who claimed to fight in both the Revolutionary War and the War of 1812, one a supporter of slavery and the other an advocate of African American equality. *The Fort Stanwix Captive,* published by Josiah Priest in 1841, tells the story of Isaac Hubbell, a veteran who was taken captive by Indians during the Revolutionary War and chose to return to service as an older man during the War of 1812. *The Narrative of James Roberts,* written by an anonymous amanuensis and published in 1858, presents the story of an enslaved man who purportedly served on the American side in both the Revolutionary War and the War of 1812, despite being held in bondage by the very nation for which he fought.

Both of these narratives share features that stretch credulity and suggest that they were written more as fantastic imitations of the genre than as objective biographies. Through this comparison, I argue that divisions among the soldiers in the War of 1812 provided a symbol of the perpetual instability faced by a nation founded on revolutionary violence. In response, a discourse about white supremacy and racial purity would be remembered in the antebellum era as the source of affiliation between men that could balance this volatility. Within these texts, the lost unity of the Revolutionary era becomes coded as racial stratification. As these narratives illustrate a cultural effort to define legitimate expressions of political violence as the exclusive right of a sovereign community of white men, they reveal how racial divisions obscured the similar forms of exploitation experienced by both white soldiers and enslaved blacks in the service of an expanding nation-state.

The book's final chapter considers Herman Melville's 1854 novel *Israel Potter,* based on that veteran's 1824 narrative. Starting with the historic Potter's pleas for recognition, Melville questions the project of narrating the history of the United States through the valorization of representative individuals. Melville emphasizes the tension in the original narrative, which emerged from Potter's status as a Revolutionary soldier stranded in England for fifty years after the war. Israel Potter was excluded from the nation he helped to found, and his narrative argues that this suffering should have entitled him to recognition and respect from subsequent generations. Melville heightens this contrast by making his fictional Potter an active participant in many of the Revolutionary War's pivotal moments and a colleague to three heroes of the Revolution: Benjamin Franklin, John Paul Jones, and Ethan Allen.

While many critics of the novel have read these three figures in distinction to Israel, I assert that we should pay closer attention to their similarities. The novel imagines the sly Franklin, the ruthless Jones, the bold Allen, and the hapless Israel each at the head of the body politic, in order to suggest that this space can be filled by anyone who lays claim to it in the United States. A writer like Potter imagines sovereignty as ultimately rooted in recognition as a representative member of the body politic, and the genre of the veteran narrative asserts that to be a member of the sovereign people is to demand acknowledgment of one's willingness to fight for that membership. Melville worries that this condition in which each subject demands his privilege as sovereign will lead not to a shared sense of political community but instead to an aggressive competition among individuals that will be hardly distinguishable from a state of nature. *Israel Potter* confronts the challenge posed by defining sovereignty as individual autonomy.

Read in context with texts like *The Fort Stanwix Captive* and the James Roberts narrative, Melville's novelization of the Potter narrative in the 1850s might appear as the culmination of a trend toward fictionality throughout the genre. Such a shift would reflect changes in the form that we would expect over the passage of time. As fewer veterans remained to tell their stories and the war faded from lived memory, a turn toward myth-making would seem likely.

As this survey of many of its most recognized titles indicates, however, this genre offered heavily mediated versions of the veteran's story right from the start. Israel Potter and Deborah Sampson both told their stories to collaborators who altered or omitted unflattering details. Hugh Henry Brackenridge blurred the line between editor and author in the narratives of Knight and Slover. These are texts that sold an audience the idea of an authentic experience of the war, yet often those experiences were narrated and composed by someone other than the veteran. Even the more truly autobiographical narratives, by Ethan Allen and Joseph Plumb Martin, feature a healthy degree of self-promotion. Although Allen and Martin might not be inventing details out of whole cloth, as Herman Mann does in *The Female Review,* they are clearly crafting a particular persona for their readers. That well-crafted persona marks the common factor that draws these examples of the Revolutionary veteran narrative together. Each example strikes a careful balance between the veteran's individual, mortal, civilian body and the collective, immortal, military body. The examples

I have chosen evince how the veteran narrative represents those two bodies in a constant tension. These examples suggest that the discursive link between popular sovereignty and military sacrifice requires a representation of the soldier that does not veer too much toward either biography (favoring the civilian body) or fiction (favoring the military body).

Each of these texts reflects on the consequences of upsetting that balance, and each, in its own way, accepts the notion that violence is integral to American sovereignty. These texts offer no easy solution to the appropriation of veteran lives within military nationalism. But in bringing the paradox inherent in the figure of the US soldier constantly forward, the genre invites consideration of how to reimagine those representations. Revolutionary veteran narratives suggest that depicting the military as the source and guarantor of United States sovereignty has never actually won veterans the kind of recognition they sought. Reckoning with that history seems a vital aspect of finding new ways to describe both American sovereignty and the American military. As the so-called War on Terror produces a new generation of veterans and continues with no clear end in sight, such a reckoning seems more necessary than ever.

1

Ethan Allen, Daniel Shays, and the Invention of a Revolutionary Hero

IN PERHAPS THE MOST famous scene from his 1779 captivity narrative, Ethan Allen describes the pivotal moment when he had led his men to capture Fort Ticonderoga, four years earlier, at the start of the Revolutionary War. Allen claimed that when the British officer in command asked him by what authority he demanded the fort's surrender, he had exclaimed, "In the name of the great Jehovah, and the Continental Congress." Scholars typically regard this purported demand as artistic license on Allen's part, but its appearance in his popular narrative no doubt helped to encourage his image as a heroic revolutionary and backcountry republican.[1] Following this famous declaration, however, is this sentence in the text: "(The authority of the Congress being very little known at that time), he began to speak again; but I interrupted him, and with my sword drawn over his head, again demanded an immediate surrender of the garrison; to which he then complied."[2] Reading this aside as Allen's explanation for why the officer was initially hesitant to surrender and why Allen chose to threaten the man with his sword raises a key question: Was the fort taken in the name of Jehovah and the Continental Congress or by the authority of Ethan Allen's sword?

Obviously, this question does not necessarily require an either/or choice. But Allen's somewhat awkward use of a parenthetical aside here appears emblematic of a basic uncertainty regarding the sources of American sovereignty. The officer at Ticonderoga questioned Allen's right as a British subject to lead a military assault on a British fort, but Allen rejected royal sovereignty to declare himself an agent of the

American people. Yet Allen wrote at a time when the body politic on whose authority he claimed to act barely existed, and such a body was even more tenuous at the moment of the fort's capture. It would appear that sovereignty emerged as much, if not more, from Allen's willingness to call his violent actions the "will of the people" than from any actual popular accord.

Allen's narrative exemplifies the fundamental tautology of popular sovereignty: the people are both the source of authority and its subjects. In the pages of Allen's text, popular sovereignty appears as a performative act that inextricably links narrative and violence. Political violence in the name of "the people" gains legitimacy through the claim to act on the people's behalf, and this claim gains its efficacy from that violence. In his famous analysis of Walter Benjamin's "Critique of Violence," Jacques Derrida described this performative tautology as the "force" of law, as how "one gives oneself the means to decide between legal and illegal violence."[3] Allen's narrative stages that decision explicitly, before an audience. By writing his narrative, Allen completed his invocation of an American people that could authorize his assault on Ticonderoga. The narrative transformed Allen's actions from the opportunistic exploits of a frontier demagogue into the bold conquests of a new national hero.

This transformation becomes more apparent when we compare Allen with another well-known New England populist. Like Allen, Daniel Shays led a local militia that forcefully demanded recognition of its sovereignty. Like Allen, Shays and his comrades also asserted that their violent acts were made by the authority of "the people." Shays even briefly pursued an alliance with Allen, before leading the ill-fated January 1787 attack on the national arsenal at Springfield, Massachusetts, that made him famous.[4] Yet Shays has become an iconic American figure only in hindsight, as during the 1780s, among many of the early republic's political elites, his name was a watchword for anarchy.[5] Given their similarities, why was Ethan Allen successful in presenting Vermont's movement toward independence as part of the American Revolution, whereas Daniel Shays failed in his argument that the same principles that had led him to resist the British in 1776 now led him to resist his state government in 1786?

Comparing Allen and Shays reveals how Allen's talents for self-presentation established him as a popular hero of the Revolutionary War, despite the fact that he spent much of the conflict either in British custody or at his home in Bennington, Vermont. In his numerous writings during the war, Allen depicted Vermont as a loyal and deserving member of the American confederation, and within his captivity narrative specifically, he presented his virtuous endurance as a testament to the patriotism of the region. Yet, by emphasizing his role in the capture of Fort Ticonderoga and by offering his captivity as a moral inspiration to the entire country, Allen also claimed the authority to represent not just Vermont but also the people of the United States. Allen's narrative models the role the Revolutionary soldier played in establishing popular sovereignty in the United States. The narrative imagines sovereignty as the product of sacrifices by national heroes like Allen.

In contrast, Daniel Shays avoided attaching a larger significance to his role as a representative of the angry farmers of western Massachusetts. Shays always emphasized his position as a delegate of a specific and limited community, and he denied claims to leadership or authority over the protesters.[6] This avoidance of fame meant that Shays also left little written record of his motivations. He thus became an open text whose meaning could be penned by others. Indeed, supposedly true accounts of Shays began to proliferate in Boston newspapers during the crisis, especially in the pro-government *Massachusetts Centinel*.[7] Shays was cast as a dangerous demagogue in many of these accounts—an American Catiline, Caesar, or Cromwell.

Shays and Allen thus appear as opposite poles within a cultural account of military service in the early republic. Both Allen and Shays participated in backcountry movements that justified acts of force as taken on behalf of "the people," yet the contrasting receptions they garnered reveal that such smaller, locally based definitions were increasingly subsumed within the continental nationalism favored by many of the framers, as the "body of the people" came to describe all citizens of the American states as a united political entity. In the pages of his narrative, Allen could appear as a brave revolutionary by blending Vermont's struggle for independence with that of the United States, in order to engage this expansive sense of the people. Shays, on the other hand, held to a more narrow sense of the body politic that emphasized local self-determination, yet this commitment would lead to accusations that he fomented a rebellion that threatened not only Massachusetts but also the entire confederation.

The attention paid to both men reveals an ideology that takes the exceptional representative, rather than the aggregate community, as the key political actor. Allen and Shays each became the best-known member of their movements—Allen by choice, Shays by circumstance. This fame reflects the beliefs of a culture of deference and hierarchy, in which it was assumed that powerful men influenced the course of social events, and it was precisely in such a culture that the reputations of Allen and Shays were shaped through their literary representations. Within the print culture of the urban Eastern seaboard, Allen the heroic revolutionary and Shays the corrupt rebel each stood as a kind of frontier doppelganger of the elite men who held political and social power.

The acts of violence undertaken in Vermont and western Massachusetts appear not as forceful demands for sovereignty by specific communities but instead can be interpreted as paramilitary acts led by a charismatic commander. The reputations of the two men became means to literally write popular expressions of sovereignty into the discourse of representative government by narrating such expressions as the work of exceptional individuals. Allen's literary self-promotion thus has the ironic effect of making him appear to be more of a disinterested patriot than Shays, who actively shunned the representative role thrust upon him. Allen and Shays, and the writing they inspired, therefore reinforced a political vision in which sovereignty would be expressed by elite delegates rather than by the people as a collective entity; this vision ultimately supported the notion of a strong national government composed of exceptional individuals whose elevation from their local communities would ideally make them most likely to act on behalf of the body of the people.

In short, the comparison between Allen and Shays indicates how the emphasis placed on the representation of individuals became a primary means of defining popular sovereignty in the broadest possible terms and of discrediting the potential use of force by small communities. The success of Allen's self-image and the ignominy of the image attached to Shays demonstrate the assimilation of local popular activism within the burgeoning continental state.

In what follows, I explore how these two men became powerful symbols in the development of a more centralized, national government. I turn first to a review of the similar contexts in which Allen and Shays gained notice, before offering an analysis of how each man's characterization in print made him a model for considering structures of representation in the new nation. The representation of both men evinces a definition of sovereignty based in the demand for autonomy. The actions of both men are placed within a script that favors individual actors, not a collective chorus.

Ethan Allen's public career began in 1770, when he purchased three lots in the New Hampshire Grants, the territory that would eventually become the state of Vermont. Many New England settlers had purchased title to this land from New Hampshire, yet the colonial government of New York claimed that the New Hampshire titles were invalid and demanded that settlers in the Grants either repurchase their land at higher prices, with New York titles, or watch it be sold off to speculators. In the early 1770s, settlers in the Grants formed a militia to defend their land claims from what they perceived as the tyranny of the "Yorkers." This militia took the name the Green Mountain Boys and elected the charismatic Allen as its colonel.

The Green Mountain Boys embarked on a campaign of resistance to New York authority, which Allen led through discourse and physical force. He authored a stream of political pamphlets that cast the leading citizens of New York as a tyrannical aristocracy. He also led extralegal protests, such as burning a building owned by New York speculators, forming a well-armed human wall to block a sheriff's posse from evicting a local family, and holding a public trial of surveyors for trespassing on land held by squatters. Through these displays of force, the Green Mountain Boys aimed to demonstrate that the residents of the region, not the government in Albany, held political authority in the Grants.

In his writings, Allen cast these acts as the justified reaction of a people being denied their legal rights by an unjust government—the same rhetoric being used across New England to explain the growing frustration with British authority. When this rhetoric turned to action, in 1775, Allen determined that the best means to demonstrate the deserved independence of the Grants would be to put aside the conflict with New York and join the other colonies in armed resistance to the British. Allen led a group of Green Mountain Boys in the first American offensive of the Revolutionary War, a bold predawn raid on Fort Ticonderoga, in May 1775. Allen captured the British garrison without firing a shot and soon enjoyed a modicum of fame throughout the American colonies.

This fame increased later that year, when Allen became a prisoner of war as a result of his capture during the failed invasion of Canada. Allen would spend the next two years and eight months being shuffled from one British prison to another, yet his time in captivity only added to his reputation and encouraged his transition from backcountry insurgent to revolutionary hero. Indeed, Allen's perseverance during captivity became a cause célèbre in the early years of the war, as evinced by a congressional order to American printers to distribute a resolution directing all American military commanders to exchange any British officers they took captive, at the rank of colonel or below, for Allen.[8] Even George Washington would use Allen as a symbol of loyalty to the American cause, in a letter where he reminds a young captive officer of the example of Allen, who had been "torn from his dearest connexions, sent to England in irons, and is now confined to the most servile drudgery on board one of the King's ships."[9] Upon his release, Allen capitalized on the heroic status his captivity had earned him around the country by publishing a narrative recounting his experiences, and this text was immediately successful, going through eight reprints during 1779 and 1780.

Having authored many pamphlets arguing for Vermont's independence, Allen was accustomed to standing as a representative of his community in print, and his narrative extended that role as Allen associated Vermont (and himself) with American independence. The fame his narrative secured him made Allen distinct from other leaders of backcountry uprisings, most of whom drifted back into obscurity after their movements ended.[10] Like most of these men, Allen came from the middling class of yeoman farmers and small speculators, yet his narrative enabled Allen to portray himself as a gentleman and an officer engaged in the struggle against the British. Stephen Carl Arch has suggested that, within the text, Allen sets the primary social distinction not between British and American but between those who recognize him as a gentleman and those who do not.[11] The man from the frontier demands to be treated the same as more urbane officers from the city. This rhetorical choice evinces Allen's belief in republican equality while also hinting at the pleasure he displays, throughout the narrative, at being viewed as an exceptional individual, apart from the common crowd. In contrast, the limited writings of Daniel Shays never seek to establish their author as anything more than a spokesman for an aggrieved community. Shays thus gained far more fame from the writings of his detractors than from any text to which he signed his name.

Shays reached his peak of infamy in the winter of 1787, after the attack at Springfield left four protesters dead and gave rise to rumors of anarchy and civil war across Massachusetts. Despite their notoriety, Shays and the men he led were only a small faction of a larger movement of court closings and protests inspired by the perceived failure of the state government to address the economic hardships faced by rural citizens. Amid the heavy burden of postwar debt, citizens of other states had obtained some relief from collection and foreclosure by petitioning for the issuance of paper money. In Massachusetts, however, a legislature dominated by Boston merchants and financial speculators refused to bow to such requests and continued to demand payments in specie. Residents of the more rural western counties responded with a campaign of closing local courthouses as a statement of popular sovereignty over a government they determined to be unresponsive to their grievances.

For many supporters of the state government, these protests were an effort by the "Shaysites" to avoid paying their obligations, to abolish private property, and to overturn the existing government.[12] Yet, while their detractors accused the protesters of rebelling against a legitimate government, the protesters saw the court closings as performing a necessary check on state power by "regulating" laws they considered unjust.[13] Many of these protesters had served in the Continental Army or in local militias and believed they had fought for a stronger voice in their own governance.[14] However, Massachusetts had developed one of the most hierarchical constitutions of the newly independent states, with property requirements for political office that ensured that only men of substantial means would hold authority—an arrangement that established the mercantile interest as a much more powerful voice in the state legislature than the rural farmers of the western counties. Many western residents also felt literally excluded from state government by the capital's distant location in Boston. Despite the ideals of self-government for which they struggled during the Revolutionary War, these men perceived themselves as shut out of governance in their state. Many protesters therefore imagined the economic burden they faced as an expression of unjust power and set out to resist it, just as they had resisted the power of Great Britain. Like Ethan Allen and the Green Mountain Boys before them, the protesters of Massachusetts imagined their actions to be part of the broader revolutionary struggle for self-determination in the American colonies.

Unlike in the case of Allen and Vermont, however, no charismatic leader arose to portray the yeomen of rural Massachusetts as heroic patriots. As noted, Ethan Allen's fame as a backcountry leader was far more atypical than the absence of such a leader in western Massachusetts. The protests in this region were spread across multiple towns and counties, and kinship ties, rather than an influential leader, carried the greatest weight in attracting participants to the movement.[15]

Furthermore, the notion of a single authoritative leader would have run counter to the goals of local self-determination pursued by these protesters. Such an idea would strongly accord with the worldview of many urban elites in the eastern part of the state, however, where a culture of deference remained powerful. Ronald Formisano has suggested that men of wealth and influence believed public affairs could only be shaped by men such as themselves, "or by men *pretending* to be like them" and their understanding of the protests thus necessitated elevating a man like Daniel Shays into a position of leadership he never pursued.[16] When Shays became the reluctant commander of the small force that assembled to resist the private army led by former Continental Army general Benjamin Lincoln and funded by wealthy Boston merchants to end the protests, he filled the need for a corrupt leader at the head of the protest movement, and he frequently would be described in eastern newspapers as the "generalissimo" or the "mushroom general" of the insurgents, who led his neighbors into anarchy.

This description made Shays a convenient symbol in the arguments of those who demanded a more powerful central government, during the Constitutional Convention later in 1787. As Jay Fliegelman has observed, the *Federalist Papers* marks the earliest appearance in print of the noun *responsibility,* which in this context describes "the condition of being answerable."[17] Through the figure of Daniel Shays, conservative elites could imagine an individual who could be held answerable for the discord in the western part of the state. For those soon to organize themselves as Federalists, the tumult in Massachusetts clearly argued for a change in government, and the example of Shays foreshadowed the danger of a corrupt despot who could overwhelm the confederation unless the national government was given greater authority.

Despite the contrasting receptions they received, Allen and Shays each achieved fame, in part, because they could fulfill this position of responsibility for what were otherwise imagined as anonymous, collective groups. The reputations that would accrue to each man through their appearances in print became a means of attaching an individual, representative voice to seemingly inarticulate masses and thus imagining those masses as potentially manageable. Such rhetoric provided a means of stepping outside the circular logic of popular sovereignty by imagining a powerful individual as the true source of the populist violence in Vermont and Massachusetts. Both men personify a kind of Schmittian decider as the sovereign. Due to their demagogic qualities, Allen and Shays were seen as having gained power over their followers and having led them into defiance of the existing law.

Misty Anderson has described the remnant of unitary majesty within ostensibly republican societies as "zombie sovereignty."[18] Paul Downes and Jonathan Elmer have each explored this persistent afterlife of monarchic sovereignty in early American culture, and I would offer Allen and Shays as further examples of the struggle to envision political authority outside such a model.[19] The representation of both men in print demonstrates a shift of the symbolic body of the sovereign, what Downes calls "that ungraspable, immortal, and avowedly trans-historical conveyer of political authority," away from the specific body of a king and into a discursive field of competing individuals.[20] As they perpetuate a focus on individual responsibility, the figures of Allen and Shays maintain an analogy of sovereignty as individual autonomy.

Placing Allen and Shays at the head of their respective movements translated the anarchic democratic potential of these movements into the favored political language of urban elites, a language based in hierarchical structure, delegable sovereignty, and representative governance by enlightened leaders. Allen and Shays offered structure for accounts of rural political violence, and as they came to signify a revolutionary and a rebel, their personas also allowed these outbreaks of violence to be interpreted in relation to the broader narrative of the emergence of an American nation. As Ed White has shown, this broad narrative has tended to emerge from the written forms of discourse found in the east rather than from the vernacular expressions found in the backcountry.[21] In this context, the notoriety attached to Shays comes into greater focus, as does the success of Allen's project of connecting Vermont to the other states by promoting his own heroic example.

Through the medium of his captivity narrative, Ethan Allen could frame his service and suffering during the Revolutionary War as an act of representation by recounting his exceptional virtue as an example to an audience he imagines as the people of the new United States of America. Allen depicts the misery of his captivity to inspire continued commitment to the war effort among his readers, and his narrative encourages this commitment by urging his readers to sympathize with his hardships. Allen informs his countrymen of the suffering that awaits if the cause of independence fails, and he makes this purpose clear in the preface to his narrative, where he writes of feeling "induced by a sense of duty to my country" to recount the "cruel and relentless disposition of the enemy." Allen offers his example as a guide for others, remarking that his readers "may deduce such inferences as they shall think proper to carry into practice" after reading the narrative.[22] By presenting his story as emblematic of a broadly national sense of purpose, Allen envisions himself as more than just the leader of a backcountry militia.

This distinction becomes more apparent throughout the text, where Allen strives to assert Vermont's independence while also illustrating its affinity with the other American states. This task required a careful balancing act, since the residents of the former New Hampshire Grants had to prove their affiliation with other Americans to argue for inclusion in the national confederation, while also asserting their difference from the residents of New York or New Hampshire to argue for independent statehood. Allen approached this dilemma by presenting his virtue as representative of the character of all the residents of Vermont. The narrative proper opens with a description of how Allen was motivated to fight the British as the result of a "sincere passion for liberty," which he had refined through reading the "history of nations doomed to perpetual slavery."[23] This opening links an emotional state to the study of written examples and thus models the value of Allen's own narrative for his readers. Furthermore, with its focus on the solitary act of reading, this passage also emphasizes an individual response to the revolutionary cause.

After establishing a focus on personal choices, in the opening pages of the narrative, Allen shifts to a depiction of the valor of the Green

Mountain Boys in the capture of Fort Ticonderoga as an example of individuals who have each chosen to stand against tyranny. Allen briefly alludes to the New Hampshire Grants controversy when he recalls the speech he made to the Green Mountain Boys before their assault on Fort Ticonderoga, in which he reminded the men that they had "been a scourge and terror to arbitrary power" for several years. Yet, within the context of his narrative, this appellation links the men he leads to the American struggle against the British and elides their earlier (and at the time of publication, ongoing) dispute with New York.[24] Allen introduces the Green Mountain Boys in the narrative not as the scourge of the provincial government of New York, a fellow colony, but rather as citizens willing to stand against British tyranny.

As I have noted, the perhaps best-known line from the narrative comes when Allen orders the commander of Fort Ticonderoga to surrender "in the name of the great Jehovah, and the Continental Congress." The Second Continental Congress would not even open its first meeting until several hours after Allen had taken the fort, yet his account of the fort's capture declares that the group he led struck a blow on behalf of a broadly defined American nation. Allen offers this assault as testament to the virtue of the men of Vermont, as they set aside local disputes to strike at a foreign enemy. By drawing attention to their willingness to align themselves with the other states, Allen casts the refusal to recognize Vermont as a member of the American confederation as a disregard for the loyalty its individual residents have already shown to the other states as a national political body. Through this depiction, Allen stresses the individual character of the residents of Vermont rather than their collective identity as a rogue frontier settlement.

As he establishes the virtuous character of the Green Mountain Boys, Allen also subtly asserts his own virtue as the leader of this brave force. Allen's self-depiction during the account of Ticonderoga's fall carefully balances his elevated status as commander of the Green Mountain Boys with respect to the republican character of this citizen militia. The clearest demonstration of this balance appears in the speech he claims to have given prior to the attack: "I now propose to advance before you, and, in person, conduct you through the wicket-gate; for we must this morning either quit our pretensions to valor, or possess ourselves of this fortress in a few minutes; and inasmuch as it is a desperate attempt, which none but the bravest of men do undertake, I do not urge it on any contrary to his will."[25]

As Daniel Williams has observed, giving a speech loud enough to be heard by eighty-three men while crouched below the walls of the enemy's fort would likely eliminate the element of surprise; thus, we can assume Allen's speech here functions more to inform his readers how to interpret his character than to record the accurate history of Ticonderoga's capture.[26] This depiction simultaneously emphasizes Allen's acceptance of an equal share in the dangers his men face and his status as their commander, who takes personal responsibility for their success. Furthermore, as he states that this attack must be a free choice for its participants, Allen reiterates the virtue of the men who chose to follow him into the British stronghold. These men are not the blind followers of a demagogue; they are loyal Americans striking a blow against foreign tyranny. Even as he celebrates the virtue of the Green Mountain Boys, Allen's wording clearly positions him at the head of this body of "the bravest of men," which suggests his own exceptional character as the most qualified and respected member of this noble group.

Within his narrative, Allen portrayed himself as a representative of the sovereign people of the United States, but competing accounts suggest that, outside the text, his claim to political authority rested solely on his position as the strongest man in the room. The two most significant alternative accounts come from Benedict Arnold, with whom Allen had been competing for command of the mission, and from Jocelyn Feltham, the British lieutenant to whom Allen made his famous demand for surrender. The accounts of these two men present Allen's attack on the fort as far more like a poorly planned rebellion by a local militia than the first offensive maneuver of a revolutionary nation.

For example, Allen's narrative makes no mention of Arnold even being present at the moment of the fort's surrender. In his report to General Thomas Gage, however, Feltham writes that he was confronted by both Allen and Arnold and that they informed him they held a joint command. Ethan Allen entered the fort at the head of the Green Mountain Boys and claimed to act on the directions of the Connecticut legislature. Benedict Arnold came to the assault with signed orders from the Massachusetts Committee of Safety, but he had been assigned to recruit men as he made his way toward the fort. In short, Allen had an army but no commission, while Arnold had a commission but no army. Omitting any mention of Arnold at this moment in the narrative suggests that Allen recognized that Arnold's competing claim to authority over the expedition would complicate the role he had written for himself as a representative of a united American people.

Both Feltham and Arnold depict Allen as more brutish insurgent than republican hero. In recounting the moment of capitulation, Feltham states that, while Arnold begged the fort's surrender "in a genteel manner," Allen demanded surrender with a sword drawn over Feltham's head and a promise to leave no man, woman, or child alive in the fort if the British offered any resistance.[27] Feltham makes no mention of an appeal to God and the Continental Congress, which is not to say that Allen didn't invoke those two institutions, but it does point to the significant difference in how Allen justifies the threat of his sword in his own account.

While we might expect a defeated British officer to take a negative view of Allen's behavior, the brutality of this threat to women and children finds support in Arnold's writing, as well. From Arnold's view, Allen and the Green Mountain Boys appear more like an angry mob than an army engaged in a justifiable war. In a letter to the Massachusetts Committee of Safety, Arnold writes that "Colonel Allen is a proper man to head his own wild people, but entirely unacquainted with military service," and he complains that "there is not the least regularity among the Troops, but every thing is governed by whim and caprice."[28] A further passage from this letter demonstrates the stark contrast between the character Allen cultivates in his narrative and Arnold's perception of him:

> I had agreed with Colonel Allen to issue further orders jointly, until I could raise a sufficient number of men to relieve his people; on

> which plan we proceeded when I wrote you yesterday, since which, Colonel Allen, finding he had the ascendancy over his people, positively insisted I should have no command, as I had forbid the soldiers plundering and destroying private property. The power is now taken out of my hands, and I am not consulted, nor have I a voice in any matters. There is here at present near one hundred men, who are in the greatest confusion and anarchy, destroying and plundering private property, committing every enormity, and paying no attention to publick service.[29]

Arnold's account erodes the claim to democratic sovereignty that Allen's narrative seeks to establish, by depicting the Green Mountain Boys as representatives of an angry multitude rather than a united people. Allen and his men are seen pursuing self-interest as they loot and plunder the fort, and, in Arnold's opinion, this disregard for public service disqualifies their actions as a legitimate expression of violence. Admittedly, neither Arnold nor Feltham can be trusted to provide a substantially more reliable account of the capture of Ticonderoga than Allen. However, their agreement that Allen's authority stemmed almost entirely from his advantage in military power underscores how Allen carefully arranged his account of the event to present his violence as carried out in the name of an American people whom he represents.

By writing himself into the role of the people's representative, Allen legitimated his claim to act as a revolutionary, not a rebel. Allen's narrative defines popular sovereignty as a performative act. This claim—that written discourse creates the sovereign body politic that it purports merely to describe—is not a new one in early American studies, with Michael Warner's hugely influential *Letters of the Republic* standing as a prominent example.[30] What makes Allen's narrative, and the larger genre of the veteran narrative it exemplifies, unique in regards to this claim is the relationship between violence and narration that these texts describe. Allen's narrative establishes a myth of origins by joining an act of violent self-assertion to an invocation of a continental body politic.

In the lectures that would be published as *The Beast and the Sovereign*, Derrida asserts that sovereignty functions as an act of narration that binds language and physical force into a cohesive power.[31] This relationship between narrative and violence appears most clearly in his discussion of the fable. Through its depiction of an anthropomorphized, nonhuman world, the fable presents its moral lessons as grounded in natural, presocietal principles. Derrida deconstructs such claims to illustrate the degree to which fables reflect natural truths that accord with what he calls "the reason of the strongest":

> The essence of political force and power, where that power makes the law, where it gives itself right, where it appropriates legitimate violence and legitimates its own arbitrary violence—this unchaining and enchaining of power passes via the fable, i.e., speech that is both fictional and performative, speech that consists in saying: well, I'm right because yes, I'm right . . . I am the most valiant and I'll strangle you if you object.[32]

In other words, the fable naturalizes the maxim of "might makes right." While his narrative lacks the talking animals that often characterize the fable, Allen's embellished depiction of his capture of Ticonderoga certainly classifies as "speech that is both fictional and performative." Only the words he claims to have said before raising his sword distinguish this act as an expression of the commonweal rather than a self-serving act of rebellion. As comparison with the accounts of Feltham and Arnold indicates, Allen's appeal to popular sovereignty in the narrative stands in contrast to his reliance on force and intimidation at the moment of the fort's surrender.

Framing this force as a fable of the nation's birth means that even if "the people" who could legitimate Allen's violence did not exist at the time of Ticonderoga, they would come into existence through reading his narrative and recognizing him as their patriotic representative. Trish Loughran has challenged the effectiveness of Benedict Anderson's well-known concept of imagined communities, the sense of national connection created through a shared print culture, for describing an early US society that lacked the infrastructure to distribute literature of any kind across the wide continent.[33] Loughran argues that writers like

Tom Paine instead spun fantasies of a continental readership to promote a Patriot cause that was far from universally accepted across the thirteen colonies.

We should read Allen's idea of audience through a similar lens. Allen creates a fantasy of representing the American people when he took Ticonderoga, when he endured captivity among the British, and when future readers encounter his example in print. Jason Frank has written that all claims to represent the American people rely on an "unrealized futurity"—a sense that "the people" always describes a broader collective than any specific temporal or empirical measure can delimit.[34] Allen's narrative orients itself toward such a sense of futurity in subtle ways.

Within his preface, Allen contextualizes his decision to write in the following terms: "Some men are appointed to office, in these States, who read the history of the cruelties of this war with the same careless indifferency, as they do the pages of the Roman history."[35] Given that Allen will inform his readers, in the first pages of the narrative proper, that reading history inflamed his "sincere passion for liberty," this passage in the preface contrasts ineffective and/or Loyalist political leaders who carelessly ignore historical precedent with a thoughtful student of history such as Allen. His contemporary history of British tyranny can play the same instructive role for Allen's audience that Roman history has played for him. Similarly, at the narrative's conclusion, Allen writes of being greeted, upon his return to Bennington, with a fourteen-gun salute, "thirteen for the United States, and one for young Vermont," and he recalls how he and his neighbors toasted "the rising states of America" in celebration.[36] At the beginning and end of the narrative, therefore, we see Allen positioning himself as part of the story of a nation that encompasses the continent. Both references imply a future in which the people of the United States recognize themselves as a common body politic joined by a shared history and shared patriotic heroes.

Throughout the narrative, Allen cultivates just such a heroic image. He frequently describes his attitude in captivity in terms that imply a concern not for his own well-being but for how his example reflects on the country at large. In the most striking example, after he had written a letter he hoped would be delivered to Lord North, complaining about his treatment, Allen describes his behavior as follows: "I nevertheless treated them [his captors] with scorn and contempt; and having sent my letter to the ministry, could conceive of nothing more in my power but to keep up my spirits, behave in a daring soldier-like manner, that I might exhibit a good sample of American fortitude."[37] By claiming to stand as a representative of the character of the continent, not just of Vermont, Allen helps to make it possible to imagine the American states as a unified nation.

As the narrative continues, it draws on the generic conventions of the Indian captivity narrative to further illustrate Allen's heroic character through a demonstration of his perseverance in the midst of his savage captors. During his captivity, Allen endures physical and verbal harassment from Indians, British officers, and Tories and finds himself kept in unsanitary cells, with little regard given to his basic needs, such as food and water. Allen presents these hardships as a test of his faith, yet he defines this faith not in the workings of providence but in loyalty to the American cause. This trial reaches its culmination near the end of the narrative, when an unnamed British officer offers Allen a commission as a colonel in a regiment of Loyalists, along with a large tract of land in either the New Hampshire Grants or Connecticut. Ironically enough, this officer tells Allen that his faithfulness to the American cause during his captivity has recommended him to General Howe; Allen replies that he should hate to lose the general's good opinion by accepting the offer.[38] Allen compares this offer to the temptation of Christ in the wilderness.

If this comparison seems slightly unexpected, coming from an author who would soon publish the deist tract *Reason: The Only Oracle of Man,* it should also remind us of the ease with which a purported republican like Allen could draw on the metaphors of sovereign transcendence. As a monarch could stand in for the absolute sovereignty of God, Allen stands in for the popular sovereignty of the American people. In this way, his ideal of representative leadership fits within the discursive frame of colonial federalism. By depicting himself as an illustration of an ethos that spans the continent, Allen not only models a more centralized form of representation, in which one person stands on behalf of a large and diverse body of constituents, but also conceives of representation as embodying a particular set of values rather than a concrete and specific set of local interests or demands.

This attention to the outstanding character of a representative will likely appear familiar to students of the early republic, as it anticipates the mode of representation advanced in one of the seminal texts of American politics, *Federalist 10*, where James Madison famously argues for the value of a large republic, led by enlightened representatives drawn from across the continent, as the best protection against the dangers of self-interested factions. Madison conceived of national representatives as an elite class capable of making the best decisions for the nation precisely because they could govern based on their own rectitude rather than on the demands of their constituents. He writes of "representatives whose enlightened views and virtuous sentiments render them superior to local prejudices and schemes of injustice."[39]

Eric Slauter has analyzed how such Federalist ideas drew on a metaphor of representation as shorthand transcription, through which the representative seeks not to capture the exact interests or precise demands of his constituents but instead uses his expertise to "transcribe" an accurate synthesis of the general will. Slauter's analysis reveals how Madison reversed the notion that representatives expressed the views of the people to assert, instead, that "the people" were expressed by their representative.[40] Suzette Hemberger has suggested a similar point, as she argues that the Federalist perspective made the national assembly the only place where the "body of the people" could actually come into existence, as the federal legislature would be the only representative body that could claim to act on behalf of the American people as a whole.[41] From this perspective, the people's representatives in the federal government become a central means of imagining a commonality among the far-flung residents of the American states, from places like the Green Mountains or the Berkshires to places like Albany and Boston.

Allen was by no means a part of the Federalist elite, nor was he always committed to American nationalism. After all, this is a man whom George Washington once speculated might need to be kidnapped to stop his flirtation with returning Vermont to the British during the Revolutionary War's later years.[42] Allen's primary goal throughout the conflict remained the establishment of an independent Vermont, and he considered an assertion of common values and virtues among American colonists as the surest means of demonstrating Vermont's fitness for membership in the new republic, a strategy reflected in the writings he continued to publish, arguing for the region's recognition as a state.[43] Yet, by presenting himself throughout his narrative as primarily an exemplar of a broadly American character, Allen also was able to separate his public persona from association solely with Vermont and to create a self-image that could exemplify the heroic revolutionary struggling on behalf of American liberty.

Ethan Allen and the Green Mountain Boys succeeded in attaching their cause to a continental sense of nationality. Daniel Shays, on the other hand, was frequently cast as an apostate of the American Revolution. Shays had fought for American liberty against Great Britain as an officer in the Continental Army, yet his detractors accused him of renouncing the principles of that service by placing personal interests above those of a freely elected government. A popular anecdote of the time condemned Shays's decision to sell a sword given to him by the Marquis de Lafayette as the act of a man who failed to appreciate "this precious symbol of his patriotism."[44] Like his rumored connection to Vermont, such stories demonstrate how Shays's name and reputation became a powerful ideological symbol throughout the early republic. Many upper-class Americans viewed Shays as an indication of the tenuous grasp the new states held on independence, with several writers even suggesting that the uprising in Massachusetts was the result of British subterfuge. As the protests in Massachusetts drew toward a critical point, Henry Lee suggested in a letter to Washington that the insurgents not only were forming connections with the "Vermontese" but also "contemplate a re-union with G. Britain."[45] Washington would take a less sensational view but still entertained the possibility of a secret conspiracy at the heart of the protests, writing to Henry Knox in February 1787 that "Shays must be either a weak man, the dupe of some characters who are yet behind the curtain, or has been deceived by his followers. Or which may be more likely, he did not conceive that there was energy enough in the Government to bring matters to the crisis to which they have been pushed."[46]

Washington appears to hold a dual perspective on Shays in this statement: either he is an impotent leader, the puppet of hidden conspirators or a corrupt mob, or he is an inept leader who could not effectively evaluate the strength of his opponent. Either viewpoint suggests Washington's underlying assumption that the protests represented a crisis in American sovereignty. The nation needed stronger, centralized leadership by elite individuals to prevent unqualified individuals from grasping power in the people's name. In an earlier letter to James Madison, regarding the turmoil in Massachusetts, Washington wondered, "What stronger evidence can be given of the want of energy in our governments than these disorders?"[47]

Imagining the tumult in Massachusetts as a problem of leadership indicates the tendency to place Shays at the head of the protests; whether Shays is a dupe or a dope, Washington frames him as the responsible party to whom the disturbances can be traced, the leader who has set his followers on a path to ruin. Placing Shays at the head of the protests introduced a specific tangibility and a distinct temporality to these events by establishing an individual as the responsible party. Upon the arrest (or execution) of this individual, the disturbance would come to an end and order could be restored.

Assertions of Shays's leadership over the protesters exemplified the threat of ambitious men using popular fervor to gain tyrannical power within the new republic. A letter to the *Massachusetts Centinel* in January 1787 presented the record of a purported interview with Shays, made by an unnamed source, and the writer offers a damning portrait of Shays as a ruthless incendiary and instigator. Shays reportedly claimed authority over ten thousand men, along with sympathizers in Connecticut, New Hampshire, and Vermont, and vowed to crush Lincoln's army before marching to Boston, which he planned to set ablaze in order to "destroy the nest of devils, who by their influence, make the Court enact what laws they please." When his interviewer asked what government Shays would establish as a replacement, he replied that "he knew no more what government to set up than he knew the dimensions of eternity."

Much like Washington's perception of Shays as an unqualified leader, this writer depicts the insurgent commander as a man wielding a power that he cannot control. This Shays has no goals other than to destroy the elected government. A bit of doggerel from the time, made in the voice of Shays, summarizes this image nicely: "In hell 'twas planned by obscure hand / All laws should fall before me, / Though in disgrace the populace / Like Persia did adore me."[48]

Just as Allen had looked to Roman history at the start of the war with Great Britain, many of Shays's detractors sought Roman analogues for the crisis. For instance, a January 1787 speech from a pro-government clergyman compares the social unrest in Massachusetts with the conditions that favored Catiline and Caesar, both of whom rose to power by appealing to the interests of the poorer classes.[49] Infamous among upper-class Americans as examples of demagoguery, Caesar and Catiline each had led armies loyal to them against Rome, just as Shays had been rumored to be building an army with which to assault Boston.[50]

Like Catiline, Shays ultimately became associated with a failed revolt, but as Eran Shalev has noted, elite Americans recognized that Catiline's failure cleared the way for Caesar's success, and the example of Shays implied the ease with which a more adroit leader could grasp power.[51] Alexander Hamilton would argue as much in *Federalist 21,* where he asks of Massachusetts, "Who can determine what might have been the issue of her late convulsions, if the malcontents had been headed by a Caesar or by a Cromwell?"[52]

Such efforts to frame Shays as an American version of some of history's most infamous demagogues point toward the broader anxiety elite American men felt about the protests in Massachusetts. Shays's Rebellion came to symbolize a potential democratic madness, in which the prosperous few would be vulnerable to demands for economic equality from the many. The focus on Shays as a backcountry Catiline encouraged the view of the Massachusetts uprising as a radical attack on liberty, property, and prosperity. Descriptions of the causes of the protests by many upper-class Americans revealed anxieties over both political tyranny and economic leveling.

In an October 1786 letter to Washington, Henry Knox declared the insurgents "determined to annihilate all debts public and private, and have agrarian laws, which are easily effected by the means of unfunded paper money."[53] Madison would share similar concerns with his father, in November 1786, writing that although the protesters "profess to aim only at a reform of their Consti[tu]tion and of certain abuses in the public administration, . . . an abolition of debts public and private, and a new division of property are strongly suspected to be in contemplation."[54] In the first contemporary history of Shays's Rebellion, George Richards Minot would write that the objective of the insurrection had been "to annihilate the present happy constitution, or force the General Court into measures repugnant to every idea of justice, good faith, and national policy."[55] Minot comments that any success on the part of the insurgents would be "destructive of civil liberty," as it would be a triumph of force over moral principle. In the midst of such fears, imagining Daniel Shays as the demagogic leader of the uprising allowed demands for greater political influence to be bracketed as the irrational and incoherent cries of a mob that had sacrificed individual autonomy to the will of a corrupt rebel. This mob could then be distinguished as an interested faction apart from the true body of loyal citizens in the state.

Yet, as many scholars have observed, the effort to cast the protesters as desperate men driven by a leveling impulse distorted the strong link these men felt between their own liberty and their property. As Knox's reference to "agrarian laws" indicates, the aggrieved men of Massachusetts, like other backcountry protesters across the American frontier, sought government policies that would protect what they saw as the source of their liberty: freehold family farms. Far from seeking the abolition of private property, these men hoped to achieve greater security for their own property by demanding that their governments protect them from the violence of Indian raids and frontier outlaws, from the burden of heavy taxes and debts, and from the economic domination of wealthy land speculators. As Alan Taylor argues, backcountry protesters did not desire a complete overhaul of the existing social structure, but they also did not accept economic inequality as a natural state and they believed their government should prevent such inequality.[56]

Close attention to the few writings Daniel Shays produced illustrates his conception of the protesters as republican citizens who have come together merely to seek "constitutional relief" from their government. However, the insistence on local priorities within these writings would be cast by Shays's opponents as indicative of his rebellion against the government, which they took to be the true representatives of the "body of the people."

Shays wrote two letters to Benjamin Lincoln, in late January 1787, after the failed attack on the Springfield arsenal, both of which were reprinted in the conservative *Worcester Magazine* as "Authentick Insurgent Papers." In both letters, Shays presents the protesters as unwilling to continue the violence and desirous of a cease-fire with Lincoln's army while they await a settlement with the state government.[57] These letters provide crucial insight into how Shays understood both the movement in which he was participating and his leadership role within it. In these texts, Shays justifies his actions as being taken on behalf of the body of the people.

For example, he opens one letter, dated January 30, in the voice of "the people assembled in arms from the counties of Middlesex, Worcester, Hampshire, and Berkshire." Shays claims that the people have taken up arms out of "that virtue which truly characterizes the citizens of a republican government," and this claim implies his belief that the people have a right to use political violence against an elected government when that government fails to respond to other means of persuasion, just as such violence was used against the British Crown. In a recruiting letter signed by Shays and others that was published alongside his letters to Lincoln, the author warns that the government seeks "to crush the power of the people at one broad stroke and render them incapable of ever opposing the cruel power, Tyranny, hereafter."

As this statement demonstrates, Shays accepts the idea of a factional divide between the government and the people gathered in protest, a point he also recognizes in his letters to Lincoln. In the first letter, dated January 25, he requests that "all troops on the part of the government be disbanded immediately," and in the second letter, dated January 30, he asks that "each army occupy the posts where they now are." In acknowledging this divide, Shays implies a belief that the people retain the power to act politically, apart from the government.

Formisano notes that this belief was a major source of contention between Federalists and Anti-Federalists during the Constitutional Convention, as the opponents of stronger national government hoped to limit the consolidation of governmental power through a bill of rights or through efforts to preserve the sovereignty of the states.[58] Although both sides held that sovereignty emerged from the consent of the governed, Federalists held that the people expressed this sovereignty indirectly, through their elected representatives. Shays's belief that the protests and the assault on the arsenal were a virtuous expression of republican citizenship, by contrast, holds to a model of more direct democracy.

Furthermore, Shays considered himself only the speaker for the people, not their commander. Throughout both letters, his use of first-person pronouns is exclusively plural. Shays does not seek to appear as a representative of the people but rather as the recorder of a collective voice. Yet, where Shays intended to present a chorus, Lincoln heard only a single actor. The general's response to Shays's missives indicates the need to position Shays as the responsible party at the head of a rebellion. Through a direct address written in the second person, Lincoln notifies Shays that he will be accountable for any subsequent violence: "You cannot hesitate a moment to disband your deluded followers; if you should not, I must approach and apprehend the most influential characters among you." Lincoln not only makes Shays answerable for the lives of his associates; he also confidently asserts his own singular authority as a military commander.

This exchange between Shays and Lincoln provides a microcosm of the struggle to balance popular sovereignty with political representation in the early republic. Shays's writings also indicate the very condition that made him such a popular symbol for his detractors. By rejecting the role of representative, Shays became available to the rhetoric of his opponents, as the lack of reliable information about him left a blank screen upon which the image of an anarchist rebel could be projected. Unlike Ethan Allen, Shays never published a personal narrative or other writings to justify his actions, so he lacked a space in which to influence public perception of his career.

As Shays's limited writings suggest, he conceived of his role as that of a spokesperson for the collective opinions of the residents of western Massachusetts. Shays and his comrades demanded a representative mode in which delegates would remain faithful to the instructions of their constituents. Yet, for Federalists, Shays would become the dominant example of how representatives could be corrupted by the demands of self-interested factions—unless they possessed an outstanding personal character. In lieu of delegates bound to their communities, Federalists sought representatives who could act as trustees for their constituents but would be beholden only to their own judgment as they made political decisions.

Ethan Allen's narrative, with its portrayal of a heroic individual enduring hardship on behalf of the nation, presented a cultural model of such a form of representation. The narrative also offered an example of a nationally representative figure from the backcountry, rather than from the eastern cities and southern estates that had produced so many members of the early nation's leadership. In this way, Allen's narrative depicted an exceptional man drawn from the ranks of ordinary Americans and thus participated in the creation of a meritocratic ideal that would encourage the transfer of political agency from communities to individuals. The development of such an ideal would make Daniel Shays representative in a manner he never anticipated.

2

Hugh Henry Brackenridge, the Crawford Expedition, and an Ideal National Army

IN 1782, WHILE THE Revolutionary War was largely concluded on the Eastern seaboard, the conflict on the western frontier grew in intensity as the struggle shifted to one between hostile neighbors: the American settlers of the broad Ohio Valley against a mixture of Loyalists, British soldiers, and multiple indigenous nations, particularly the Shawnee, Wyandot, and Miami. The American side would suffer one of its most infamous defeats, in June of that year, when a militia expedition led by William Crawford, a colonel in the Continental Army and a longtime acquaintance of George Washington, was routed by a mixed body of Indians and Loyalists. Planned as a surprise offensive against the Wyandot towns near present-day Sandusky, Ohio, the expedition's slow progress allowed the Indians ample time to organize an effective ambush, and the American militia was put to a disorganized and hasty retreat after two days of fighting. Crawford himself was captured and burned at the stake after being beaten and tortured for several hours.

Accounts of the failed expedition quickly made their way eastward, but the most prominent version of these events would not appear until the next year, when Hugh Henry Brackenridge published the narratives of Dr. John Knight and John Slover, the surgeon and a scout from the expedition, respectively, who had been taken prisoner and then managed to escape execution. These narratives were serialized in the Philadelphia newspaper the *Freeman's Journal* and would be reprinted as a pamphlet soon after.[1] In a letter to publisher Francis Bailey, Brackenridge claims that he recorded the oral narrative of Slover, while

Dr. Knight gave his account in his own hand. Brackenridge published the narratives together with his own brief memoir of Crawford and an appendix arguing against Indian land claims in North America.

Given Brackenridge's heavy involvement in the production of these narratives, the individuality and authenticity of Knight's and Slover's accounts is nearly impossible to ascertain.[2] The line between editor and authors has blurred into obscurity. Knight, Slover, and the deceased Crawford become appropriated within Brackenridge's nationalist rhetoric. I read these narratives of the Crawford expedition as part of a single text, prepared by Brackenridge, that suggests how the figure of the suffering Revolutionary soldier could be deployed to distinguish violence committed *in the name of* the people from violence committed *by* the people.

In the appendix to the narratives, Brackenridge lays out a vision of American expansion into indigenous territory, which he justifies by asserting the lack of civilization among the Indians—a condition evinced in large part by what he describes as the inhuman manner in which they fought their wars. Yet, to Brackenridge, the raids on Indian towns by small militias of white settlers were essentially indistinguishable from such inhumanity and thus undermined the development of an orderly society on the frontier.

In particular, he was critical of the killing of ninety-six Delaware converts to Christianity, including women and children, during a Pennsylvania militia raid on Gnadenhutten, a settlement established by Moravian missionaries in the Ohio territory. This venture was widely condemned as a massacre, but it also initiated calls for a more organized military operation into Ohio to prevent Indian raids in reprisal—calls that were answered in the form of the Crawford expedition. Popular opinion at the time suggested that Crawford's torture and execution were retaliation for the murder of the Gnadenhutten settlers, framing the two events as part of a cycle of violence on the frontier. For Brackenridge, this cycle emerged in part from the reluctance of citizens to subordinate their will to violence into a broader conception of national identity that would stretch beyond their immediate frontier setting.

The Crawford narratives remain a largely overlooked area of Brackenridge's oeuvre, but these texts grapple with a persistent concern in his writing after his move to the frontier: the problem of separating popular sovereignty from popular violence. Brackenridge most famously dealt with this question in the 1790s, when he became involved in the protests over the federal excise tax on distilled spirts that we know as the Whiskey Rebellion. He published an account of his involvement, *Incidents of the Insurrection in the Western Parts of Pennsylvania, in the Year 1794,* and throughout that work, Brackenridge worries that the most immediate method for many citizens to express sovereign power would remain participation in moments of political violence. *Incidents of the Insurrection* suggests that, both for the protesters and for the federal militia eventually sent to suppress them, violence or the threat of violence established a feeling of empowered participation within the body politic.

This line of thinking can be traced back to the Crawford narratives and its response to the frontier violence between indigenous groups and settler militias at the Revolutionary War's end. As he would ten years later, in *Incidents of the Insurrection* Brackenridge sought to encourage the expression of sovereignty through discourse rather than force. Like Ethan Allen's narrative, the Crawford narratives engage an ideal of military heroism, yet whereas Allen aims to inspire with his example, Brackenridge uses the failed Crawford expedition to issue a warning to the ordinary American: leave warfare to the professionals.

By placing the Crawford expedition in context with the Gnadenhutten massacre, Brackenridge evokes the reciprocal violence on the frontier to suggest the need for an authority from outside the region to bring that violence to an end. The narratives of Knight and Slover work as ideal vessels for conveying this need and for imagining the body that could meet it. Like the Allen narrative, these texts present their protagonists, as well as the Crawford himself, as having suffered patiently on behalf of the American cause. Also like the Allen narrative, Brackenridge transforms the unsuccessful war experiences of his subjects into a patriotic ideal for his reading audience. Crawford's failed expedition led to his death, and Knight and Slover were nearly executed themselves, but as representative symbols of a Revolutionary army, their sacrifices take on greater meaning. The hardships of Knight and Slover at the hands of uncivilized Indian captors and corrupt Loyalists set them as examples of an American identity that crosses geographic lines to imagine a common people united by principles.

Within the Crawford narratives, Brackenridge tries to discover a means to describe an American people that goes beyond the racial opposition of the backcountry. Although he accepts the racist rhetoric of Indian-hating, he also recognizes how this rhetoric destabilizes frontier settlements. Such rhetoric perpetuates an underlying conflict between local demands for sovereignty and the development of a stronger continental political culture. Through the figure of the Revolutionary martyr, Brackenridge aimed to inspire a nationalism that would encourage the individual to recognize himself within a community bound by shared values and ideas rather than by its physical strength. Brackenridge recognized a community fused into a multitude that he hoped to reorganize as part of a larger people. In these efforts, his writing searches for a conception of sovereignty distinct from violent demands for autonomy and security.

The Crawford narratives reveal how Brackenridge sought to encourage a culture of national military heroes that would provide a stable model of political violence in the early United States. The written propagation of examples like those of Knight, Slover, and Crawford, who could be depicted as representatives of a continental nation, established a popular narrative of the national government as the legitimate heir to the sovereign violence of the Revolutionary moment and drew emphasis away from local militia expressions of force. As Brackenridge's account of the Whiskey Rebellion suggests, however, this model of violence carried strong implications for how the sovereignty of the people and their role as citizens would be understood. Over the course of this chapter, I will trace Brackenridge's thoughts on popular political violence, from the end of the Revolutionary War to the Whiskey Rebellion, as a means of analyzing how the figure of the Revolutionary soldier, particularly the Continental Army soldier, became a cultural trope that could resolve the inherent tension between the license of a sovereign and the restraint of a citizen, in terms of access to force.

Through the Crawford narratives, Brackenridge sought to reduce the chaotic frontier violence of 1782 to the stark and simple terms of a clash between civilization and savagery. These texts depict the Indians of the region as the primary aggressors in that conflict, with Brackenridge offering graphic examples of the torture and abuse experienced by Crawford, Knight, and Slover. While he acknowledges that white settlers also participated in the violence, Brackenridge asserts that the Indian possessed an inherently murderous and vicious character that made peaceful coexistence impossible. In his appendix to the narratives, he maintains that the best outcome after the war with the British would be to drive the Indian nations as far west as possible, with the eventual goal of abolishing them through extinction.[3]

Brackenridge's racism should by now be familiar to most readers. Christopher Looby has referred to Brackenridge's "genocidal wish" toward Native Americans, and Lynn Haims has remarked that "Brackenridge's mistrust and contempt for Indians were hardly a secret" even in the author's own time.[4] As I will demonstrate, however, attention to Brackenridge's racism should also account for his concern about the populist rage and frustration among many white settlers in the region. A review of the correspondence among some of the Continental Army officers stationed in the backcountry during this time reveals that extreme violence was by no means restricted to only one side of the conflict. These officers recognized the will of an angry multitude in acts like the Gnadenhutten massacre, and they worried that such anger could overwhelm efforts to administer the region from afar. Such concerns proved valid, as proposals for new states and independent governments circulated among the region's settlers.

Within this tense atmosphere, Brackenridge published the story of a martyr to the American cause. The death of a virtuous soldier had featured prominently in some of Brackenridge's earliest writing about the Revolutionary War, the plays *The Battle of Bunker's Hill* (1776) and *The Death of General Montgomery in Storming the City of Quebec* (1777).[5] In these plays, Brackenridge offers the Revolutionary martyr as a unifying symbol. Such a symbol would ideally provide an additional form of affiliation for frontier settlers, which would channel the energy of racial resentment into an expanded sense of nationality. For Brackenridge, the Revolutionary martyr hopefully would dilute populist anger into a broader stream of continental nationalism.

Knight's narrative offers a detailed account of the virtuous suffering of Crawford, while also advancing Brackenridge's anti-Indian sentiment. Knight vividly describes the torture of Crawford, which included being beaten with sticks, burned with hot coals, blasted with gunpowder, and having his ears cut off. Crawford was then burned at the stake, and Knight was promised the same treatment but managed to escape while being escorted to another town for execution. Slover testifies to witnessing similar treatment of other captives and recalls his own near-death experience, when only a sudden rainstorm prevented him from being burned at the stake.

In addition to their memories of torture and execution, both Knight and Slover observe grisly violence being carried out not just by Indian warriors but also by women and children. Slover recalls seeing all the inhabitants of the town where he was held beating a naked captive who was being forced to run the gauntlet, and Knight remembers seeing an older Indian woman decapitate a prisoner, whose head was then kicked around on the ground by young boys. During the account of Crawford's execution, Knight describes "an old squaw (whose appearance every way answered the ideas people entertain of the Devil)" dumping a load of hot coals and ash on Crawford's back and head, near the end of his torture.[6] Along with these scenes, both Knight and Slover recall the dismemberment of the corpses of prisoners and the public display of body parts and scalps within the Indian towns. Both accounts imply that the Indians conducted warfare as part of communal life, with women and children participating in the violence alongside the warriors.

Cultivating this impression supports Brackenridge's larger effort to depict the Indian as unfit for civilization. For Brackenridge, the abuse of these prisoners is bad enough, but the shock of such behavior is compounded by the participation of those who should be the most virtuous members of society. Such behavior becomes the basis for Brackenridge's claim of Indian savagery and inhumanity. He writes, near the end of his appendix to the narratives, that Indians "have the shapes of men and may be of the human species, but certainly in their present state they approach nearer the character of Devils" and that the "tortures which they exercise on the bodies of their prisoners, justify extirmination [*sic*]."[7]

In 1970, Daniel Marder sought to explain Brackenridge's racism as he claimed that the author's "hatred of the red man is not racial; it is self-defense."[8] Most scholars today would likely recognize the false binary within this assessment. Rather than an either/or explanation, Brackenridge's desire for security in a setting where violence remained ever present was intertwined with his perception of the Indian as a dangerous racial Other. He felt a need for self-defense because he accepted an ideal of racialized savagery. He writes in the appendix that "these nations are so degenerate from the life of man, so devoid of every sentiment of generosity, so prone to every vicious excess of passion, so faithless, and so incapable of all civilization, that it is dangerous to the good order of the world that they should exist in it."[9] Though Brackenridge would criticize the event, his racist rhetoric clearly comes from the same ideology that would justify the genocidal violence on display at Gnadenhutten.

Brackenridge was among those who condemned the killing of women and children in the Moravian attack, which he describes, in a footnote to Slover's narrative, as "unjustifiable inexcusable homicide."[10] As his slightly legalistic phrasing here suggests, though, his objections to the massacre emerge more from political than from moral grounds. He appears to have felt little or no qualms over the deaths of native people, even if they were converts to Christianity. Brackenridge portrays the Indians as a constant threat to the security of frontier settlements, and in the preface he attached to the narratives, he declares that "the nature of an Indian is fierce and cruel, and . . . an extirpation of them would be useful to the world, and honourable to those who can effect it."[11] It's this question of "who can effect it" that leads Brackenridge to disapprove of the attack on the Moravian settlements. He rejected the vigilantism underlying the Moravian attack, even as he shared the racist ideology of its perpetrators.

The Gnadenhutten massacre became infamous as a result of the brutality shown to an otherwise nonthreatening set of victims. Gnadenhutten had been established ten years earlier, in 1772, as a Moravian settlement of German missionaries and Delaware converts, on the banks of a tributary of the Muskingum River. In late 1781, British-allied Wyandot warriors forcibly relocated the residents of Gnadenhutten to a new village along the Sandusky River to prevent the Christian Indians from providing aid to the United States. In February 1782, with food running low in the new village, around one hundred of the Gnadenhutten residents returned to their old village to salvage the remains of their unharvested crops. It was while they were in the midst of gathering these crops that the militia arrived.

A force of around 160 volunteers, led by David Williamson, had set out from western Pennsylvania to investigate claims that the Moravian settlement had been providing material support to Wyandot and Shawnee raiders attacking white settlers. The primary accounts of what transpired once the militia arrived come from the diaries and histories produced by the Moravian missionaries John Heckewelder and David Zeisberger, along with their presiding bishop, George Henry Loskiel.[12] Based largely on the testimony of two boys who managed to survive the attack, these accounts assert that the militia approached the village in friendship, promising to assist the residents who had suffered for their perceived loyalty to the United States. These professions of kindness proved to be a pretense, however, with the militia ultimately deciding to execute ninety-six unarmed men, women, and children. The victims were separated by gender, led into separate buildings, called "slaughter-houses" by the militia, and then killed with a blow to the head from a cooper's mallet.[13]

Brackenridge's concern about the Gnadenhutten massacre stemmed from the ability of an American militia to commit extreme acts of violence with no imprimatur save its own will. This event represented not only an expression of racial antagonism against Indians but also a rebuke to the authority of the continental government to provide security on the frontier. The settlers who assembled in this militia wanted the Continental garrison at Fort Pitt to provide a more aggressive response to the local Indians, including those who had converted to Christianity, whom the militia believed were supplying the raiding parties of more hostile Indians.

Much like the residents of western Massachusetts who would follow Daniel Shays, many people in western Pennsylvania and Virginia felt themselves alienated from more elite, urban interests in the East. They felt particularly aggrieved over the lack of attention the continental administration seemed to pay to securing the lives and property of citizens on the frontier. Ed White has described white settler life on the northwestern colonial frontier as marked by an anxiety produced by the reality of disconnected settlements and the perception that the Indians of the region lived in cohesive societies that could easily overpower them.

In response to this anxiety, White argues, residents of the backcountry imagined themselves fused together by resistance to perceived threats from both the Indians to the west and the urban elites to the east. He cites as a classic example the Paxton Boys—the pre-Revolutionary Pennsylvania vigilantes who attacked their Indian neighbors and then threatened to attack the colonial government in Philadelphia when their actions were censured. White describes this fusion as part of a drive toward nationalism that arises not from the imagined identification with a community of readers, famously described by Benedict Anderson, but from the shared perception among frontier residents, both white and Indian, that they were engaged in an existential struggle against the members of the opposite group. The identification as a nation—the identification as a cultural, political, and military collective—emerges as a strategy of self-preservation against an Other that is imagined to already be fused into a coherent group.[14]

White's analysis makes clear the imbrication of racism and self-defense in Brackenridge's view of Native Americans. As the example of the Paxton Boys indicates, however, such identification also posed the fused groups of the frontier in opposition to the urban centers, positing a locally defined sovereignty against the legal authority of administrators in the east. The fused nationalism of the backcountry claims sovereign authority through an aggregation of individual demands for security. It does not strive for the representative consensus associated with "the people."

Such an ideology thus challenged attempts by urban elites in the East, who sought to manage the resources of the frontier efficiently by claiming representative authority over the region. For many frontier settlers, the Continental Army embodied the will of such elites. Assessments of the Gnadenhutten massacre by historians Rob Harper and Leonard Sadosky have elucidated this context, in which frontier populism chafed against continental administration. Sadosky argues that the 1781 removal of Daniel Brodhead from command at Fort Pitt developed from local perceptions that the patrician Brodhead, with his diplomatic treatment of the Delawares in the region as allies against British-allied tribes, was utterly unfamiliar with the situation faced by Pennsylvania farmers, who saw all Indians as potential threats.[15]

Harper asserts that General William Irvine, the commander of the Western Department of the Continental Army at the time of the massacre, never brought its perpetrators to any punishment out of hesitation to lose the support of the local populace.[16] Reporting on the massacre in an April 1782 letter to George Washington, Irvine presents the region as having collectively fallen into anarchy, writing that "things were in greater confusion than can well be conceived. The country people were, to all appearance, in a fit of frenzy."[17] Instead of punishing or even simply censuring the militia, however, Irvine sought to understand their motivations. In a letter to his wife, Ann, shortly after the massacre, Irvine attempted to come to terms with the fears that drove locals to such brutality: "People who have had fathers, mothers, brothers or children, butchered, tortured, scalped, by the savages, reason very differently on the subject of killing the Moravians [that is, the Moravian Indians], to what people who live in the interior part of the country in perfect safety do. Their feelings are very different."[18]

In the same letter, Irvine would go on to request that Ann make no comment whatsoever regarding the massacre, since her opinions might be taken to reflect his, and at the moment of writing, he was striving to keep his thoughts on the massacre concealed.[19] Irvine's strict neutrality on the massacre illustrates the tense political climate within the region during early 1782 and speaks to the challenge he faced—to maintain order in the region while also encouraging the perception of the Continental Army as representatives of the people and not as a professional force disconnected from the concerns of ordinary settlers.

Irvine's correspondence from the months around the Gnadenhutten massacre and the Sandusky expedition reveals how these events were part of a larger struggle over subordinating the interests of backcountry nationalism within a continental sense of nationality. Irvine not only faced the challenge of maintaining the loyalty of the local farmers and settlers he was tasked to defend; he also had to worry about the discipline of his own soldiers. In the months before the Gnadenhutten attack, Irvine and Washington discussed the possibility of a Continental attack on the British at Detroit, yet both agreed that Irvine's garrison at Fort Pitt was, for many reasons, insufficient for such an attack, with the attitude of the troops being a central one. Irvine warned Washington, in a letter of February 1782, that the soldiers at Fort Pitt were too disordered and disgruntled to even maintain their own fort. Within this assessment, one comment in particular reminds us that the Continental soldiers also were likely swayed by the currents of populism within the region: Irvine laments to Washington that the troops have been stationed in one place for too long and, as a result, "they have formed such connections as make them tenacious of the rights of citizens, while they at the same time retain all the vices common to a soldiery."[20] Two months later, in his report to Washington, Irvine would observe that the Gnadenhutten massacre had "added to the then mutinous disposition of the regular troops, had nearly brought on the loss of this whole country."[21]

This last statement was no mere flourish of hyperbole, either. In the same letter, Irvine warns that "new states are much talked of," an idea he would also express to William Moore, the president of the supreme executive council of Pennsylvania.[22] Irvine speculated that such plans for new states were motivated either by secret Loyalist ambitions or (more likely, in his opinion) the desire for easy access to new tracts of land, yet the fact that such conversations were taking place in a setting where the authority of continental institutions appeared weak and the authority of local groups appeared strong demonstrates the larger problem of imagining popular sovereignty apart from a rhetoric of forceful self-assertion. As White's account of group fusion implies, expressions of force allowed frontier settlers to experience their own unity and to assert their sovereignty over the territory they had claimed. Assembling in militias or other crowd collectives defined the sovereign authority of a disconnected settler populace by literally creating a body of the people and by marshaling the strength to hold the land taken in the name of that people.

Here again we see the tautology of popular sovereignty. Yet the example of the Pennsylvania frontier in 1782 reminds us that claims of sovereignty, especially in an American context, remain inextricable from the appropriation of indigenous land. Scholars such as Mark Rifkin and Jayan Nayar have demonstrated that conceiving of sovereignty purely as a quality of political and legal authority or legitimacy ignores the reality that claims of sovereignty always entail drawing borders within geographic space and defining the very discourses by which those borders can be imagined.[23] For a Continental Army administrator like William Irvine, the Gnadenhutten militia posed the problem of making these territorial claims on too small a scale. To preserve access to western lands for future development and investment, sovereignty over the frontier needed to reside with the largest sense of the people. Encouraging the proper scale for US sovereignty necessitated creating new ways for white settlers to experience their strength.

In light of such a need, Irvine imagined the Sandusky expedition as a means of exerting continental authority over the violence of the backcountry. In a letter to Moore in May 1782, Irvine states that "a volunteer expedition is talked of against Sandusky, which, if well conducted, may be of great service to this country. If they behave well on this occasion, it may also, in some measure, atone for the barbarity they are charged with at Muskingum."[24] In order that this expedition might redeem the massacre at Gnadenhutten, Irvine sought to ensure that it would be seen as an expression of the will of the people of the United States, not just of the settlers of the frontier. He gave written directions to the militia that, while their main object was to protect the region, they were also to consider themselves "acting in behalf and for the interest of the United States" and that they should always have in view "the law of arms, of nations, or independent states." Furthermore, Irvine took pains to make sure Crawford, a commissioned Continental officer, would be elected to command the mission.[25] In addition, he sent his aide-de-camp, John Rose, a disgraced Russian nobleman also known as the Baron Gustav Heinrich de Rosenthal, to serve as an advisor to the mission. The presence of Crawford and Rose, ideally, would provide the discipline that had been lacking at Gnadenhutten.

Crawford's leadership would stand in contrast to that of David Williamson, who commanded the militia at Gnadenhutten and whom Rose described in his journal as a minor demagogue during the mission. Rose compared Williamson to Caesar and noted that the local leader knew "too well how high he is in the opinion of the people in general." Williamson's popularity among his neighbors was on display at the beginning of the Sandusky expedition, when he was very nearly elected to command of the mission over Crawford. Rose reported to Irvine that the mission would likely have collapsed from the start, had not Williamson "cheerfully submitted to be second in command."[26]

As in the contrast between Ethan Allen and Daniel Shays, the comparison between Crawford and Williamson speaks to a larger tension between narrow and broad conceptions of popular sovereignty. From Irvine's plans in response to the massacre, we can see his hope that a successful expedition led by a Continental Army officer would transfer the trust and authority placed on men like Williamson onto figures such as himself and Crawford. Unfortunately for Crawford, however, he replaced Williamson not only at the head of a local militia but also as a target of vengeance for the massacre.[27]

To Brackenridge, the Gnadenhutten massacre demonstrated the potential for anarchy on the frontier, in the absence of the institutional structures provided by a strong central government. Such a government could provide disciplined and organized troops who would conduct warfare on rational and humane principles, in contrast to the irrational and uncivilized slaughter employed by the militia at the Moravian settlements. The narratives of Knight and Slover, therefore, seek to encourage a sense of nationalism that connects the desire for frontier security and the antipathy toward Indians with a loyalty to a continental government. In demonstrating the loyalty of their protagonists to an ideal of an American nation, and the failings of the militia force that marched to Sandusky, these narratives sought to inspire a recognition that institutions such as a standing Continental Army could best offer security to the nation.

Patrick Griffin has asserted that a sense of belonging to a larger commonwealth emerged among frontier settlers in response to the racist violence of the frontier, as they accepted state authority in exchange for protection from Indians.[28] Brackenridge's rhetoric in the narratives of Knight and Slover indicates how this acceptance of a central government as the best means for creating frontier security ran, in many ways, against the popular will of the region. This rhetoric locates sovereignty in a shared narrative of political values embodied by men like Crawford, Knight, and Slover. Brackenridge seeks a sense of affiliation that goes beyond the racial antipathy of group fusion, while accounting for how the desire for security and the projection of force inspire the formation of political communities. Acknowledgment of the Revolutionary martyr becomes a means to invite white settlers into this narrative of sovereignty.

Much like Ethan Allen's narrative, the narratives of Knight and Slover cast their protagonists, along with Crawford, as symbolic representatives of the nation, to establish a sympathetic connection between the audience and a country imagined to encompass all of the independent states. Brackenridge deploys these figures in response to assertions of local sovereignty. As both victims of Indian violence and participants in a failed militia campaign, Knight, Slover, and Crawford evinced the need for a stronger and more regulated army in the region, which could guarantee white access to western lands.

Brackenridge's argument here parallels a popular shift in thinking about the role of the citizen-soldier in the early United States. As Charles Royster has shown, in the opening days of the Revolutionary War, the virtue of the American soldier was imagined by many as an equal counter to the professional skill of the British soldier.[29] By the war's later years, however, many had recognized the need for a well-trained, disciplined force whose men would serve with greater continuity and permanence than the short enlistments for which militia could be assembled. The narratives of Knight and Slover offer a further illustration of this need, and their setting, on the line between the end of hostilities with Britain and the acceleration of hostilities with the Indians, suggests a continuing need for skilled soldiers ready to fight the enemies of the United States.

The tragic example of the Crawford narratives demonstrates the shortcomings of the militia system, even as it celebrates the character of the American men who make up such a system. This focus on character rather than military accomplishments stands as a common aspect of Brackenridge's treatment of all three men, as Crawford, Knight, and Slover are distinguished for their unwavering commitment to the American cause. Crawford stoically accepts his brutal death. Knight and Slover endure the taunting and temptations from their Indian captors and their Loyalist allies. In this way, the three figures model a patriotic culture based more in shared values than in direct assertions of power. Brackenridge theorizes sovereignty as participation within a political community bound by shared values rather than by communal strength.

Of the three major characters within the narratives, Knight plays the smallest role as a paragon of American virtue, but his significance as a symbolic marker of nationality becomes essential to framing this story as one that carries meaning beyond the frontier of western Pennsylvania. Knight's role as a surgeon largely kept him out of combat, and Slover mentions in his account that the physician was" a weak, little man," yet he serves an emblematic function within the text primarily through his reaction to the intense stress of his captivity. This reaction becomes a marker of national difference, with Knight's patient resolve being set in contrast to the self-interest of the infamous Loyalist interpreter Simon Girty.

In the midst of his execution, Knight states that Crawford called out to Girty and begged to be shot. Girty claimed to be unarmed and then "laughed heartily, and by all his gestures seemed delighted at the horrid scene." Girty then told Knight to prepare for a similar fate and warned him that he "need not expect to escape death, but should suffer it in all its extremities." After mocking the suffering of Crawford and Knight, however, Girty seems to abruptly change tone, asking Knight whether he (Girty) would be safe, should he be captured by the American forces. Knight emphasizes the radical turn this topic gave their conversation by describing his response as follows: "Being at that time in great anguish and distress for the torments the colonel was suffering before my eyes, as well as the expectation of undergoing the same fate in two days, I made little or no answer."[30]

Girty's questions introduce a distinction between the sympathy of Knight, who had become emotionally overwhelmed by the scene of Crawford's torture, and the craven self-concern Girty expresses. Parker Brown maintains that the Knight narrative distorts Girty's behavior during this moment, specifically by accusing Girty of mocking the abused Crawford, when accounts from other captives suggest that this response was actually made by Simon Girty's younger brother, James. Brown attributes this error more to Knight's memory than to Brackenridge's editing, but he notes that it forms part of a gross misrepresentation of Girty's actions during Crawford's captivity. Other sources indicate that Girty worked to negotiate Crawford's release, up to the point of being threatened himself, yet Knight's narrative makes no mention of these efforts.[31] Appearing as a cowardly and nakedly self-interested figure may have distorted the character of the actual Simon Girty, but it perfectly suited the effort by Brackenridge to draw a sharp distinction between corrupt Loyalists and true Americans.[32]

While Dr. Knight marks a political line between Patriots and Loyalists, John Slover's narrative adds a racial element to its ideal of national character, through Slover's status as a white man who had largely grown up among Indians. In a short aside, after he first recounts being taken captive, Slover describes how he had lived for twelve years among the Miami and Shawnee, from the age of eight to twenty. Slover recalls that one member of the party that captured him recognized him from his childhood, addressed him by his Indian name, Mannuchcothee, and criticized him for fighting against the Indians.

Slover's subsequent treatment by his captors further suggests that he was initially seen as something of a lost son. Unlike the two men with whom he is captured, Slover received no immediate torture or abuse. He was held without any physical restraints on his person, and he states that only his lack of shoes kept him from escaping long before he was sentenced to death. On the whole, he describes the early days of his captivity as comparatively mild, observing that during this period he was "treated with some appearance of kindness." Slover notes that the warriors of the town where he was held met in council for fifteen days after his arrival. Each night, Slover claims, he was invited to join the warriors in their war dances but always declined because he "believe[d] these things to be the service of the devil."[33] In this small detail, Slover's captivity represents a trial of temptation like that of Ethan Allen, with the scout facing the option of saving his own life by abandoning the American cause.

This portrayal gains strength through the description of the factors that led to Slover's death sentence. The benign treatment he initially describes receiving from his captors came to an end largely due to the arrival and instigation of Loyalists like the Girty brothers. In addition to the Girtys, Slover encountered Matthew Elliot and Alexander McKee—men whom Brackenridge portrays as some of the most infamous Tories of the western frontier. In footnotes, Brackenridge describes McKee as an Indian agent for the British, who broke his parole after being captured and "continued to incite [the Indians] to make war against us," and he calls the Girtys and Elliot members of "that horrid brood called Refugees . . . whom the Devil has long since marked for his own property."[34]

James Girty, who purportedly laughed as William Crawford was tortured, appears to be the impetus for the turn in Indian behavior toward Slover. Slover states that Girty and Elliot refuted his truthful explanation of Cornwallis's defeat, which he had provided to his captors, and then reported that Slover had admitted to them of plotting his escape. After these encounters, Slover claims, "the enemy began to alter their behavior towards me." Furthermore, the decision to execute Slover came after the arrival of McKee, who brought word from the British in Detroit that they should discourage the Indians from taking any prisoners and encourage them, instead, to be merciless toward Americans. When the time came for Slover to be executed, the warriors who led him to this fate were accompanied by another Girty brother, George, who cursed Slover and told him that he would "get what [he] had deserved many years."[35]

These brief negative depictions of men who have crossed racial lines to work with the Indians provide a further marker of national difference within the text. They serve as converse images of Slover, who could easily occupy the liminal position in which the Girtys, Elliot, and McKee dwell. Like them, Slover retained fluency in Indian languages and culture. And, as his early treatment suggests, his captors were perhaps willing to adopt Slover as one of their own. Slover steadfastly refused to cross this boundary, however, and his loyalty further solidifies the contrast between the two sides and establishes such loyalty as part of the broader qualities of virtue that Brackenridge associates with the Revolutionary soldier.

Implicit within the contrasts between Knight and Slover and these Loyalists lies a distinction between civilization and savagery. This comparison indicates Brackenridge's belief that white men living on the frontier can easily cross the line into behavior that he considers savage. Read alongside his criticism of the Gnadenhutten massacre in the appendix, the depiction of Loyalists in the narratives of Knight and Slover offers a warning of the corrupting potential of backcountry life. Throughout the narratives, Brackenridge insinuates a link between a continental army, agricultural development, and national character. His anti-Indian rhetoric in the appendix argues that, by failing to improve the land through freehold agriculture, Indians lived in a more primitive state of society. Colonial writers such as William Byrd and Robert Beverley had long described the corrupting influence of a life organized around hunting rather than farming, and Crèvecoeur's *Letters from an American Farmer* provides a famous example contemporaneous to Brackenridge, when Farmer James writes that a life devoted to the chase makes the backwoodsman indolent and unsociable.[36]

Brackenridge shared such beliefs, noting in the appendix that "to live by tilling is *more humano,* by hunting is *more bestiarum.*"[37] Such an attitude might also explain a strange digression in Knight's narrative: in the midst of recalling his escape, the doctor begins to offer vivid details about the landscape. His tone sounds a bit like that found in a promotional tract, as he catalogs the abundance of trees he observed, makes notes of the many potential water sources he passed, and comments on the richness of the soil. Knight even mentions that "wells might easily be dug in all parts" of a ridge he crossed, a clear indication that his observations evaluate the land for future settlement.[38]

These details from Knight served as an invitation for the industry of upright yeomen farmers—provided such farms could remain safe from conflict. Without consistent security, agricultural settlement in the West would be much less economically feasible than trapping furs or trading with the Indians. These lifestyles make the individual little better than the beasts of the forests, in Brackenridge's opinion. Only by opening this land for farming can the virtue of its residents be ensured, which necessitates protecting small farms with garrisons of disciplined and trained men.

Crawford's characterization as a heroic martyr solidifies the need for such an army. In the short memoir he wrote of Crawford, Brackenridge presents the fallen officer as an accomplished soldier and a courteous citizen. This section offers the most explicit claims for Crawford's military heroism within the text, with Brackenridge citing Crawford's service as an officer in two wars and his career as an Indian fighter. In balance to this picture of Crawford as an experienced old warrior, the memoir also calls him "a man of good judgment, singular good nature, and great humanity, and remarkable for his hospitality, few strangers coming to the western country, and not spending some days at the crossings of the Yachaghany [Youghiogheny] river, where he lived."[39] This brief account sets Crawford as a personification of the citizen-soldier ideal: a virtuous man who freely volunteers to defend his home but does not relish war or allow his military service to corrupt his humane treatment of his fellow citizens.

In order to be sure that his audience reads the failure of the Crawford expedition as tied to the failings of the militia system rather than to a failure of leadership, Brackenridge emphasizes a key moment that distinguishes Crawford from his soldiers. This moment came when Knight encountered Crawford in the midst of the chaotic retreat from the battlefield. As the main body of the force rushed away, Crawford lagged behind, searching for the family members that had served with him: his son John, along with his son-in-law and his nephew. He asked Knight to stay with him, and this decision to fall back from the main force led to the two men's eventual capture.

Crawford's search for his relatives sets him in contrast to those members of his force who break ranks to begin the retreat at their own hurried pace. This contrast is made explicit in the text by the ordering of Knight's narrative. The paragraph describing Crawford's efforts to find his family follows immediately on a paragraph that concludes with the retreat losing order and the force largely abandoning seven severely wounded men who could not fend for themselves and were to be kept at the center of the march. This passage marks Crawford's only criticism of his troops in either narrative. Knight recalled that the colonel "exclaimed against the militia for riding off in such an irregular manner, and leaving some of the wounded behind, contrary to his orders."[40] The retreat from Sandusky exemplifies the popular criticism of militia soldiers as unreliable and lacking the experience and discipline to set aside thoughts of their own security in the stresses of battle.

Yet the moment of retreat also speaks to the effect Brackenridge's publication of these narratives had in polishing Crawford's reputation. Brackenridge presented Crawford as a national hero, despite the expedition's failure. As Brown suggests, "Crawford attained in death a stature that, had he survived the expedition, he surely would not have enjoyed," thanks to Brackenridge's dissemination of these narratives.[41] Had he lived, Crawford would have been the commander of a routed force that had retreated from its purpose in disarray. Indeed, Brown cites the prevalence of a rumor that persisted in western Pennsylvania for many years after the battle: that Crawford had abandoned the army during the retreat.[42] The colonel did lag behind the evacuating army to search for his family members, according to Knight. His distressed search for his relatives could be interpreted as placing personal needs above the good of the whole. As a result of Crawford's death, however, this search adds a poignant note to Brackenridge's text and contrasts the loss of discipline and the flight to self-preservation among some of the militia to Crawford's dogged refusal to leave his son and other kinsmen. It also represents another example of Brackenridge's implicit criticism of the multitude. The militia acts not as collective, motivated by sacrifice, moving toward a common purpose, but as a group of individuals all simultaneously pursuing their own security.

The narratives of both Knight and Slover present the failed retreat as the primary factor that led to the capture and execution of Crawford. Slover's narrative rebukes the militia even more sharply than does Knight's, stating that the "men broke and rode off in confusion, treading down those who were on foot, and leaving the wounded men who supplicated to be taken with them."[43] Such accounts find support in the daily journal Rose maintained to provide Irvine with a thorough report about the mission. In his initial letter to Irvine, Rose downplayed the problems of the retreat, stating simply that confusion was inevitable during a retreat under fire, even "in a body trained to the strictest discipline."[44] In his journal, however, Rose forcefully criticizes the evacuation, blaming the loss of order on the decision by one militia captain, John Hardin, to break from the agreed-upon plan of retreat. Rose claims that Hardin was motivated "by fear and rascality united" and that his leading a body of men out of order led to the opposing forces opening fire on the retreating Americans, which in turn spurred the militia's chaotic flight to safety.[45]

Rose's criticisms do not stop with Hardin, though. In contrast to the heroic depiction of Crawford found in Brackenridge, Rose provides a far more measured portrait of the doomed colonel. He praises Crawford for his bravery and endurance as a soldier and his kindness and affection in personal life, much as Brackenridge does. But Rose also offers a less flattering assessment of Crawford:

> At a council: he speaks incoherent, proposes matters confusedly, and is incapable of persuading people into his opinion, or making use of their weak sides for his purposes. He is somewhat capricious: yet easily and indiscriminately led by people, who have once gained an ascendency over him—jealous of his military knowledge, and superiority, but a mere quack in the profession of a soldier. No military genius; and no man of letters.[46]

Rose's criticisms extend to the other officers on the expedition as well, and his journal offers multiple examples of the general mismanagement of the mission in the form of poor planning and perpetual disorganization. In fact, Rose asserts that Crawford had no intention of actually fighting but instead guided the mission to be a circuitous march that would distract the enemy and satisfy settler demands for action against the Indians. He also claims that most of the militia were primarily interested in an opportunity for plunder and similarly wanted to avoid combat.[47]

Rose's blunt appraisals further indicate that Crawford's reputation would have been tarnished had he returned home in defeat. Crawford's death thus looms large in the representation of the expedition. Survival might have made him the target of blame for the defeat, but death made him another name on the roll of fallen patriots and a clear example of the need to aggressively confront the Indian threat.

Crawford's death, Knight and Slover's captivity—these hardships made these veterans more effective symbols for Brackenridge's national fable. Like a kind of observer effect, merely putting Knight and Slover together in a single text appropriated their stories within Brackenridge's vision of Revolutionary martyrs.

In 1832, another member of the militia, Angus McCoy, gave his account of it as part of a pension testimony. McCoy states as a short aside that Crawford abandoned the army during the first night of the retreat, "taking with him Slover the pilot, Harrison his son-in-law, and Dr. Knight."[48] Knight's and Slover's narratives directly contradict McCoy here, since neither mentions being in the company of the other at the time of their capture. McCoy does not actually claim to have witnessed the three men together but instead repeatedly emphasizes that his account is what he "understood" to have happened, to use his term.

McCoy's account implies that Knight and Slover became linked together in the popular vision of the Crawford expedition regardless of their own testimony. That linkage strongly suggests the influence of Brackenridge's pamphlet. McCoy might have never seen a copy of the text, but its multiple editions and reprints in the fifty years after the expedition likely made it part of a general understanding of the failed mission. McCoy's testimony implies that Crawford, Knight, and Slover had become broad characters in a cultural narrative, even while they appeared as specific individuals. McCoy even references a later encounter with Slover, in the years following the expedition, but this meeting seems only to confirm the version of events that McCoy has received. The facts of the Crawford expedition ultimately became less significant than the cultural symbolism it could perform.

Together, Crawford, Knight, and Slover became personifications of the virtue of American soldiers, acquired through their suffering rather than through their less than impressive accomplishments in battle. Their hardships illustrated the need for an army that combined such virtue with the discipline and skill to maintain order in moments of crisis. In death, Crawford provided a backcountry example of the kind of sacrifice that was associated with Revolutionary martyrs such as Richard Montgomery and Joseph Warren, both of whom featured prominently in the two plays Brackenridge published early in the war.

Jason Shaffer has included these plays in an analysis of how depictions of the patriotic martyr created a cycle of death and mourning that could be resolved by the audience taking up the unfinished work of the hero's sacrifice. Sarah Purcell has described the adoration paid to the Revolutionary martyr as part of a process of establishing a national identity based in the veneration of shared symbols.[49] Both of these strains of thought emerge in the portrayal of Crawford—Crawford the martyr's death at the hands of a purportedly bloodthirsty and uncivilized enemy offers a symbol of national sacrifice to the American community while also demonstrating that the work he set out to accomplish, the subjugation of the Indians, remains unfinished. In the specific case of Crawford, these two points become interdependent, as completing Crawford's work necessitates founding a stronger nation that can be personified in the form of a powerful, disciplined army.

Brackenridge's writing would continue to posit a stronger national army as a unifying symbol for Americans in the decade after the Revolutionary War. His work in the years of the Northwest Indian War and the Whiskey Rebellion maintains a belief that local definitions of popular sovereignty must be subordinated to a broader sense of the nation if the frontier is to become stable. He published several comments on the ongoing conflict between the United States and the Indians of the Northwest Territory (the broad region west of the Appalachian Mountains and north of the Ohio River), particularly as US militias began to suffer a string of defeats to the confederacy of Indians led by the Miami chief Little Turtle. For example, in a discussion of the futility of treaties during this conflict, detailed in the third volume of his long, picaresque novel *Modern Chivalry* (1793), Brackenridge's narrator declares himself to be "one of those who not only approve of the present war against the Indians, but also of the principle on which it is carried on, viz. by a body of regular and well disciplined troops."[50]

In early February 1792, Brackenridge published two articles in the *National Gazette* of Philadelphia, the paper edited by his college classmate Philip Freneau, advocating an aggressive response to the conflict and an expanded military presence in the region. In the first of these articles, Brackenridge rejected the opinions of those who "advocate what is called a defensive war" and argues that the best means of security in the West would be to establish a garrison at Presque Isle in Lake Erie, from which a stronger American army could use the lake to transport troops throughout the region and begin a full-scale campaign to destroy the Miami towns. His second article reiterates this point and claims that if defenders of the Indian understood the savagery of the race, they would turn their sympathy to the many white settlers who have been killed or tortured.[51]

Jeremy Engels has argued that, in these two articles, Brackenridge uses the threat posed by Indians to encourage western residents to see themselves as protected by the powerful army only the federal government could provide, at a time when many in the West felt the government's authority primarily through the unpopular excise tax on distilled spirits.[52] This tax caused protests throughout the western parts of the United States as local residents demanded from their political representatives in government greater recognition of their economic hardships and asserted the right to maintain their own sovereignty against the dictates of the federal government. The articles in the *National Gazette* further the effort that we find in the narratives of Knight and Slover, to imagine a national culture through the idealization of a continental military. Reading these articles as a continuation of that line in Brackenridge's thinking also indicates how his repeated calls for a stronger federal army arose from concerns about the anarchic potential of local expressions of self-determination.

Through a rhetoric of military sacrifice, Brackenridge sought to inspire a greater sense of nationhood that would rein in the chaotic expressions of frontier populism. In their calls for a professional army to fulfill Crawford's martyrdom, the narratives of Knight and Slover provided cultural encouragement to place legitimate political violence solely in the hands of the national government, and this placement reveals a larger discourse that subordinated the radical autonomy that the individual citizen might claim.

As we have seen in the examples of Vermont and western Massachusetts, Americans in the early republic widely shared a belief in the sovereignty of the people, but they differed markedly in what kind of role the people could play once they formed a government. Christian Fritz has summarized three capacities for the people within US constitutionalism: the people can act as a sovereign that creates, revises, or abolishes the law; the people can act as the "ruler" by choosing representatives to run their government, as a king chooses ministers; or the people can act as the "ruled," the subjects of government who are entitled to approve or criticize its actions.[53] Fritz notes that, in disputes such as Vermont's independence movement, Shays's Rebellion, and the Whiskey Rebellion, Americans were divided over whether the people retained that second capacity, to act as the ruler, once they had established a constitution. In one view, the people continue to hold the right to assemble, and to use force if necessary, to achieve redress from a government they have brought into being. In the other, the people have given the right to revolutionary political violence over to that government. The Revolutionary martyr provided a symbol through which the people could imagine themselves embodied by a continental military that preserved the physical force they have ceded.

Sympathy or anger on behalf of the martyr became a means of experiencing loyalty toward the concept of a continental nation and the strong central government necessary to protect such a nation. Brackenridge's depiction of Crawford exemplifies the broad discourse Christopher Castiglia has called the "federalization of affect," which encouraged individuals in the early United States to redirect the emotional connections that once bound local allegiances inward to imagine "sites of correspondence between individual bodies (character, personality, even biology) and state interest."[54] The Revolutionary martyr provides an affective base upon which a broader sense of nationalism can be built. As a symbol, Crawford discouraged the direct action of frontier violence, because his expedition was a failure. Instead, through his patient suffering, he embodies a particular emotional response toward an idea of the United States. Brackenridge uses the example of Crawford to outline a mode of popular sovereignty based in the affective response of individuals to a representative figure. The figure of the Revolutionary martyr models a consensus in which individual citizens' recognition of his suffering becomes a thread that binds them into a collective.

Like the perception of danger that encourages the fused nationalism of the frontier, Brackenridge's use of the martyr urges the individual from an interiorized experience toward social formation. Yet Brackenridge hopes to replace fear with something like a shared aesthetic response. The Crawford narratives impel readers to acknowledge

Crawford, Knight, and Slover as representatives of a continental nation, but they also ask readers to recognize themselves making this acknowledgment. In their capacity to imagine Crawford as their representative, individual citizens can instantiate a community distinct from the rational political discourse of eastern elites and the populist fervor of western settlers.

Brackenridge uses the figure of the martyr to inspire what Elizabeth Maddock Dillon, in a reinterpretation of Kant, has called a *sensus communis,* a "shared terrain of aesthetic value . . . that creates community (as well as exclusions from it) rather than one that emerges from it." Paul Gilmore has described Brackenridge's belief that the aesthetic realm could provide a space for reflection that acknowledged both individual rights and concerns over the anarchic potential of those rights. Dana Nelson argues that *Modern Chivalry* displays Brackenridge's belief that self-government requires the deliberation and creativity inherent in literary practices, practices that allow for "continuing dissensus rather than unified harmony."[55] In the Crawford narratives, and in much of his subsequent writing, Brackenridge sought to imagine sovereignty as a space of representation among citizens rather than as the assertion of autonomy underlying the populist violence of the frontier. *Incidents of the Insurrection,* in particular, features Brackenridge's most developed writing on the challenge of balancing popular sovereignty and populist violence.

The Crawford narratives and *Incidents of the Insurrection* share Brackenridge's underlying effort to imagine the limited sovereignty of the individual citizen. The later work, however, displays Brackenridge's conscious effort to offer writing and literary discourse as an expressive alternative to force and violence. Brackenridge describes his purpose in writing *Incidents of the Insurrection* as primarily to correct the widespread notion that he was a ringleader of the insurgency. He frames this act of writing as an expression of his agency as a republican citizen. As he states in a speech to his protesting neighbors, recorded in the text, "We are known to the government by representation only, and not by force." But as he submits *Incidents of the Insurrection* to its audience, he also acknowledges his subordination to the perception of the public: "It is possible I may not be able to remove the misconception of every one. I am aware how difficult it is to change opinion, even with the best cause on my side."[56] For Brackenridge, this gradual and often frustrating effort to change opinions through written discourse and public discussion should be the model of democratic citizenship. Yet, as moments like the protests of 1794 or the Gnadenhutten massacre a decade earlier revealed, writing is a privilege that not all citizens can access, whereas violence is always at hand.

At the core of the contrast between writing and violence that Brackenridge draws throughout *Incidents of the Insurrection* rests competing understandings of the origins of popular sovereignty. Does sovereignty flow from the people's willing subordination of their own interests for the commonweal, or does sovereignty emerge from the aggregation of self-interested individuals into a general voice? Brackenridge favors the former path. His emphasis on writing as the ideal expression of sovereignty reveals a conception of popular sovereignty as a centripetal force: the individual citizen must join his own voice and will with that of his neighbors in the messy process of representation and debate, toward a shared consensus. The violence he encounters during the protests, however, implies a more centrifugal movement for sovereignty. Sovereignty is expressed through an assertion of the individual will to power that becomes the shared rallying cry of the multitude, whether that cry is for war with the Indian or for freedom from an unjust tax (or for the preservation of the laws of the United States).

Paolo Virno uses this metaphor of centripetal and centrifugal force to describe the difference between the social formations that he calls the People and the Multitude: "The people are the result of a centripetal movement: from atomized individuals, to the unity of the 'body politic,' to sovereignty . . . The multitude, on the other hand, is the outcome of a centrifugal movement: from the One to the Many."[57] For Brackenridge, the contrast between the people and the multitude corresponds with the difference between writing and violence as expressions of sovereignty.

In a key moment from *Incidents of the Insurrection,* Brackenridge recounts the rise of "Tom the Tinker," the popular pseudonym that was attached to many advertisements and newspaper articles released during the protests, threatening anyone who complied with the excise tax. Brackenridge notes that Tom the Tinker became a source of affiliation for the protesters: "It was not now, Are you Whig or Tory? but, Are you a Tom the Tinker's man? Every man was willing to be thought so; and some had a great deal of trouble to wipe off imputations to the contrary."[58]

As a form of representation, Tom the Tinker does not emerge from consensus or even a majority vote, as would an elected official. Instead, Tom the Tinker functions as an oppositional viewpoint that proliferates itself like a virus through the people. Tom the Tinker illustrates a self-division within democratic citizens, as no one individual wants to claim to *be* Tom the Tinker. Instead, the writers who invoke this name position Tom the Tinker as a commander to whose leadership the people must submit. As an example of this rhetoric, Brackenridge includes the text of an advertisement found posted in a Pittsburgh tavern: "In taking a survey of the troops under my command, . . . I find there were a great many delinquents. . . . It will therefore be observed, that Tom the Tinker will not suffer any certain class, or set of men, to be excluded the service of this my district, when notified to attend on any expedition, in order to obstruct the execution of the law, and obtain a repeal thereof."[59]

Tom the Tinker defines sovereignty as a mask that individuals can claim without accruing any personal responsibility to themselves. Through Tom the Tinker, everyone is empowered but no one is accountable. For Brackenridge, this lack of accountability creates the conditions for political violence to occur, and he compares the climate in western Pennsylvania during the height of the protests to a return to the state of nature, at one point sardonically remarking that "the government is gone to the devil, the courts are overthrown, all law is at an end, [and] . . . the strong hand must manage all things."[60] Like the violence of the frontier militia, Tom the Tinker draws its power as each individual assumes access to the power of the group. The imagined idea of being a collective creates the actual power of that collective. As with any mob, individuals feel empowered because they are part of a large group, not because they have established a true consensus.

In response to this anarchic climate, Brackenridge turns to writing as a form of representation that demands, rather than alleviates, individual accountability. *Incidents of the Insurrection* stands as his public testimony about his involvement in the protests, and one aspect of his purpose in writing can be seen as providing his neighbors with an example of the ideal balance between individual assertion and civic subordination. Part of his attempt to repair his reputation through this work involves recalling the numerous occasions when he sought to disrupt the mob mentality of the protesters by encouraging practices that would make individuals publicly responsible for their actions. For instance, Brackenridge supported a general amnesty for the nearly seven thousand protesters who met at Braddock's Field, outside Pittsburgh, on August 1, 1794. He hoped this amnesty offer would encourage the nonviolent opponents of the excise tax to work as a check on the more aggressive protesters. By requiring individuals to personally sign an amnesty agreement, Brackenridge believed that this strategy would reduce the fusion of the protesters into an unthinking mob.[61]

He also worked within the protest movement to establish layers of bureaucracy, such as committees of correspondence that would, as he states, "take the business out of the hands of the multitude, as speedily as possible." He notes that it would be a mistake to suppose that the protesters were led by anyone in particular, such as David Bradford, the Washington County lawyer who had become a Daniel Shays–like figure at the head of the revolts. Rather, Brackenridge asserts that "it was the mass of the people that commanded and it was the fear of them that operated on the minds of the more conspicuous individuals."[62] Recording personal opinions and voices in writing, whether in the form of amnesty statements or as resolutions opposing the excise tax, presented what Brackenridge considered to be the best means of encouraging his neighbors to act as individuals.

Ironically, however, it was this effort to organize the opposition and to encourage it to follow the logic of representative republican government that would make Brackenridge himself a purported leader of the insurgency. Much of this perception stemmed from a letter he sent to Tench Coxe in Philadelphia, in which he described the prevailing mood in the western part of the state and included the claim that "should an attempt be made to suppress these people, I am afraid the question will not be, whether you will march to Pittsburgh, but whether they will march to Philadelphia." Brackenridge writes that he heard frequent rumors that the soldiers of the advancing federal militia sent by President Washington to end the protests sought to do him harm, regardless of the political or legal resolution to the conflict. He cites, for example, a rumor that, while on the march, the troops were stabbing their bayonets into bushes alongside the road and calling the bushes Brackenridge. In response to these rumors, he observes that "the example of the Jacobins in France had infected the mass of the army, just as much as it had the people here in Tom the Tinker's time."[63] Much as William Irvine had reported with regard to the troops at Fort Pitt, in 1782, Brackenridge finds that the very soldiers he would idealize as the embodiment of continental political culture are not immune to the immediate sense of meaning and power provided by populist violence.

Confronted with this threat, Brackenridge writes that he decided that his fate depended not on the authority of the officers but on the general sentiment toward him among the troops, who might act without license to attack him. With this idea in mind, he prepared a short handbill to be circulated through the army so that he could address the multitude as individuals. In this statement, Brackenridge asks to be presumed innocent until proven otherwise and suggests that his extralegal killing would tarnish the honor of the brave volunteer soldiers.[64] This effort to mitigate the wrath of the army toward him only made matters worse, however. Many officers refused to accept any copies of the handbill, and Brackenridge came in for even more criticism after the federal official he asked to distribute the handbills sent them among the troops without the officers' consent. Although Brackenridge acknowledges that this breach of protocol would not have been his first choice for distributing the handbills, he refutes the claim that he had no right to even make such a statement to the army.

In rationalizing his publication of the handbill, Brackenridge invokes many of the communication practices William Warner has described as "the protocols of liberty": open access, virtuous initiative, and a general address to the people.[65] Brackenridge argues that private letters to individual officers "could not be generally communicated," and he frames his handbill as a way to speak to his fellow citizens directly. Brackenridge also knew that he would be seen as having violated the military protocol of a chain of command when his handbill was distributed freely among the troops and not disseminated through their officers. Nonetheless, Brackenridge states that he "had considered this army as consisting of citizens, and . . . did not conceive any greater impropriety, in addressing them in a camp, by a handbill, than in their counting-houses, or upon their farms, in the gazette of Philadelphia, Trenton, or Richmond."[66]

For Brackenridge, the protocols of liberty should structure communication among republican citizens at all times, yet he finds that his countrymen in the militia believe that a different set of protocols takes precedence during the crisis. Protocols such as the chain of command and the suppression of dissenting viewpoints rely on a hierarchal authority backed by physical power. Brackenridge imagines the free circulation of information as the primary means for republican citizens to express their participation with a collective sovereign. Yet, for the federal militia and for the protesters in western Pennsylvania, it appears that assembling in force represents a more direct method of claiming sovereign power.

This encounter and, ultimately, much of Brackenridge's thinking about organized violence in *Incidents of the Insurrection* suggests the challenge of unsettling the sense of opposition to an enemy that underlies popular sovereignty. *Incidents of the Insurrection* reveals Brackenridge's anxiety that both sides in the Whiskey Rebellion imagined organized violence as an expression rather than a protection of their sovereignty. Ultimately, both the conflict with the Indian nations and the Whiskey Rebellion exemplify sovereignty as a declaration of political boundaries via force.

In response to this conception, Brackenridge can only offer the less immediate exchange offered through writing. Yet even his own efforts to imagine sovereignty as a space of representation participate in a culture of Revolutionary violence—we might ask how different evoking the name of William Crawford actually is from invoking the name of Tom the Tinker. Late in *Incidents of the Insurrection,* Brackenridge laments that one of his political rivals in Pittsburgh "mistook a figure for a threat," and this phrase seems a suitable description of the problem that persists within his theories of writing and popular sovereignty.[67] This problem of misreading provides a reminder of the challenge of balancing the will to power, inherent in demands for sovereignty, with the patience and reflection necessary for self-government.

3

Joseph Plumb Martin, Deborah Sampson, and the Soldier's Two Bodies

HUGH HENRY BRACKENRIDGE sought to encourage a sense of continental nationalism through the celebration of Revolutionary soldiers who sacrificed their own security to protect the commonweal. But as his experiences during the Whiskey Rebellion demonstrated, claiming the mantle of the Revolutionary War could inspire the violent tendencies within American self-government as easily as calm them. The figure of the soldier stood as both a model of representative sovereignty and an example of the violent demand for autonomy. In the decades following the war, the meaning of this figure would continue to shift, particularly in the pages of the veteran narratives that began to appear with regularity throughout the early nineteenth century.

In this chapter, I turn to these narratives that respond to the Revolutionary War as part of national history rather than as an ongoing event. These texts indicate that the central tension found in earlier narratives from Brackenridge and Ethan Allen—how to imagine revolutionary violence as the protection of the will of the people and not the expression of a multitude's demands for autonomy—remained unresolved throughout the early national era. More specifically, these narratives indicate that the ideal of the veteran as a heroic martyr gave rise to a mythic view of the Revolutionary soldier that diminished recognition of the actual individuals who served.

As in earlier examples from Brackenridge and Allen, these post-Revolutionary texts offer the veteran as a representative of a broadly imagined continental nationalism, but they also offset this interest in the body politic with a much deeper interest in the human body. Allen and Brackenridge present intense suffering during the war at a second-hand remove. Many of these later narratives, in contrast, tell of physical hardships directly and in detail. Rather than Allen observing starving young prisoners of war or Brackenridge editing Knight's account of Crawford's execution, postwar narratives often grant audiences an unmediated view of their misery. In many cases, these narratives were autobiographical and written in the voice of the veteran. And with their later publication dates, many of these narratives reflect on how those individual experiences of suffering failed to be included within the history of the Revolution.

A writer like Joseph Plumb Martin, likely the best-known example from this era, takes direct aim at the idealized view of the Revolutionary soldier as a selfless patriot, which formed in the early republic. During this postwar period, the histories of David Ramsay and Mercy Otis Warren attained their cultural prominence, and overtly commercial texts such as Mason Locke Weems's famous biography of George Washington sold a vision of the Revolution as the work of noble and heroic men. The title of Martin's narrative reveals his determination to provide, in contrast to such elevated accounts, an ordinary private's view of the war: *A Narrative of Some of the Adventures, Dangers, and Sufferings of a Revolutionary Soldier; Interspersed with Anecdotes of Incidents that Occurred Within His Own Observation. Written by Himself.*[1] As this title indicates, Martin emphasizes his personal experience of the hardships involved in military service. He recounts the brutality of combat in his occasionally graphic descriptions of the death and injury he witnessed. He also recounts the tedium of army life in his descriptions of the long hours spent on the march or in camp. Martin presents his narrative as a corrective to histories of the war that focused only on large battles and famous generals, and it exemplifies the many similar texts that sought to challenge a mythic view of the war that honored the veteran as a source of American sovereignty while ignoring the veteran as a specific individual.[2]

This approach can be seen in Martin's account of the infamous retreat from Kip's Bay, on the eastern side of Manhattan, in September 1776. This defeat of the American forces has been remembered as a moment when even the famously reserved Washington lost his self-control; many accounts of the day claim that the commander in chief rode about beating officers and enlisted men alike with his riding crop while screaming at men to stand their ground.[3] Martin vows to refrain from joining in all the "inkshed" over the Kip's Bay affair, however, since the battle had become a subject for "anecdotes, jests, imprecations, and sarcasms"—far more than it deserved. Martin does share one brief story, though, which he claims to have read in multiple printed accounts of the battle.

> A certain man or the friends of a certain man have said that this certain man was sitting by the highway side when the Commander in Chief passed by and asked him why he sat there. His answer, as he or they say, was "that he had rather be killed or taken by the enemy than trodden to death by cowards." A brave man, he! I doubt whether there was such another there that day, and I must doubt whether he himself was there under such circumstances as he or his friends relate. Every man that I saw was endeavoring by all sober means to escape from death or captivity.[4]

This anecdote illustrates Martin's concern, throughout his narrative, with how the story of the war had been and was being told. The anecdote contrasts the majority of soldiers at Kip's Bay with some small number of virtuous patriots who held firm in their commitment to the American cause. However, Martin dismisses the scene of the proud soldier by the roadside as a likely fabrication. He asserts that the real distinction in this account of Kip's Bay is not between cowards and heroes but between fact and fiction. Martin offers his narrative as the unglamorous reality experienced by ordinary soldiers, who were motivated as much by self-preservation as by their patriotism. In his telling, the brave man on the side of the road symbolizes an impossible ideal that detracts from the experiences of the actual men who fought in the war.

Of course, not all postwar veteran narratives actively challenged the myth-making around the Revolutionary War. Other veterans were more willing to identify with myth over reality. While Joseph Plumb

Martin rejected the man on the roadside as imaginary, the subject of another popular narrative effectively sought to prove that he could have been that soldier.

Robert Shirtliff appears as a model private in his 1797 narrative, which was written for him by the Massachusetts printer Herman Mann. He displays many of the virtues desired in an enlisted man—loyalty, obedience, sobriety, chastity—to the point that one modern biographer has even suggested Shirtliff was something of a "bootlicker."[5] Of course, Mann had more incentive than most writers of veteran narratives to establish his subject as a model of virtue, since "Robert Shirtliff" was actually the identity created by Deborah Sampson Gannett, the most famous woman to serve during the Revolutionary War disguised as a man.[6] Throughout Sampson's narrative, *The Female Review,* Mann seeks to prove that, in spite of the suspicions her cross-dressing might raise about her character, Sampson remained a chaste example of republican womanhood during her time in the army.

Along with her impeccable moral behavior, Mann's fictionalized version of Sampson also displays courage and calm under fire, whether she's fighting Loyalists in the neutral ground around New York or challenging Indians on the frontier. While the historical Sampson undoubtedly did her best to be a good soldier to avoid drawing unwanted attention to herself and her disguise, Mann's literary depiction stretches the likely truth of her service into a fantastic adventure story that borrows from many genres of eighteenth-century popular literature.[7] The literary Sampson thus becomes less the record of a unique individual soldier than another character within a nationalist fable of origins.

Martin and Sampson may be viewed as contrasting textual responses to the kind of idealized Revolutionary soldier that is personified by Martin's anonymous roadside patriot. Both Martin and Sampson appear as literary personas that acknowledge that their physical bodies cannot align with this imagined ideal, but they differ in how their narratives respond to that dissonance. Sampson's female body does not match the expectation of soldiers as male, so her narrative suggests that her virtuous performance as a soldier offset her transgression of gender norms.[8] Martin's male body fits within cultural expectations for a soldier, but his narrative implies that such expectations often amount to a fantasy actual men cannot fulfill. Where Sampson's narrative evokes a transcendence of the physical body by its protagonist, Martin's narrative doubles down on the validity of the material experience of its subject.

These narratives share an understanding of the Revolutionary soldier as having two bodies: a discursive military body that can be publicly celebrated for its contributions to the war and a physical civilian body that may or may not receive the same level of recognition and acknowledgment. If we think of the citizen-soldier of a republican government within the frame of the king's two bodies in medieval European law, we can imagine the American soldier as both a citizen endowed with sovereignty and a military subject who submits to that sovereignty. However, Elizabeth Samet has noted that "whereas the king's two bodies worked by and large in concert . . . , the soldier's civilian and military bodies, equal and potentially incompatible, seemed destined to always exist in a state of civil war."[9]

That conflict structures the postwar veteran narrative. These texts always carry two versions of the veteran: a young man who fought and an older man telling the story of that fight. The soldier's younger self appears as a source of American sovereignty through his military sacrifices. The older self appears to its contemporary audience as a reminder of those sacrifices. The narratives of both Sampson and Martin assume that the celebration of the military body—the veteran in youth—has come largely at the exclusion of the civilian body—the veteran at the time of writing—from the republican *demos.* As a woman who served in drag, Sampson's account makes that condition literal, since her civilian body was explicitly not recognized as that of a citizen. Yet Martin's narrative suggests that this split between the soldier's two bodies ultimately affects all veterans.

The postwar veteran narrative indicates how the figure of the Revolutionary soldier became a means of imagining a political community, of creating a discourse of American sovereignty, just as Ethan Allen and Hugh Henry Brackenridge envisioned. However, placing the soldier at the heart of US sovereignty does not solely reflect either the consensus of a people or an attempt by government to define the lives of its subjects. The discourses of military heroism and patriotic nationalism that run through Allen and Brackenridge evolve toward forms of power that do not fit easily within the terms of traditional sovereignty or the biopolitical perspectives associated with Giorgio Agamben. When the military body is sundered from its association with a specific, individual body, soldiers can be considered as an abstract, aggregate class, as in Martin's anecdote of Kip's Bay, with its unnamed patriot and retreating masses. The narratives of Martin and Sampson assert that a mythic view of the Revolutionary War distinguishes soldiers from their civilian capacities as citizens and renders the veteran purely an element of a war machine.

If we consider some of the language commonly applied to the military, such as "boots on the ground" or "foot soldiers" or even the most basic description of military equipment as "arms," we can see how the discourses that organize large groups of individuals into highly coordinated units often invoke a rhetorical dismemberment. In many of the ways we describe soldiers, they cease to represent distinct individuals but instead appear as simply a collection of body parts and biological drives that can be marshaled toward a violent purpose.

Political theorists François Debrix and Alexander Barder have described such discourses as "agonal sovereignty," in an effort to analyze modes of power that, in a break from biopolitical perspectives, appear unconcerned with dictating the conditions of life and death. Debrix and Barder argue that, unlike biopolitical sovereignty, agonal sovereignty focuses not on defining the lives of those within and without the state but instead takes the perpetuation of conflict and the production of warring bodies as its primary goals. Agonal sovereignty is unconcerned with narratives of security and threat that take the greater preservation of the state as their motivation. Instead, it describes moments of force and violence that seek only to reduce the individual to its bodily components, either through rampant acts of destruction or through discourses of reification and categorization, and thus to enable the continuance of a state of war.

Debrix and Barder define this concept through examples relevant to an early twenty-first-century context, such as US drone missile strikes against "enemy combatants" or the grotesque executions of rival gang members and civilians by the Mexican criminal organization Los Zetas. Agonal sovereignty may then seem an anachronistic concept to apply to an eighteenth-century context. However, postwar veteran narratives such as those of Sampson and Martin evince how this theoretical approach might reposition our understanding of the representation of Revolutionary War violence.

Unlike biopolitical modes of sovereignty, acts of agonal sovereignty are not concerned with defining and controlling life and do not ultimately express the authority of a centralized state. The concept thus serves as a useful way to consider the inchoate quality of sovereignty in the early United States, when that power was expressed as both a discursive ideal of the popular will and a material reality of organized violence. Agonal sovereignty seems to reconcile these two tendencies within a narrative of military struggle that finds the source of political authority in the people's ability to enforce their will through violence.

In this chapter, I analyze how the postwar veteran narrative perpetuates a divide between the soldier's military and civilian bodies and how such a model encourages a discourse of agonal sovereignty that spreads that divide throughout the body politic. I begin by describing the contrast between the youthful soldier and the aged veteran in the text of the postwar narrative. In many examples, the veteran argues for a recognition that he feels he and/or his comrades should have received. But as these claims for recognition draw on an assertion of the merit of the veteran's military service, they continue the celebration and valorization of the veteran as an ideal rather than as a specific individual. The genre participates within agonal sovereignty, even as it critiques the effects of this discourse.

Martin's narrative, for instance, tries to reassert his individual humanity against such a discourse. His autobiographical text strives to remind its audience of the human costs of war, and he demands that readers appreciate how veterans willingly chose to accept these costs. Martin insists that the particularity of the civilian body remain part of any representation of the veteran. I then focus on Sampson's narrative and how she becomes the perfect subject of agonal sovereignty. In the text of *The Female Review,* Deborah Sampson's military body can be almost entirely severed from her civilian body. Herman Mann presents her as an idealized republican soldier in scenes of heroic valor and patriotic virtue. Sexless and selfless, the literary Sampson represents the reproduction of subjects through agonal sovereignty rather than through birth, marriage, or naturalization. At the same time, however, Mann struggles to account for Sampson's cross-dressed civilian body. Thus, in Mann's inability to reconcile Sampson's two bodies, the narrative might offer a space to imagine the recognition of veterans in a way that does not perpetuate the claims of agonal sovereignty.

Martin and Sampson (along with Israel Potter, perhaps) are likely the most famous examples of the postwar veteran narrative. Their literary personas attained such fame through neatly contrasting approaches: Martin represents the typical soldier, whereas Sampson's gender makes her an exceptional figure. Originally published in 1830, Martin's first-person account of his service remains in print today in multiple editions, and as the title of one of those editions, *Ordinary Courage,* reveals, the narrative opened a window into the experiences of the common soldier of the Continental Army. Martin's narrative has been a widely cited source on the Continental Army for historians of multiple emphases, from the military to medicine, from social history to sports history.[10]

While Martin represents the mean, Sampson's story turns on its protagonist being far from average. The tale of a young Massachusetts woman disguising herself as a man to join the Continental Army has attracted readers across generations, from Sampson's first appearance in print in a brief *New York Gazette* article in 1784 to twenty-first-century novelizations of her life for popular audiences.[11] In the most thorough scholarly biography of Sampson, Alfred Young claims that although she was far from the only woman to serve in drag, she was the most willing to demand recognition for that service.[12] That demand for recognition began with a successful petition to the Massachusetts legislature for back pay, in 1792. Karen Weyler has described this as the moment when Sampson realized that she could use print to shape public opinion of her military service.[13]

This realization inspired Sampson's lengthy collaboration with Herman Mann. Beginning with the publication of *The Female Review,* in 1797, Mann would subsequently act as a speechwriter for Sampson, crafting the address she would deliver as part of her lecture tour through New England, in 1802, as well as writing an unpublished first-person manuscript in her voice, in 1829, which purported to contain details and facts which Mann had lacked in 1797. Judith Hiltner asserts that, throughout these works but especially in *The Female Review,* Mann created his own textual version of Deborah Sampson: "a 'genteel' and nonthreatening Amazon tailored to embody early national ideology . . . with merely a contingent relation to the actual Middleboro, Massachusetts, woman who enlisted for unknown reasons near the end of the Revolutionary War."[14] Where Martin's narrative grounded its protagonist in what it presented as an unflattering reality, Sampson's textual persona floated freely away from fact.

Martin's appeal as the norm and Sampson's appeal as the exception both emerge from a larger pattern of representing the Revolutionary soldier as a model of national character. This image marked a distinct switch from concerns about paid soldiers and standing armies at the time of the war. For many American republicans, the Continental Army had represented the dregs of society—young men without property or families who looked at military service as an economic opportunity. Charles Neimeyer has documented that those most likely to join the Continental Army were "those least strongly connected to communities," such as "African Americans, ethnic minorities, and 'free white men on the move.'"[15]

In the years following 1783, however, the reality of soldiers who were at the margins of American society came to be overshadowed by an ideal of the selfless freedom fighter. Biographies of famous officers, such as John Marshall's five-volume life of Washington, William Gilmore Simms's *The Life of Francis Marion,* or David Humphreys's

The Life and Heroic Exploits of Israel Putnam, presented these men as paragons of virtue. Popular accounts of moments such as the Battle of Bunker Hill or the winter at Valley Forge found this character among the ordinary soldiers of the war. Early US historians such as Mercy Otis Warren, Salma Hale, and George Bancroft claimed Valley Forge as a monument to the endurance and commitment of the American soldier.[16] Israel Putnam's legendary command at Bunker Hill to hold fire "until you see the whites of their eyes" was taken as evidence of steadfast American resolve against a more powerful foe. Ray Raphael has argued that the legend around Bunker Hill preserved an ideal of the war as a close-up, face-to-face struggle among men rather than the impersonal reality of an artillery bombardment.[17]

Raphael's assertion underscores how the reputation of the Revolutionary soldier was transformed. Accounts that celebrated the virtuous character of the soldier favored the mythic archetype over the specific individual. Such accounts draw on the immortal, representative quality of the soldier's military body over the physical reality of the civilian body. Thus, while both Martin and Sampson sought recognition for their service, the contrast between their narratives indicates a distinction in the quality of that attention.

The structure of the veteran narrative in the decades after the Revolution depends on a distinction between the veteran as a living man and his youthful self that participated in the war. This split becomes the defining trait that distinguishes postwar examples of the form from earlier models like that of Ethan Allen. The appeals made by these retrospective narratives turn on the tension produced between two competing chronotopes within the narrative, to use M. M. Bakhtin's concept of the interaction between place and time that structures literary representation.[18] The primary chronotope within the veteran narrative follows the veteran's experiences during the war. In this chronotope, the veteran appears active in the assertion of US sovereignty, as a soldier fighting (or being held captive by) the British.

The secondary chronotope of the text emerges from the framing of the narrative as a history being told to a contemporary audience. In this second chronotope, readers imagine an aged veteran whose suffering and service have been largely overlooked and who feels disempowered within the nation. Asserting that the soldier in the first chronotope established US sovereignty encourages a split in which that soldier becomes a transcendent symbol of sovereign authority while the veteran in the second chronotope demonstrates the limitations of a material civilian body.

This narrative division reflects the trope that John Resch calls "the suffering soldier," a view of Revolutionary soldiers as both brave republican warriors (as young men) and as impoverished and infirm veterans (as older men). Resch credits this trope with overturning skepticism about paid soldiers in the early nation by promulgating support for the Continental Army as a republican institution. Poverty and deprivation became badges of honor that marked a veteran as loyal citizen-soldier, not a paid hireling.[19] In this way, the veteran's lack of recognition after the war represents a continuation of the sacrifices he made as a soldier. The suffering of the veteran's civilian body perpetuates the immortality of the military body.

We can see this rhetoric at work in the many postwar narratives that depend on the veteran's hardships for their commercial appeal. As Herman Melville's novel tells us, Israel Potter's 1824 narrative falls into this category. So does the 1828 narrative of Andrew Sherburne, who served aboard a privateer's crew during the war and was twice taken captive by the British. Sherburne's narrative was released in a second edition in 1831, with an additional chapter that directly depicts its author peddling his book in New York City, including a distinctive visit to a custom house, where one potential buyer rejected Sherburne as little more than a beggar while another praised him as a source of American liberty.[20]

Not all veterans framed their stories in such stark economic terms, of course. Benjamin Tallmadge, the young officer who had been in charge of George Washington's network of spies in New York, the Culper Ring, addressed his narrative to his children, and it was not published until decades after his death. Francis Brooke's narrative describes his casual (and privileged) indecision about finding a profession after his career as an officer ends with the war, and like Tallmadge,

Brooke imagined his primary audience to be his family and paid little heed to the commercial prospects of his text.[21] Brooke and Tallmadge might stand at the opposite end from Sherburne and Potter on the range of motivations that led veterans to tell their stories. But, like the narratives of Martin and Sampson, they share the underlying assumption of all veteran narratives: that the military service of their protagonists deserves an audience's recognition.

This demand appears most pronounced in those narratives that, like Sampson's, appeal for compensation for veterans after the war or, like Martin's, criticize the inadequate compensation soldiers received at the time of the war. For example, Martin recalls the lack of payment he received as a Continental soldier, writing that "the country was rigorous in exacting my compliance to my engagements to a punctilio, but equally careless in performing her contracts with me, and why so? One reason was because she had all the power in her own hands and I had none. Such things ought not to be."[22] Martin's comments reveal a feeling of alienation from the body politic that his military service purportedly helped to found. Martin and other veterans critique a view of the Revolutionary War that celebrates famous officers and reduces individual soldiers simply to patterns of troop movement.

The impetus behind all veteran narratives, whether written to entertain a commercial audience or to enlighten a familial audience, whether written by the actual veteran or prepared by an amanuensis, was to bring greater attention to the contributions of one specific soldier. But, in making this appeal, the genre inevitably becomes a means of participating within the culture of Revolutionary heroism that divides the veteran into an immortal military body and a mortal civilian body. The form of the veteran narrative and its content exist in a perpetual tension; the genre tries to preserve the individual humanity of the veteran at the same time that it feeds the mythos that renders the veteran pure symbol. If the veteran achieved great valor in combat, such as when Lemuel Roberts single-handedly stormed and captured a British blockhouse, then that valor demonstrates the will of a people determined to achieve victory.[23] If the veteran suffered intense hardship, such as the squalid misery of the many sailors forced into the close confines of the

Jersey prison ship, then that misery attests to the indomitable drive of a people who would be free.[24] If the veteran records the indifference he faced from the countrymen for whom he fought, then that disregard marks a decline from the heroic spirit of an earlier age.

In all these cases, the veteran's relationship to sovereignty is not as a member of a collective people but as a warring body that demonstrates the power of the nation. From this perspective, the living civilian body of the veteran becomes ultimately unnecessary to the cultural expression of sovereignty because the military body of the soldier can survive as a symbol as long as the nation can exercise military force. The civilian body becomes necessary only in its inherent vulnerability, through its capacity to suffer and become an object of violence. A dead body killed in war or an aged body living in poverty can serve the same ideological purpose as a heroic soldier by attesting to the authority of the sovereign. Thus, even as the genre overtly argues for the veteran's recognition within popular sovereignty, its formal reliance on the violence of the Revolutionary War as the source of sovereignty reiterates the divide between the military body and the civilian body.

Debrix and Barder's concept of agonal sovereignty provides a means to analyze the effect of this tendency to separate the civilian body from the military body within the veteran narrative. If the military body loses its recognition as a distinct, living individual and instead represents the expression of sovereign power, then the civilian body can be seen primarily as a physical object that serves that power. Debrix and Barder describe how the horrors of war and violent conflict pose a threat to what they call the "ontological dignity" of the subject: "a dignity that typically presents itself as or is maintained through an insistence on singularity, individuality, and uniqueness of being." They theorize agonal sovereignty as a mode of power that emerges from horrific violence and that takes the erasure of the subject's individual integrity as its goal. Agonal sovereignty does not aim to establish a political state or to define the role of citizen, as in traditional accounts of sovereignty. Nor does it seek to regulate the life of the subject, as in biopolitical revisions of sovereignty. Instead, Debrix and Barder write that:

> Within agonal sovereignty, the dominant logic is neither about protecting individual or collective bodies, nor about the opposite principle, that of planning and carrying out the elimination of certain forms of life. Rather, agonal sovereignty . . . evokes the real (or virtual) possibility of a pulverization of these two prior political logics and, in fact, reveals their indistinctiveness in the face of endless scenes of immanent terror, emergent violence, and unsaturated horror.[25]

The dissociation of the military body of the veteran from the civilian body encourages a cultural narrative of endless struggle, in which the nation's soldiers are an ever-present force and all civilians can potentially become warriors. By placing the Revolutionary War at the center of American sovereignty, the veteran narrative as a genre imagines both a people acting collectively and the possibility of perpetual war and violence. Imagining the war as an ongoing debt or obligation within US culture makes agonal expressions of power the shadowy double of popular sovereignty.

The veteran's demand for individual recognition, for representation within a project of communal sovereignty, invokes the violence that also tends toward the erasure of all such individuality. As we might expect from perhaps the best-known example of the genre, Martin's narrative provides the most sustained example of this tension. The narrative demands Martin's recognition as a self-willed individual participating freely in the Revolutionary struggle, based on the intense suffering he endured. It provides some of the most vivid depictions of the human costs of the Revolutionary War, as Martin expands the definition of violence beyond the battlefield.

Reading his narrative through the lens of agonal sovereignty emphasizes how he sought to define the suffering of camp life as coterminous with the violence of combat. Martin often presumes that his audience holds an ideal of the Revolutionary soldier that his memoirs do not uphold. We see this assumption in moments such as his commentary on the hunger the army experienced during the winter of 1780:

> I do solemnly declare that I did not put a single morsel of victuals into my mouth for four days and as many nights, except a little black birch bark which I gnawed off a stick of wood, if that can be called victuals. I saw several of the men roast their old shoes and eat them, and I was afterwards informed by one of the officers' waiters, that some of the officers killed and ate a favorite little dog that belonged to one of them. If this was not "suffering" I request to be informed what can pass under that name. If "suffering" like this did not "try men's souls," I confess that I do not know what could.[26]

Tree bark, shoe leather, a beloved pet—all of these "meals" represent the soldier being driven by self-preservation into behaviors that are physically or morally repugnant. In contrast to the stark appeal to pathos in the content of this passage, though, Martin employs a formal diction that almost seems ready for the courtroom. The language of this passage implies that Martin expects a skeptical response from his reader, as if he expects the reader to dismiss such stories of hunger as unworthy of preservation in the history of the Revolutionary War. Implicit in such comments throughout the narrative is a contrast between Martin as a specific, individual, human soldier and a patriotic, selfless military ideal who met these challenges with a stoicism Martin cannot maintain. The roadside patriot from Kip's Bay haunts Martin throughout the narrative.

The narrative demonstrates that both fighting and deprivation in war lead to the same result: a disregard or even disdain for the individuality of the subject. The narrative takes the recovery of this individuality as its goal by insisting on Martin's choice to go to war and experience the suffering he describes. Against the agonal violence Martin underwent during the war, the text reiterates his integrity as an autonomous subject. Yet that claim to autonomy ultimately relies on the will to violence that threatens Martin's ontological dignity in the first place.

Martin's extended account of his service at Fort Mifflin might provide the narrative's most direct description of the dehumanizing effects of combat.[27] Martin recalls the stress and danger caused by the nearly constant bombardment the British rained on this small island fort in the Delaware River, which guarded the approach to Philadelphia. He remarks that the muddy filth of the encampment made finding a place for even a moment's rest nearly impossible. Martin notes that he went almost entirely without sleep in the two weeks before the fort's eventual surrender. In a scene that resonates with Debrix and Barder's attention to violence that dismembers the individual subject, Martin describes his reaction to the death of an artillery sergeant who was shot while raising a signal flag within the fort—a task for which Martin had been preparing to volunteer:

> The sergeant then came down and had not gone half a rod from the foot of the [flag] staff when he was cut in two by a cannon shot. This caused me some serious reflections at the time. He was killed! Had I been at the same business I might have been killed, but it might have been otherwise ordered by Divine Providence, we might have both lived. I am not predestinarian enough to determine it. The enemy's shot cut us up. I saw five artillerists belonging to one gun cut down by a single shot, and I saw men who were stooping to be protected by the works, but not stooping low enough, split like fish to be broiled.[28]

Martin underscores the unpredictability and the inherent vulnerability of combat here, as he reflects that the dismembered body of the sergeant could have easily been his own. The randomness of death in battle sends the generally secular Martin into a moment of theological speculation that quickly resolves into acceptance of his ultimate powerlessness in such a situation.

Martin's reflections on the lack of human agency in battle are underscored by descriptions that emphasize the loss of bodily integrity his comrades experienced in death. The sergeant and the other men in this passage do not just die; their bodies are pulverized. Martin's simile of "fish to be broiled" implies that their humanity disappears as their bodies are reduced to bloody chunks of meat. Near the end of his account of this battle, Martin comments that "our men were cut up like cornstalks," suggesting that the fighting has transformed soldiers into corpses that bear more resemblance to harvested produce than to living human beings.[29]

Furthermore, within the context of Martin's immediate experience of the war, these deaths have no clear meaning. As he notes, Fort Mifflin was largely overlooked in the history of the Revolutionary War. For example, John Frost gives the fort's defense only passing reference in his 1838 history, simply mentioning the "terrible cannonade" that destroyed the fort's walls and forced its garrison to evacuate. Salma Hale notes that the fort was "bravely defended" but provides no details regarding that defense or the suffering it entailed. Closer to the time of the battle, Brackenridge offered a brief history in *United States Magazine,* but this account was similarly devoted more to the artillery bombardment than to the soldiers: "The spectacle was magnificent . . . a river covered with ships,—four great fire ships in blaze, floating on the water,—the islands and the main covered with smoke and fire."[30]

The siege of Fort Mifflin exemplifies the impersonal, almost industrial quality that was the reality of many Revolutionary battles, as opposed to the idealized myth of man-to-man struggle that Raphael finds in the popular version of Bunker Hill. Martin's narrative serves as one of the few means to preserve the humanity of the soldiers who died there. When the sacrifices of soldiers like the defenders of Fort Mifflin are forgotten, they become neither sovereign nor subjects within the body politic. Instead, Martin's narrative suggests that the soldier becomes mere flesh that serves a war effort. Scenes like this one, where soldiers are reduced to broken and fragmented corpses for reasons largely forgotten, represent how agonal sovereignty takes hold within conditions of war. When the military body of the soldier can be represented through a larger ideal, the specific physical body can be disregarded.

Death and injury threaten the material life of the subject, but Martin demonstrates how the conditions of war place the subject within a field of power wherein the notion of an individual, rights-bearing subject is itself at stake. Debrix and Barder argue that this reduction of the individual into nothing but an expendable body distinguishes agonal sovereignty from both the traditional modern account of sovereignty and the biopolitical revisions of that account offered by Foucault and Agamben:

> In the context of agonal sovereignty, objects of power (to the extent that it may even be said that agonal sovereignty has objectives or objects) are no longer human subjects, citizens, selves (as was the case with modern power), or even life, humanity, or the species (the identified objects/objectives of biopolitical power). Rather, what agonal sovereignty targets are body parts, fragments of lives, bits and pieces of singular human experience and flesh and their always readily reopened wounds or scars. Once again, it is the individuality, singularity, or uniqueness of the human experience, condition, or essence, in a word, of being, that agonal sovereignty wishes fiercely to confront and attack.[31]

Debrix and Barder argue that even Agamben's influential concept of the *homo sacer,* the figure who is not recognized by the state but whose biological existence remains governed by state power, fails to capture the degradation inflicted by modes of agonal sovereignty.[32] As in traditional accounts of the subject-as-citizen, the model of the *homo sacer* implies recognition of a unique individual who could bear rights, even as those rights have been denied by sovereign power.

It would be tempting to read the figure of the Revolutionary War veteran as an example of the *homo sacer.* The veteran's claim to stand at the origin point of US sovereignty while also claiming to be overlooked and excluded from sovereignty parallels Agamben's notion of the *homo sacer* as simultaneously included and excluded from the demos. Yet, as Debrix and Barder argue, Agamben's biopolitical model understands sovereignty as a vertical configuration of power that locates a Schmittian decision-maker at the top of the body politic. Such a model fits well with a narrative like Ethan Allen's. Allen's self-portrayal as both a sovereign figure who declares a state of exception at Ticonderoga and a maligned prisoner of war evinces the transformation of traditional sovereignty into biopolitical sovereignty that Agamben describes. But, as we have seen, Allen's narrative maps a sovereignty that flows along hierarchal lines of authority. A narrative like that of Joseph Plumb Martin invests less in making its protagonist a representative of the nation and recalls a more decentralized experience of violence. Unlike Allen or William Crawford, Martin appears less the victim of British cruelty than the subject of the inherent brutality of warfare itself.

Agonal sovereignty describes the discursive and material practices of war, in which particular lives mean nothing and are subsumed within an objective of mass destruction. Debrix and Barder assert that this theoretical lens magnifies how "sovereign power . . . is received and perceived as a series of decentered, discontinuous, and disembodied performances of force, violence, terror, and horror."[33] Recounting his war experience represents a means for Martin to reassert autonomy against such force. In his efforts to define the suffering he endured as a Revolutionary soldier, Martin struggles against the loss of individuality he experienced during the war. He asserts that he willingly chose this degradation as a sacrifice on behalf of the common weal—an assertion that stakes Martin's claim for inclusion within a collective, sovereign body politic. For Martin, that claim is all that separates his suffering from the dehumanizing chaos of war.

Martin's narrative posits recognition of the soldier's suffering as essential to resisting the horrors of war. Perhaps his most telling example occurs when he writes of his return to the battlefield at White Plains, in 1778, two years after the famous clash there, in October 1776. Martin writes that he and a few comrades walked across the same field where they had fought years before and observed the results of the conflict:

> We saw a number of graves of those who fell in that battle. Some of the bodies had been so slightly buried that the dogs or hogs, or both, had dug them out of the ground. The skulls and other bones and hair were scattered about the place. Here were Hessian skulls as thick as a bombshell. Poor fellows! They had, perhaps, as near and dear friends to lament their sad destiny as the Americans

> who lay buried near them. But they should have kept at home; we should then never have gone after them to kill them in their own country. But, the reader will say, they were forced to come and be killed here, forced by their rulers who have absolute power of life and death over their subjects. Well then, reader, bless a kind Providence that has made such a distinction between *your* condition and *theirs.* And be careful, too, that you do not allow yourself ever to be brought to such an abject, servile and debased condition.[34]

If the scene at Fort Mifflin demonstrates how war reduces human bodies to mere chunks of flesh, then Martin's commentary on White Plains amplifies the political resonance of such treatment. Martin again depicts dismemberment as a consequence of battle. Reflecting on the scattered fragments of deceased soldiers, Martin questions the distinction between the forms of sovereignty that separated these soldiers in life. The narrative erases a line between the idealized citizen-soldier of the United States and the denigrated Hessian mercenary.[35] After expressing sympathy for the dead Hessians and recognizing the grief their deaths must have caused their families, Martin pivots to an unsentimental attribution of agency to the dead men—he holds the Hessian soldiers responsible for their own deaths by implying that they chose to come fight in the American colonies. Martin's retort to his imagined reader, who counters that the Hessians were the subjects of despotic power and lacked such agency, emphasizes the underlying fragility of the distinction between popular sovereignty and absolute sovereignty. His free reader could just as easily end up a Hessian corpse. In fact, as this scene displays, many Americans who believed themselves to have the agency the Hessians lacked now lie equal to the foreign soldiers in death. As in his account of Fort Mifflin, this view of the dead inspires a spiritual reflection from Martin. He defines the distinction between American freedom and Hessian servitude as essentially a product of belief, and as his conclusion to the passage warns, maintaining that belief requires a perpetual act of recognition by American citizens.

While Martin's warning focuses on a line between self-governance and despotism, the implications of the passage speak to a deeper concern. The key opposition here is not between liberty and tyranny, nor between the living and the dead. Martin's anecdote undermines both those sets of distinctions. Rather, the underlying point of division here is between the unmourned Hessians and the American dead that Martin sought to remember during his visit to the battlefield and that his narrative brings to his audience's attention. Martin argues for the necessity of remembrance as the foundational act that gives the horror, suffering, and death of war ontological and political meaning.

Adriana Cavarero has theorized that the feeling of horror emerges through confronting the body with the possibility of its own dismemberment or dissolution. She writes that "death may transform it [the body] into a cadaver, but it does not offend its dignity or at any rate does not do so as long as the dead body preserves its figural unity, that human likeness already extinguished yet still visible, watchable, for a period before incineration or inhumation."[36] The scattered bones of the Hessian soldiers disturb Martin not as a sign of his possible death but as a marker of a meaningless death shorn of all dignity. He expresses sympathy for the degradation of the German soldiers as human bodies robbed of their individual unity and thus of their personal integrity, yet he also associates the revolting spectacle of these corpses with the loss of political agency. American deaths transcend the horrors of war and the threat to individual humanity if they are remembered as deaths made willingly, in the service of self-government. Without such recognition, the discourse of agonal violence faced by the Continental Army leaves its soldiers as unlamented as the Hessian bodies Martin finds on the battlefield-turned-graveyard.

Martin's account demonstrates the confluence of multiple forms of recognition within the genre of the veteran narrative. Many veterans wrote to earn an income through book sales, but such economic recognition became intertwined with political recognition as a source of US sovereignty. Recognizing the value of the veteran's story meant accepting the significance of his sacrifices in bringing the nation into existence. As Martin's commentary on the Hessian dead suggests, this political recognition should also extend to an ontological recognition of the individual soldier as a self-possessed individual who could freely choose to make such sacrifices on behalf of the common weal. Personal autonomy becomes the key to establishing ontological dignity.

Yet Martin argues throughout the narrative that the divide between the military and civilian bodies of the veteran allows for recognition in a political register without necessitating attention to the economic or the ontological. Soldiers can be acknowledged for their participation within a collective military body while the needs of their individual civilian bodies are ignored. The military body of the veteran can provide recognition within popular sovereignty, and the veteran can be praised for the sacrifice of his autonomy as a soldier.

However, this rhetoric of sacrifice by no means ensures that such autonomy will be restored to the veteran after the war. Martin's narrative confronts an aporia within the genre's request for recognition. Veterans like Martin ask to be acknowledged for their individual humanity. They ask to be seen not solely as part of an immortal military body but also as specific mortal bodies. The genre perpetually argues for the immortality of the military body in its insistence on the sacrifice made by these mortal bodies. By reiterating the civilian body's loss of autonomy, the veteran narrative cannot help but inspire the fable of the virtuous, suffering soldier.

For instance, in a telling passage near his narrative's conclusion, Martin accuses his country of failing to recognize his human individuality in a very specific, very corporeal way:

> Almost every one has heard of the soldiers of the Revolution being tracked by the blood of their feet on the frozen ground. This is literally true, and the thousandth part of their sufferings has not, nor ever will be told. That the country was young and poor, at that time, I am willing to allow, but young people are generally modest, especially females. Now, I think the country (although of the feminine gender, for we say "she" and "her" of it) showed but little modesty at the time alluded to, for she appeared to think her soldiers had no private parts. For on our march from the Valley Forge, through the Jerseys, and at the boasted Battle of Monmouth, a fourth part of

> the troops had not a scrip of anything but their ragged shirt flaps to cover their nakedness, and were obliged to remain so long after.[37]

The image of the Revolutionary soldier's bloody footprints presents another example of agonal sovereignty's tendency to reduce the individual to mere fragments of flesh. Bloody footprints demonstrate the soldier's suffering, yet they are literally separated from the actual soldier in pain. Even as Martin seeks to counter this mythic view of the Revolutionary past, however, he demonstrates his own participation within that discourse by offering a different example of heroic sacrifice.

Martin amplifies the rhetoric behind the bloody footprints trope in his claim that many veterans lacked pants, as well as shoes. He makes this claim through an extended metaphor of the country as an immodest young woman. Martin's appeal for economic and/or ontological recognition becomes conflated with an assertion of his masculine autonomy—autonomy that he sees as under threat from a country he personifies as something of a coquette. Martin asserts, in particular, that the country has behaved as if "her soldiers had no private parts." Soldiers become either eunuchs or automatons, in this metaphor. The idea of the "private part" here suggests those parts of the body that, unlike the arms or feet, belong solely to the individual and not to the army. Martin argues that the nation has treated its soldiers as sexless bodies that can be sent to war, rather than as individual men. Yet this metaphor also insists that a particular part of those bodies entitles the soldier to the dignity he feels has been denied. As he reiterates his autonomy over his flesh, Martin implicitly accepts the logic of agonal sovereignty, that his ontological integrity can be reduced to that flesh.

Martin's expectation of bodily autonomy as a man becomes clearer when his narrative is compared with *The Female Review.* Deborah Sampson's body could be transformed in exactly the way Martin imagines in his metaphor of the immodest young woman. As a female soldier in drag, Sampson could be seen as having no private parts—in the sense of having no sexual organs and in the sense that her sexual organs belong to the public. Mann depicts the first sense directly within the text as a means to achieve the correct understanding of the second sense. Throughout the narrative, Mann portrays Sampson as a chaste young woman (and an impotent young man), to argue that, despite her violation of gender norms, she remained capable of being a faithful republican wife and mother and not the promiscuous girl her cross-dressing might imply. Through this characterization, Mann develops a view of the Revolutionary soldier as a sexless body and illustrates how agonal sovereignty reproduces subjects not only through physical violence and horror but also through the demands for political recognition that we find within the veteran narrative. Rather than social reproduction through marriage, Sampson's narrative models the reproduction of warring bodies.

Unlike Martin or other male veterans, Sampson's military and civilian bodies are divided not only by time but also by gender performance. *The Female Review* asserts that the adventurous young woman who disguised herself as a man has matured into a demure wife and mother. In his effort to establish Sampson's virtue and chastity, Mann essentially creates a fictive persona in many places within *The Female Review.* He places Sampson at battles she could not have seen and gives her adventures she could not have had. While the historical Deborah Sampson served only around eighteen months, in 1782 and 1783, in the Mid-Atlantic theater of the war, Mann's literary Sampson ranges from Cornwallis's surrender at Yorktown to the streets of Philadelphia to an expedition into the Ohio frontier.

The liberties Mann takes with Sampson's story create perhaps the most vivid illustration of the split between the soldier's military and civilian bodies. That contrast becomes so distinct in many places in the narrative that Mann might as well be describing two different people. Hiltner has observed that, in some of the narrative's more adventurous scenes, "It is as if Mann . . . forgets temporarily that the subject of his memoirs is a woman." Ann Fabian calls such a depiction a common feature of female transvestite narratives, stating that such texts frequently follow the generic conventions of masculine narratives.[38]

I would push Hiltner's and Fabian's observations even further. It is not that Mann forgets Sampson is a woman so much as he forgets that she is human at all. Mann portrays his subject as a mythic figure of the Revolutionary past who combines two sometimes opposing personas: Deborah Sampson, a complex woman who served in the Continental Army, and Robert Shirtliff, a fantastic archetype of the republican citizen-soldier.

Like Samet's account of the civil war between the soldier's two bodies, *The Female Review* struggles to resolve these two protagonists into a consistent characterization. The very prose of the narrative often reflects this struggle. Mann writes in a tortured style that can make the subjects of his sentences unclear. His prose frequently bounces between chronotopes to refer to Sampson in the past at one moment and in the present at the next. When added to his complete fabrication of entire sections of the narrative, this tendency makes it difficult to develop any real sense of the woman who told him her story. For example, Mann comments on Sampson's participation in an assault on a pair of British redoubts at Yorktown:

> Was not this enterprise, alone, in a female, worth the attainment of liberty? Yet, where is the fair one who could again hazard it! Methinks I see the crimson cheek of the female turning pallid, her vigorous limbs relaxing and tottering in the rehearsal of this eventful scene. Yet, let no one imagine I have painted it to the life. The fact is simply narrated; and the proper coloring is left for those peculiar inmates of the female benevolent and heroic breasts. I hasten to drop the scene.[39]

This passage provides a representative sample of Mann's twisted syntax and verbose diction. Presumably, the antecedent for "the female" in the third sentence of this passage refers to Sampson, and this line describes Sampson's reaction as she narrated this passage to Mann. Yet Mann's wording leaves this interpretation ambiguous because he presents this physical reaction to the traumatic memory as a vision he imagines rather than a fact he recalls. Did Sampson actually have this reaction in the interviews that must have preceded the narrative, or is this purely Mann's idea of how a virtuous woman should respond to this story?

Further muddying the water here is Mann's address to his audience. Who are the "peculiar inmates" he describes? Does he mean Sampson's intimate circle of relations? Or does he mean readers who share the kind of benevolent and heroic qualities he attributes to Sampson? Why is Mann hesitant to depict the scene in detail?

The short answer, at least for the last question, is that Deborah Sampson did not actually serve at Yorktown. The general consensus among scholars holds that Sampson enlisted in the army in mid-1782, more than six months after Cornwallis's surrender. Mann's decision to place her at the famous battle displays how he creates an idealized soldier as much as he records the life of an actual woman. The attack on the British redoubts at Yorktown would no doubt have been an inviting moment to showcase Sampson's virtue. This clash became notable due to the involvement of Alexander Hamilton and the Marquis de Lafayette, who commanded the two units that attacked the redoubts. Also, despite having orders to take no prisoners, the American forces accepted the surrender of the redoubts' defenders. This combination of famous officers and American magnanimity made the clash an appealing anecdote for early US historians.

Hiltner cites David Ramsay and William Gordon as Mann's main sources for most Revolutionary battles, and his depiction of this attack accords with their accounts.[40] Mann makes Sampson part of this moment, to associate her military service with the highest ideals represented by the Revolutionary army. He praises Sampson as an exceptional woman fighting to attain liberty. At the same time, he insinuates that Sampson should never have been in such a situation, describing the stress even the memory of this clash still causes her. The way in which Mann can be read as praising and criticizing Sampson here reiterates the divide between her military performance and her civilian body. Robert Shirtliff courageously participated in this heroic moment, even as Deborah Sampson trembles at its recall.

Mann's depiction of Sampson reminds us that both the military body and the civilian body can only appear in narrative as representations. Where Martin and other veteran writers demand to be recognized as specific men, Mann felt free to craft both Sampson's civilian and military personas. Sampson's history becomes pure text, ungrounded in the imperfections of a particular body. Mann thus presents Sampson as the ideal example of a patriotic myth that imagines the military body of the soldier as his access to sovereignty. Sampson's appeal for recognition cannot carry the implicit call for individual recognition as a citizen within popular sovereignty, as made by Martin and other veterans. Because of her transgression of gender expectations, Sampson's narrative cannot demand the kind of economic or ontological recognition sought by Martin. She can only be acknowledged as part of the aggregate military body that established US sovereignty.

Her exclusion from full citizenship thus allows Mann to depict Sampson's civilian body as totally subordinate to her military body. Mann portrays Sampson in ways that highlight how her virtuous character as a woman stood her well in the army. She appears in the text as a model soldier—quite literally, in one anecdote from her time serving as General John Paterson's waiter:

> The General's attachment towards his new attendant was daily increasing. Her martial deportment, blended with the milder graces and vivacity of her sex and youth, filled him with admiration and wonder. Anxious to avail himself of every advantage to inspire his troops with emulation in the cause of their country, it is said, perhaps justly, that when he saw a delinquency or faintheartedness in his men, he often referred them to some heroic achievement of his smock-faced boy, or convinced them by an ocular example. . . . Hence it seems he was led to conceive that such an assemblage of courage and refinement could exist but in the superior order of his sex; and that such a youth was highly calculated to shine either in the sphere of war, or in the profession of a gentleman of taste and philosophic refinement.[41]

Here Mann attributes the positive impression Sampson has made on her commander to her presentation of both masculine and feminine characteristics. He claims that General Paterson believed Sampson could achieve greatness both socially and militarily because of the "refinement" her femininity added to her masculine courage.

From a modern point of view, we might say that Sampson appears as a model soldier to her commanding officer because she presents an androgynous subject who embodies the most valued traits from the binary gender roles of her society. Yet Mann quickly adds further commentary to this anecdote to attenuate the subversive potential of Sampson's androgyny. He directly addresses the narrative's female readers, informing them that "whilst you see the avidity of a maid in her teens confronting dangers and made a veteran example in war, you need only half the assiduity in your proper, domestic sphere, to render your charms completely irresistible."[42] Mann warns young women to remain in their socially prescribed roles and not to follow Sampson's example, despite the praise she earned. Where some might read Sampson's military success as an argument for an expanded public role for women, Mann takes the opposite tack and suggests that her traditionally feminine qualities made her a better soldier. Rather than implying that women deserve greater equality, Mann's rhetoric implies that men might become more submissive to authority.

Mann creates out of whole cloth several scenes of Robert Shirtliff in action. Sampson appears calm, deliberate, and decisive in these anecdotes. She maintains loyalty to her comrades, defends the innocent, and punishes her enemies. In short, she appears the perfect citizen-soldier. Mann took the greatest liberty with Sampson's character in the scenes where his story was unmoored from her actual experience. Young notes that Mann invents his least reliable plot points for the period between the summer of 1783, when Sampson was hospitalized with the illness that led to the discovery of her secret, and October 1783, when she was discharged from the army.[43]

Sampson's service on an expedition against British-allied Indians on the western frontier stands as the most notable example. This expedition follows a tangent of Sampson joining an expedition into the Ohio country with Colonel Benjamin Tupper. Tupper would become one of the early settlers of Ohio in 1788, but this expedition, in 1783, appears to be entirely fictional. As such, this subplot closely follows the conventions of other frontier narratives and relies on the threats of devious Indians and an inhospitable landscape as challenges to its protagonist.[44] Sampson survives physical hardship, outwits and outshoots her Indian adversaries, and rescues a captive young white woman during these frontier adventures.[45]

The idealized military body Sampson's narrative evokes is a literal fiction, but this military body becomes the guarantee of the virtue of her civilian body. Presenting Sampson as a soldier of impeccable courage, discipline, and decorum allowed Mann to allay the suspicion that a cross-dressing woman would join the army to work as a prostitute or to continue a relationship with a lover. Elizabeth Ellet alluded to the prevalence of such suspicions in her 1848 history, *The Women of the American Revolution,* where she states that "there is no reason to believe that any consideration foreign to the purest patriotism, impelled her [Sampson] to the resolution of assuming male attire, and enlisting in the army."[46]

Sexual relations motivated many of the popular examples of women warriors during the late eighteenth century. *The Female Soldier; or, the Surprising Life and Adventures of Hannah Snell,* appeared in 1750 and told the story of Hannah Snell, a British woman who donned drag to follow into the army the husband who had abandoned her.[47] Two prominent novels of the early republic also featured women whose romantic feelings led them to the military in drag: the anonymous *History of Constantius and Pulchera, or Constancy Rewarded* (1794), and Charles Brockden Brown's *Ormond, or, The Secret Witness* (1799). As Sandra Gustafson has argued, however, Mann provides Sampson with a different motivation—she acts not out of love for a man but out of love for her country.[48] Mann states this idea directly at one point in the narrative:

> Neither the rigor of a parent to induce her marriage with one whom she did not dislike, nor her own abhorrence of the idea of being considered a female candidate for conjugal union, is the cause of her turning volunteer in the American War; as may hereafter

> partly be conjectured by an anonymous writer. This must be the greatest obstacle to the magic charm of the novelist. She did not slight love, nor was she a distracted inamorata.[49]

Mann acknowledges that Sampson makes an unconventional romantic heroine. Her story cannot easily be placed within a paradigm that defines the female soldier through her relationship with a man. Instead, Mann argues that Sampson's love of liberty was a different form of conjugal union where "her love extended to all." The expansive love that Mann describes here could be read as the kind of commitment to the commonweal that we expect from republican rhetoric. Yet Mann's use of the language of romance and marriage to describe Sampson's patriotic impulses suggests how agonal sovereignty might create warring bodies in more ways than just violence.

In a plotline common to stories of women warriors, Mann presents Sampson as attractive to many women in her male guise. He comments extensively on Sampson's relationship with a wealthy young woman from Baltimore who became infatuated with Robert Shirtliff. Mann attempts to disperse the homoerotic charge of this relationship, writing that, had the young woman known that Shirtliff was Sampson, her attraction would have likely "subsided into a calm, and have drooped, like the rose or lily, on its dislocated stalk."[50] Greta LaFleur has analyzed Mann's reliance on a botanical idiom to explain Sampson's sexual behavior as unusual but not unnatural, and we see that approach here, as Mann dismisses the possibility that the Maryland woman's sexual desire could be anything more than a case of mistaken identity.[51]

He further dismisses the prospect of lesbian desire in his account of Sampson's flirtations with the girls of her uncle's village, following her discharge from the army, when she spent the winter living under the name of her younger brother and continuing to pass as a man:

> But her correspondence with her sister sex!—Surely it must have been that of sentiment, taste, purity; as animal love, on her part, was out of the question. . . . Worse, indeed, it might have been, had any one entered against her—not a bill of ejectment, but a system

> of compulsion, for having won of her a large bet in a transport of bliss, after Morpheus had too suddenly whirled away two-thirds of the night—still refusing to satisfy the demand![52]

In some of his most obscure prose, Mann implies that any woman who actually sought to consummate an attraction to Robert Shirtliff would have been highly disappointed.

As LaFleur's research has shown, *The Female Review* clearly has much to offer to the history of sexuality in the early United States. The full range of those implications is beyond the scope of my analysis, so I want to focus less on what such scenes reveal about Herman Mann's attempt to understand the sexual behavior of Deborah Sampson and more on what they tell us about his invention of Robert Shirtliff as a Revolutionary symbol.

Mann ties sex to procreation and insinuates that, because Sampson could not reproduce with other women, "animal love, on her part, was out of the question." Through his disavowal of same-sex desire, Mann reiterates the divide between the civilian Deborah Sampson and the soldier Robert Shirtliff. Sampson's military body attracts other women, but her civilian body cannot fulfill such attractions. Mann effectively envisions Shirtliff as the sexless automaton from Martin's metaphor of half-naked soldiers. Deborah Sampson Gannett could become a proper republican mother in her civilian capacity. But as a soldier, Sampson embodied a patriotic ideal that reproduces through a rhetoric of military sacrifice and heroism.

Her characterization in *The Female Review* thus demonstrates the larger motivations Debrix and Barder ascribe to agonal sovereignty as a mode of power: "The agonally heroic war machine performs sovereignty functions and tasks for the purpose of being able to produce more and more warring bodies (making potential warriors of us all, irrespective of whether we are friends or enemies) and more and more instances of combat, violence, death, destruction, terror, and horror against human bodies and lives whose identity does not really matter."[53]

Sampson appears as a subject who can be reproduced through a discourse of war and heroism rather than through social bonds like marriage or naturalization. The sexual associations readers place on Sampson as a young unmarried woman are redirected toward her military service. This shift goes beyond Mann's emphasis on her chastity. Sampson takes on a kind of maternal role even in drag, as her choice to enlist becomes a contribution to bringing the nation into being. Rather than creating a nation through child care, as a republican mother, Sampson's example of military sacrifice encourages the further production of agonal subjects. Ellet suggests this shift in a brief line from her profile of Sampson: "She . . . bitterly regretted that as a woman she could do no more, and that she had not the privilege of a man, of shedding her blood for her country."[54] Instead of transferring her blood to her descendants through motherhood, Sampson wants to spill her blood for the Revolutionary cause.

This language of shedding blood in the nation's defense is familiar patriotic rhetoric. It also echoes the claims of agonal sovereignty over human bodies. The nation emerges from the transformation of the civilian body into a military body, where the individual no longer maintains ownership of his or her bodily integrity. The physical body becomes mere parts that support the immortality of the military body. Again, Sampson appears as the ideal subject of such discourse. Whereas a soldier like Martin protests this separation of the civilian body from the military body, Sampson could be portrayed as the embodiment of this split.

Given the paradox of recognition that agonal sovereignty produces for the Revolutionary veteran, we should not be surprised to find Joseph Plumb Martin turning to additional forms of recognition and to other means to assert his ontological dignity. Like many ordinary white men during the early nineteenth century, Martin found such a means in his racial identity. As we will see in chapter 4, the rhetoric of white male supremacy and the discourse of Revolutionary military heroism made a potent alliance in the antebellum period.

Martin makes few comments on this topic over the course of the narrative, but in these rare moments he reveals an investment in his status as both white and male. This commitment to white male supremacy emerges from scenes Martin presents as moments of levity. In one example, Martin relates a racist joke he observed a wagon master make to a woman about a young African American boy sitting by the fireplace of her home: "'Mother, is that your son that sits in the corner?' 'My son!' said she. 'Why, don't you see he is a Negro?' 'A Negro! Is he?' said the man. 'Why I really thought he was your son, only that he had sat there until he was smoke-dried.'"

In another example, Martin recalls his reaction upon encountering an interracial couple who sold liquor out of their home:

> "My dear," said the lady, "this soldier wishes for a quart of rum." I was thunderstruck . . . I took my canteen and hastened off as fast as possible, being fearful that I might hear or see more of their "dear-ing," for had I, I am sure it would have given me the ague. However agreeable such "twain's becoming one flesh" was in that part of the Union, I was not acquainted with it in that in which I resided.[55]

In each example, Martin links casual racism with criticisms of female virtue. The first example creates its frisson as humor through the implicit threat of miscegenation. The second example makes that threat explicit. Martin presents the idea of a white woman in a sexual relationship with a black man first as amusing, then as revolting.

Behind Martin's levity lurks a fear that he can be replaced, that the social privilege of his body might be taken away just as the sexual privilege of that body appears to have been lost in these anecdotes. Read in the context of his narrative's appeal for recognition, we can see Martin's anxiety that his body counts as nothing outside of its capacity to serve the military needs of the nation. White male supremacy enabled him to reassert the absolute primacy of that body, to maintain that the body he gave to the army and the nation is recognized as his property. Such ideology maintained the integrity of Martin's unique individual body. It allowed him to see himself as more than just feet that can march and arms that can kill.

Martin sees recognition of his choice to suffer as essential to his being included within popular sovereignty. Sampson's appeal for recognition demonstrates how that claim always enables the veteran to be claimed within agonal sovereignty. But Sampson's narrative also demonstrates how we might imagine forms of recognition that don't insist on the priority of the civilian body. Instead, her narrative, by making the divide between chronotopes more extreme, by casting the soldier and the veteran as essentially distinct bodies, allows us to recognize the essential differences between the military body and the civilian body and to locate dignity in each outside of the rhetoric of sacrifice. We can see both bodies as deserving of recognition while resisting agonal sovereignty's claim that the civilian body deserves recognition because of the military body's sacrifices.

4

Isaac Hubbell, James Roberts, and the Fantasy of a White Army

AMONG THE MANY veterans of the Revolutionary War who published narratives, Jonathan Burnham, a colonel in the New Hampshire line, provided perhaps the most glowing account of the war's results, in his 1814 text: "Then we had our independence from Great Britain, and peace and plenty and the love of the whole world, and were the happiest nation in the world." Though Burnham may have been guilty of a small measure of hyperbole, his rosy recollection of the United States following the Revolution stood in stark contrast to his feelings about the war that he found the nation fighting at the time of his writing—his narrative closes with the frustrated claim that "America is undone, for if we should take Canada it is not worth the life of one man, to America."[1]

Burnham was not alone in describing the War of 1812 as a decline from the glorious era of the Revolution. Other Revolutionary War veterans, such as Samuel Dewees and David Perry, expressed a similar sense of disappointment about a second war with Great Britain and the domestic tension between Federalists and Republicans that accompanied it. Dewees, a fifer, even claimed to have served in both wars, which is a reasonable claim, given that he joined the Continental Army as a young orphan and was in early middle age during the War of 1812. As in Joseph Plumb Martin's narrative, the frustration expressed in these texts indicates how many of the nation's first veterans imagined the Revolutionary War as a moment of collective virtue that had been forgotten as younger Americans pursued their self-interest at the expense of the common weal.[2]

The popularity of such claims helps explain the appearance of two narratives of questionable authenticity that drew from the well of post-revolutionary disillusionment. Isaac Hubbell and James Roberts, two obscure veterans of the Continental Army, also claimed to be veterans of both the Revolution and the War of 1812. Their narratives shared the concern that the later war represented a compromise in national virtue. However, these texts display many fictional elements, given the many bold claims and historical inaccuracies they present. Both narratives openly admit the presence of an amanuensis. Josiah Priest, a prolific author of sensational literature for the popular press, adapted Hubbell's story, and an unnamed collaborator recorded Roberts's experiences.

Priest's tale differs in significant ways from the other written accounts of Isaac Hubbell's war experiences, and no evidence of James Roberts exists apart from the narrative published in his name.[3] Yet, in their fictional qualities, both texts provide unique insight into the ways that the Revolutionary War and the War of 1812 were represented and understood during the years leading toward an even greater national struggle. These two texts demonstrate how the trope of national decline from the Revolution could be put to competing ideological purposes amid the fight over slavery during the later antebellum period. What these narratives lack in historical reliability they make up for in their demonstration of the efforts of antebellum writers to reshape American history in order to narrate the nation's violent past as a warning to an increasingly troubled present.

While these texts agree that the War of 1812 marked a symbolic end to the promise of the Revolutionary era, they describe this moment through contrasting emotions. The narratives of Hubbell and Roberts respond to a nationalist discourse that envisioned liberty as the product of the collective strength of a continental body politic. Both narratives implicitly assume an ideology of popular sovereignty that remembers the violence of the Revolution as an expression of the will of the American people—with that people defined not as an aggregation of local political communities but as the association of men from across the colonies joined in communal resistance.

The collective will to political violence appeared as the most concrete expression of popular sovereignty, but, like Martin's narrative, these texts imagine this collective will to be the product of the subordination of the individual to the common weal. Military service offered a compelling model of this subordination, and both narratives emphasize the individual act of submission to military authority as a means of describing a commitment to the nation. However, in the racial contrast between the white Hubbell and the black Roberts, these narratives also suggest that such a commitment only gains legitimacy through a discourse of white supremacy and racial purity.

Read together, these two narratives indicate that racial difference has provided the ideological underpinnings of the history of American revolutionary violence by imagining the legitimate expression of this violence as the sole domain of the united white men of the United States. Josiah Priest framed Isaac Hubbell's experiences in 1812 as a lament over the loss of the national unity that Priest attributed to the Revolutionary conflict. He found this unity embodied in the Continental Army, and the narrative concluded in dismay that the army assembled for the second Anglo-American war lacked the fraternity that Priest associated with the army that had won the first.

Priest told Hubbell's story as that of a white man who abandoned his military service to live as an Indian before ultimately recognizing the error of his ways and returning to the normative racial order—an order figured by Hubbell's membership in the army. Such an ideal anticipated Priest's later writings as a proslavery apologist and indicated his desire to locate the ideology of white supremacy within the nation's founding moment.

The James Roberts narrative presented its protagonist as a freed slave who served in the armies of George Washington and Andrew Jackson while still in bondage. For Roberts, his service in the War of 1812 established that the liberty he helped win in 1783 extended only to white men. The narrative reads both the Revolutionary War and the War of 1812 as false promises of freedom in order to challenge the founding notion of revolutionary violence in the United States. As it depicts the broken promises of freedom made to a black man who had served in two wars, as well as the mistreatment and disregard for white soldiers in the War of 1812, the narrative implies that revolutionary violence in the United States had not assured liberty and inclusion in the body politic for those who fought. The Roberts narrative argues that such violence had instead served the imperial interests of America's political and economic elites—it describes war and slavery as mutual expressions of domination and finds little distinction between the battlefield and the cotton field.[4]

Both texts were published several decades after the Revolutionary War, with Hubbell's story appearing as Priest's 1841 pamphlet *The Fort Stanwix Captive* and Roberts's narrative seeing print in 1858. Given this wide time gap from even the latest events in the narratives, it should be unsurprising that both stories feature their share of inaccuracies, but these narratives go beyond errors in memory and present plots that border on the fantastic. Priest told Isaac Hubbell's story as a frontier romance in which the brave white soldier is adopted by his Indian captors and marries an Indian "princess." After being taken captive by the British and separated from his wife, Hubbell was reunited by chance with his Indian bride as he attempted to escape to Boston, only to see her tragically drown, along with his mixed-blood son, as they row out to the boat that will take them to safety. James Roberts was presented as a purportedly 104-year-old former slave who fought along with his master in the southern theater of the Revolutionary War and was promised freedom in exchange for his service in Jackson's army at New Orleans, where, as a sixty-year-old man, he killed six British soldiers in close combat. Roberts also claimed to have argued for a veteran's pension, with both President Pierce and President Buchanan—as a centenarian.[5]

As authentic records of the voices of veterans of the first US wars, the narratives of Roberts and Hubbell appear less than reliable. However, as cultural fantasies of the history of US political violence, these two texts reveal how a stable form of that history emerged through the interaction of the ideology of white male supremacy with the valorization of the American citizen-soldier. Both narratives approach the memory of the nation's first wars as an opportunity to self-consciously arrange that memory into a history that forwards the political argument their authors present. Josiah Priest rearranged the facts of Isaac Hubbell's life to create a romantic fiction of the progress of white civilization and the tragic disappearance of the Indian; the author of the James Roberts narrative told the fiction of Roberts's life as a lost set of facts that overturns the celebratory history of American nationalism. In both narratives, these fantastic elements bring sharper contrast to the ways in which each text locates race at the center of the nation's revolutionary origins. Neither Hubbell nor Roberts fits the ideal of Revolutionary heroism that developed forward from Ethan Allen's narrative. Yet the contrast between their representations displays how white supremacy provided a notion of unity that was essential to the fable of a sovereign people.

The Fort Stanwix Captive draws on two discourses that promoted national identification in the early United States: the commemoration of the American Revolution and the advancement of theories of white supremacy. Both discourses evolved over the course of the decades between 1800 and the start of the Civil War.

The remembrance of the Revolutionary War imparted a sense of national identity almost from the moment the war ended. Public orations and private toasts, especially on the Fourth of July, celebrated the achievement of liberty from Great Britain. Written tributes and ceremonies of mourning marked the sacrifices of American patriots lost to the cause. As we saw in chapter 3, new American histories, such as those by Mason Locke Weems, Mercy Otis Warren, and David Ramsay created a class of heroic Founding Fathers. The wide array of cultural practices for remembering the Revolution as the moment of origin for a new nation allowed Americans to imagine themselves bound by a common identity that was unique from Europe, and also transcended local distinctions among the states.

During the same years that the nation developed a shared sense of history, many Americans speculated that such unity could only be maintained in a racially homogenous country. In his 1785 *Notes on the*

State of Virginia, Thomas Jefferson famously described his belief that people of African descent were by birth inferior to those of European descent and that African Americans should be removed to Africa because they would be less capable of citizenship in the new nation. Many writers during the next decades would further Jefferson's belief that the races could not coexist. The antebellum era would see a proliferation of discourses that sought to demonstrate that white supremacy was the justified result of historical, natural, and/or divine forces. Liberty was held to be the unique motivation of the Anglo-Saxon race, which had carried this drive from the shores of Britain to the New World. The pseudoscience of phrenology arose out of ethnological comparisons between races to claim that the Caucasian race was distinguished by a greater cranial capacity and thus by greater intelligence. Supporters of slavery advanced interpretations of the Bible that sought to prove God's intention for the white race to be elevated above others.

Such discourses intended to defend in theory a situation that existed in fact: the United States was a nation that extended its benefits nearly exclusively to white men. Identifying as a white man deemphasized class distinctions between the lower classes and the elite by investing all white men with a sense of autonomy that distinguished them from nonwhites and women. Like the commemoration of the American Revolution, white supremacist discourse offered a means of identification that transcended regional and economic divisions among men.[6]

Much of the argument of *The Fort Stanwix Captive* emerged from its effort to draw these discourses together to reimagine national history in a way that would justify white supremacy as a basis for social unity. The narrative's mixture of two popular nineteenth-century literary genres suggests the intersection of these two strands of thought. Priest's deployment of Revolutionary-era commemorative rhetoric appears readily within the text, as he depicts Isaac Hubbell as a forgotten hero of the struggle for nationhood. The text shares the generic features of many veterans' narratives published throughout the nineteenth century, depicting a protagonist who proudly served during the Revolutionary War only to be mistreated or unacknowledged by his countrymen in later years. Priest's engagement with racist discourses of the time occurs more subtly, as *The Fort Stanwix Captive* blends the conventions of the veteran narrative with the traits of a historical frontier romance in the mode of James Fenimore Cooper (or of the sections of *The Female Review* set in Ohio). Hubbell's choice to intermarry and live as an Indian is a decision for which he is symbolically punished over the course of the story, primarily through the deaths of his Indian wife and child. Hubbell's intermarriage also interrupted his service in the Continental Army, yet Hubbell appears to redeem this decision by returning to serve in the War of 1812.

This return served to position Hubbell in contrast to subsequent generations of Americans and implied a decline in national virtue. Despite his dalliance with the Indians, Hubbell symbolized a disinterested commitment to the nation that Priest implied had been lost by 1812. The narrative concludes with a final scene of Hubbell, "full of the old fire of the war of Independence," returning to the army in 1812. This second service ended abruptly, however, when a younger officer, who had "taken offence at the old man's stories about his deeds in the Revolution," struck Hubbell on the head with a heavy wood cane.

In the immediate context of the narrative, this attack suggests a decline in the character of the nation's soldiers, as the man whom Priest called "a monument to heroism and courage" is assaulted by a "ruthless envious fool." This officer appeared to gratify his emotions of jealousy toward Hubbell rather than respecting the bonds of military camaraderie or the figurative debt that he owed to the older man as a veteran of the Revolution. Through this conclusion, *The Fort Stanwix Captive* distinguishes between the Revolution and the War of 1812, indicating a decline of the fellow feeling that bound individuals into an American nation, which Priest sought to locate in the memory of the earlier war. As a commemoration of the Revolution, *The Fort Stanwix Captive* called on its readers to rally around the common sacrifices made by men like Hubbell and to avoid the selfish disregard for such efforts shown by the younger officer.[7]

This appeal to respect the Revolutionary past stemmed from Priest's presentation of Hubbell at the end of the narrative as an example of disinterested republican virtue. Motivated by the same spirit that led him to war in 1776, Hubbell returned to serve his country once again, in 1812. By depicting Hubbell as both a brave young soldier who accomplished many daring tasks in battle during the Revolution and an older veteran who received the scorn and abuse of a younger generation in 1812, Priest incorporated a cultural image John Resch has described as "the suffering soldier," a dual-faceted figure that simultaneously emphasized the Revolutionary veteran's bravery and endurance during the war and his infirmity and deprivation after its conclusion. Emerging through the many personal narratives and pension testimonies given by Revolutionary veterans during the years after the war, the image of the suffering soldier became a celebration of the heroic sacrifices of those veterans and, Resch argues, encouraged a shift in national memory regarding the Continental Army. Negative portrayals of this force as a collection of social dregs and mercenaries, motivated only by enlistment bounties, gave way to an idealized view of these soldiers as virtuous republican warriors fighting on behalf of the American people. The motif of the suffering soldier allowed soldiers of the Continental Army to be perceived as having made a disinterested defense of the will of the people, even if they enlisted out of economic self-interest.

Standing armies of professional soldiers that would be beholden to the will of their patron had long been considered a danger to liberty in republican thought, but the reality of fighting a prolonged war often made such soldiers essential. As a result, Americans sought ways to imagine the soldier of the United States that emphasized his autonomy and independence, even as they acknowledged the subordination necessary for military discipline. Unlike the European hireling, the American soldier was imagined to serve not out of obligation to a powerful commander but out of what Elizabeth Samet terms "a liberal obedience" based in his personal commitment to the cause for which he fought. Even though the soldier of the Continental Army received financial compensation for his efforts, he could be imagined to have freely chosen to defend the common good on behalf of his countrymen.

This liberal sense of free choice would erase distinctions between a virtuous militia and a potentially corrupt standing army. Part of the utility of the trope of the suffering soldier comes from how this conception of military service deemphasized any questions about the motivations of an individual soldier in favor of attention to his affiliation with the national cause. A soldier might have enlisted out of purely self-interested reasons, such as enlistment bounties, a desire to escape an overbearing parent or master, or simple boredom, but his affiliation with the army that fought in the Revolution marked him as a disinterested patriot.[8]

In this rhetoric, the soldiers of the Revolutionary War exemplify an idealized moment of national consensus. In *The Fort Stanwix Captive,* Priest both laments the loss of that unity and advances what he saw as the best means to regain it. In place of the struggle for independence from the British, Priest imagined white supremacy as the bulwark to support commitment to the common weal. The narrative casts the Continental Army not just as an example of national solidarity but also as an embodiment of an ideal moment of white male unity. This racial argument developed in large part through the depiction of Isaac Hubbell's earlier lapse from the disinterested sense of service he embodies at the story's end. Hubbell's intermarriage figures as both a pursuit of his own self-interest and a crossing of racial boundaries. Priest emphasizes the tragic deaths of Hubbell's wife and son so that the protagonist appears as a white man who chose to live as an Indian and suffered negative consequences as a result of that decision. Unlike the officer of 1812, though, the text presents Hubbell correcting his lapse in virtue—in this case, by returning to a racially homogenous nation, represented by the Continental Army.

Over the course of the narrative, Hubbell's career follows a plot of the rise, fall, and ultimate redemption of a forgotten Revolutionary soldier. The early sections of the text present Hubbell not only as a common soldier but also as an exceptional and heroic patriot, to stress his subsequent decline among the Indians. Like many of the subjects of veteran narratives, Hubbell is introduced to readers as a young man swept up in the patriotic fervor of the opening shots of the war. Priest describes Hubbell joining a local militia after being inspired by the Boston Tea Party—an event that the narrator states "roused in a moment the slumbering fires of the bosoms of all true patriots, throughout the country and produced the great resolve that America should be free." Hubbell went on to serve in the regular army and participated in the failed invasion of Canada as well as in the Battle of Monmouth. Priest depicts Hubbell as a significant participant in the latter battle, claiming that General Washington handpicked Hubbell for a dangerous individual mission that involved driving a wagon toward a squad of British light horse in order to provoke a chase that would lead the enemy cavalry into an American ambush. Priest asserted that this mission was essential in initiating the entire battle and that Washington had personally chosen Hubbell because the general recognized him as "one of those fear-naught kind of men."

This claim illustrates both the unreliability of Priest's story as a record of Hubbell's service and the degree to which Priest aimed to present the veteran as an idealized Revolutionary hero. In contrast to Priest's heroic tale, the historical Isaac Hubbell made no mention of the Battle of Monmouth in his application for a federal pension in 1820. Furthermore, he stated that he was a member of Goose van Schaik's Second Regiment of the New York Line. This unit was not included in the advance force Charles Lee led against the British at the start of the battle. It therefore seems likely that the scene of Hubbell bravely serving as bait to lead the enemy into a trap was pure invention by Priest. That invention set Hubbell within the discourse of the suffering soldier by firmly establishing his patriotism and his self-sacrificing commitment to the American cause in the early days of the war.[9]

Such a depiction grounded the subsequent theme of Hubbell's personal decline as he chose not to attempt to escape from his Indian captors but instead accepted adoption into the tribe. Priest made it clear that this decision emerged because an Indian lifestyle granted Hubbell far more material and social privilege than he had known before. The narrator states that Hubbell "had now made up his mind to remain for life among the Indians, as he saw from the position he had acquired among them that he could possess himself of wealth and importance; and besides that he loved Estaloee [his Indian wife] as he had never loved before." As the son-in-law of the chief of his adopted tribe, Hubbell chose the comforts of high status among the Indians over the privation he would continue to face as a soldier in the Continental Army.

Although Priest clearly shows Hubbell as having maintained his physical and social superiority over the Indians, besting the tribe's runners in sport and winning the hand of the chief's daughter, his subsequent suffering in British captivity and the death of his Indian family implied that this privileged lifestyle was unsustainable. The hardships of his life apart from the army suggested that Hubbell had been symbolically punished within the narrative for choosing to pursue his own self-interest rather than maintaining his commitment to the national struggle. Further, the story coded this choice of self-interest as an act of racial transgression and a violation of the norms of white manhood.[10]

When the plot of Priest's text is compared with other accounts of Isaac Hubbell's war experiences, it becomes much clearer that Priest arranged the plot to define Hubbell's intermarriage as a choice of self-interest over military commitment. In addition to *The Fort Stanwix Captive* and his federal pension application, Hubbell's story can be found in Walter Hubbell's 1881 genealogical history of the Hubbell family. The three accounts of Hubbell's experiences offer slightly different versions of his escape from captivity. The unreliability of an aged man's memory may be the simplest explanation for these differences, but the contrasting details here can also be a window into Priest's intentions as he prepared Hubbell's story for a commercial audience.

The History of the Hubbell Family and his pension application agree that Hubbell initiated his efforts to escape from the Indians; both assert that he escaped directly from the tribe. Conversely, *The Fort Stanwix Captive* suggests that Hubbell was unwillingly removed from the tribe when he was claimed by the British as a prisoner of war. Indeed, shortly before describing this capture, the narrator remarks that "Hubbell, as he informed the writer, had now made up his mind to remain for life among the Indians." In contrast, the Hubbell family history claims that Isaac Hubbell snuck away from his Indian captors due to "a constant yearning to see again his friends and relatives" in Connecticut. Priest thus gave greater attention to Hubbell's decision to intermarry and to live with the tribe as an indication of the veteran's abandonment of the national struggle and his deviation from an ideal of racial purity.[11]

This deviation received further emphasis from another key distinction among the accounts of Hubbell's captivity. Priest dramatized Hubbell's story to emphasize the veteran's conscious decision to live as an Indian and to repudiate such an impulse. The narrative implies that Hubbell's decision to gratify his interests by going native could only end in tragedy. In Priest's version, Hubbell was miraculously reunited with his Indian wife and child during his escape from British captivity in Montreal. His wife had joined another tribe to be closer to the place where her husband was a captive, and they met each other by chance when he was detained by this band. Hubbell was ransomed to his wife, and they agreed to make their way to Boston. Just when things seemed about to change for the better, Hubbell's wife and child drowned in a canoe accident as the family attempted to row out to a Boston-bound ship.

In *The History of the Hubbell Family,* however, Hubbell left his Indian captors with his family by his side. His family still perished when their canoe overturned, but the account here rendered this event as an unfortunate accident rather than the final tragic blow to a pair of star-crossed lovers, as depicted by Priest. This revision places *The Fort Stanwix Captive* squarely within the literary vein of historical romance that became popular in the era between 1820 and 1850. Writers such as Cooper, William Gilmore Simms, and Lydia Maria Child published novels during this period that worked to forge a national literature from the colonial and revolutionary past. Such fiction frequently incorporated frontier settings to imagine the nation's history as the progress of civilization moving westward into the wilderness, and often included Indian characters condemned to die or otherwise fade into obscurity before the advance of a white society.

Lucy Maddox has argued that such literature reflected a popular binary in nineteenth-century American culture: Indians were destined for either extinction or civilization; they could not continue to exist as separate nations apart from the United States. Priest drew on such a line of thought by presenting Hubbell as having willingly chosen to live among the Indians and then enduring the tragedy of losing his wife and child before ultimately returning to white society. Child's *Hobomok* offers a comparable literary theme, depicting a Puritan woman who married an Indian man after she believed her white lover had died. When it is revealed that the deceased lover is still alive, the Indian husband nobly sacrifices his own happiness by departing for the West, leaving his wife to a new (white) husband and leaving his mixed-blood son to be raised as a white man. As in Child's novel, the interracial marriage in *The Fort Stanwix Captive* cannot be sustained. Further, the choice of self-interest, which Hubbell appeared to make, became associated with a more primitive culture and way of life that the story implied must fade into oblivion.[12]

By deploying the trope of the vanishing Indian, Priest defined the United States through a contrast between a fading population of Indians and an expanding population of white Americans. Though he did not address this idea directly in *The Fort Stanwix Captive,* this rhetoric underscored that the decline of the Indian nations allowed for the territorial expansion of the United States. As a white American civilization advanced into lands held by Indians, the institution of the nation, especially its power to direct military force, secured these lands for future settlement. We have seen the association of a national army with the seizure of Indian lands as early as the narratives of the Crawford expedition. Such land represented a potential source of property for the soldiers who served during the Revolution, many of whom were recruited specifically through the promise of land grants upon the completion of their service. This land could provide greater economic opportunity and social autonomy for those who served.

Traditionally, the republican citizen-soldier has been distinguished from the mercenary or the soldier in a standing army through reference to property ownership. The citizen-soldier owns property and fights alongside his neighbors to defend it. As J. G. A. Pocock has written in summary of the Renaissance ideal of this individual, in order to value the public good, a soldier must have a home of his own and an occupation apart from making war, as only then will he have any motivation to end the fighting quickly. Unlike a professional soldier, an independent, property-holding citizen would be uninterested in maintaining a state of perpetual war that would threaten his home and disrupt his livelihood. Furthermore, the citizen-soldier's independent property allowed him to avoid becoming the pawn of a corrupt tyrant and to go to war with a clear sense of purpose in defending the common good.

As we have seen, however, such an ideal could not be realized during the Revolutionary War, and the Continental Army included many men who served precisely because they were not property holders. But, as men choosing to serve in the army that makes the acquisition of future lands possible, soldiers without property could see their labor as an essential contribution to the commonweal. Gregory Knouff has argued that Revolutionary-era militia requirements that mandated that all white, male inhabitants of a community be available for potential service played a key role in encouraging the perception of white men, regardless of class, as political actors within the public sphere in the years after the war. What a text like *The Fort Stanwix Captive* suggests is that, in place of actual property, the commitment to the nation became a source of autonomy for American soldiers.[13]

But this commitment only gained value if the soldier could imagine himself as freely choosing to submit to military discipline—a choice that Priest suggests was coded in racial terms. In place of land or other capital, the American citizen-soldier's control over his own labor became the property that established his independence, and his racial identity as a white man became the guarantee that he enjoyed full title to this property.[14]

Through the deaths of his Indian wife and child, the story presented as its climax a final hardship that ultimately brought Hubbell to a state of symbolic repentance, highlighting his restoration to an unintegrated racial order. Isaac Hubbell returned to his place in the Continental Army just prior to its disbanding, and he received an honorable discharge along with his comrades. This detail reasserted Hubbell's equality with his fellow soldiers, following his intermarriage, especially since Priest wrote that Washington himself was present for Hubbell's return and the commander in chief "gave orders that the brave soldier should do no duty, but remain at his leisure, till the army should be disbanded, receiving his rations as the rest received theirs in his regiment." Hubbell's return figures within the text as a moment of redemption, as Washington's order that Hubbell should receive equal treatment to his fellow soldiers erases his transgression of racial boundaries and recertifies his status as a white American male—a status the text highlights through reference to Hubbell's marriage to a white woman after his discharge.

This moment also indicates that Hubbell's dalliance away from the American fold has ended; he has returned to the service that defined him as a virtuous member of a republican body politic. However, this service now appears less as the kind of physical activities that Hubbell undertook before his captivity and more as a passive form of affiliation. Instead, Hubbell's redemption appears to emerge from his solidarity with his fellow soldiers. More than actual military service, this sense of camaraderie factored as the antithesis to Hubbell's racialized pursuit of self-interest. As Hubbell's example illustrates, the free choice implicit in liberal obedience always threatens political stability, since individuals can choose to pursue their own interests over those of the nation. In response to such instability, Priest's story furnished a cohesive sense of affiliation within the nation by casting race as the source of the unity that bound the Revolutionary generation into a sovereign people.[15]

By reading the ways in which *The Fort Stanwix Captive* integrates white supremacy into the Revolutionary past, we can observe how Priest ultimately framed the story's 1812 conclusion as a cautionary tale for his audience in the 1830s. Isaac Hubbell's character arc of initial virtue declining into self-interest closed with his redemption in the institution that Priest treated as the embodiment of white, male unity, the Continental Army. In contrast to this depiction of a Revolutionary-era soldier correcting his lapse in virtue, the epilogue of Hubbell's tale portrays an officer of 1812 violating the bonds of white male solidarity and provides no moment of redemption or remorse. Priest presented the Revolutionary generation as flawed but ultimately heroic, whereas the generation that fought in 1812 symbolized a national decline.

A brief consideration of Priest's later career indicates his concern that this loss of collective virtue had only accelerated from 1812 onward. Although the conflict between Hubbell and the rude officer would not appear to relate directly to racist or white supremacist discourse, this scene of one white man infringing upon the rights of another enables us to trace a line to Priest's concern about the growing influence of the abolitionist movement. Priest presented the attack on Hubbell in 1812 as foreshadowing the discord over slavery that he found in his own time, which he would describe more fully in his biblical defense of slavery, published two years after *The Fort Stanwix Captive*. In that text, Priest argued that abolitionists failed to recognize the ancient grounds of African inferiority and that continued division over slavery would eventually lead the sections of the United States into civil war.

Maintaining white supremacy thus became essential to the integrity of the nation, in Priest's view. He contended, at one point, that the English actively encouraged the end of African slavery out of a desire to cause dissension between the American states, in the hope that such division would produce a civil war and allow the English to claim unmatched authority over the continent once again. He therefore accused abolitionists of tacitly collaborating with the "bitterest enemy" of America. At one point in the text, Priest drew a line from Abraham, Lot, Job, and Moses to Washington in order to cast American slaveholding as an extension of biblical precedent. Like the biblical patriarchs, Priest noted, Washington observed the divine intention for some to be masters and some to be slaves. The nation Washington established can thus be characterized in part by slaveholding, as could the nation of Israel.

This reference set slaveholding as one means of providing the United States, a nation formed in the rupture of revolutionary violence, with a continuous history emerging from the ancient past. Respecting that past thus required maintaining white supremacy. Like the officer who strikes Hubbell, abolitionists ignored the collective commitment to the common weal that Priest attributed to the Revolutionary era. Read from the perspective of Priest's defense of slavery, *The Fort Stanwix Captive* can be interpreted as an effort to locate white supremacy in the historical origins of the nation. To address the divisions within his contemporary society, Priest proffered a fantasy of racial solidarity as the common history of the nation.[16]

Of course, this vision of national history not only obscured the contentiousness of an earlier era but also advanced a false image of racial homogeneity within the American forces during the Revolutionary War. Although a larger number of African Americans joined the British following the offer of emancipation made by the royal governor of Virginia, Lord Dunmore, in 1775, the Patriot cause was not without support from black men and women. On the American side, black men were initially barred from combat roles and were limited to serving as laborers, but as the fighting dragged on and the initial enthusiasm for war cooled among many white men, most states began recruiting blacks as soldiers to meet the pressing need for manpower. This need eventually led the American political and military establishment to accept both free and enslaved black men into the army, with many states offering manumission to those who would enlist, thus creating a dual purpose for many African American soldiers, who fought for both national and personal independence. The James Roberts narrative presented its subject as evidence of the failure of many of these soldiers to achieve the personal independence, even as they valiantly fought to gain the national, and launched a bitter critique of the cultural history of American freedom as the product of the brave sacrifices of white patriots.[17]

Despite its factual inaccuracies, the Roberts narrative framed itself as a historical corrective to this popular myth of revolutionary violence by asserting that the contributions of black soldiers have been erased from US history because those contributions contradict the ideal of this violence as the achievement of liberty. More specifically, the Roberts narrative uncouples the ideas of liberty and sovereignty within US Revolutionary discourse. African American soldiers neither gained citizenship nor enjoyed autonomy as a result of their service. Such examples sought to overturn a prevalent line of thought in the antebellum period, which cited the absence of a large-scale revolt by the enslaved in the United States as evidence that blacks lacked the will to fight against slavery as whites had fought against the British.

François Furstenberg has argued that many early national civic texts proffered a simple vision of slavery as a choice; one could actively resist being enslaved, even to the point of death, or one could passively accept a life in bondage. The Revolution demonstrated that whites had earned their freedom through violent resistance. Ignoring African American contributions to this war excluded blacks from this reward and allowed a belief that those who were held as slaves had assented to their condition. In its depiction of its protagonist, and in the graphic anecdotes of acts of resistance it recounted, the Roberts narrative countered claims that African Americans had passively accepted subjugation. However, the Roberts narrative sought not only to remind its readers of the sacrifices made by African Americans in the cause of liberty but also to demonstrate that such sacrifices only established a sovereign power that continued to deny black men their liberty.[18]

In its claim to present the history of a forgotten black veteran, the Roberts narrative fits within a larger context of historical recovery among African American writers during the antebellum period. Many of these works sought to locate African American claims to liberty within the rhetoric of the American Revolution. In 1829, David Walker published his *Appeal to the Coloured Citizens of the World*, an indictment of the cruelties endured by both enslaved and free blacks in the United States. He would end his argument by quoting from the Declaration of Independence and its assertion of universal equality in order to ask how far the nation had fallen from this ideal: "Compare your own language . . . extracted from your Declaration of Independence, with your cruelties and murders inflicted by your cruel and unmerciful fathers and yourselves on our fathers and on us—men who have never given your fathers or you the least provocation!"[19]

Several African American writers took the implications of Walker's reference to the Declaration of Independence even further, arguing the similarity between black struggles against slavery and the struggle for American self-government. The 1850s would see the publication of works like Frederick Douglass's novella *The Heroic Slave* and William Wells Brown's novel *Clotel, or the President's Daughter,* both of which deliberately posed stories of enslaved characters struggling for freedom as historical parallels to the nation's Revolutionary origin. Like Walker's appeal, these works of fiction aimed to display the distance between Revolutionary ideals of liberty and the reality of a slaveholding society.

A more specific line of argument within such antislavery thought worked to reassert African American claims to liberty based on the service of black soldiers during the Revolutionary War. In 1855, African American historian William C. Nell published *The Colored Patriots of the American Revolution,* a state-by-state collection of examples of black military service on behalf of the United States, from the Revolution to the War of 1812 and beyond, which sought to prove the invaluable role of African Americans in the nation's conflicts. William Lloyd Garrison recorded multiple examples of this argument in an 1861 publication that included excerpts from abolitionist speeches, comments from members of Congress regarding the bravery of black soldiers during the Revolutionary War, brief anecdotes describing African American men who served, and discussions among the Founders on the necessity of enlisting African American soldiers to defeat the British.

In 1858, Nell helped to revive a Boston civic tradition of marking March 5 to commemorate the five men killed by British soldiers on that day in 1770, the date remembered as the Boston Massacre and considered the prelude to the Revolution. The renewed commemorations placed special emphasis on the role of Crispus Attucks, a black sailor believed to be the first man shot during the struggle. Nell's emphasis on Crispus Attucks revealed a desire to remember African Americans as essential contributors to the Revolutionary struggle, and not just peripheral actors. This desire could also be found in the popular notion that an African American soldier provided Andrew Jackson with the idea to use cotton bales as the keystones of the makeshift ramparts his army assembled on the field of battle at New Orleans.

Such ideas reflected a larger movement to establish a distinctly African American history that would provide a sense of communal identity while also asserting the unrepresented contributions of this community during the nation's founding. Having acknowledged the rhetoric of revolutionary violence, African American writers argued that blacks had been co-participants along with whites in the defense of American liberties and that, as a result of this loyal service to the common weal, they too should enjoy the personal autonomy and political sovereignty that had become the nearly exclusive property of white men.[20]

The Roberts narrative clearly draws on this current of thought in its forceful depiction of a black veteran of two American wars who remains in slavery, his service unacknowledged. The narrative combined elements of the autobiographical slave narrative, as Roberts recalled the horrors of plantation slavery, with the argument of the Revolutionary veteran narrative, as Roberts protested that his time at war had been unappreciated. Unlike *The Fort Stanwix Captive,* however, the Roberts narrative made no distinction between 1783 and 1815; it claimed that Roberts's service in both wars had the same ultimate effect, which was to make the chains of slavery tighter for African Americans. By presenting the Revolution and the War of 1812 as equivalent illustrations of white racism toward blacks, the Roberts narrative denied both the ideal of social unity during the Revolution and the idealization of its veterans exemplified in texts like those of Josiah Priest.

Although the Roberts narrative can easily be located within a culture of antebellum African American historiography, solid details about its publication history remain elusive. The narrative was published in Chicago in 1858, though within the text Roberts implied that he had prepared an edition as early as 1856; he described giving his story to president-elect James Buchanan, during a personal meeting. Roberts also stated that his narrative was written by an unnamed black amanuensis, and he expressed what he calls the satisfaction "of knowing and seeing one of my despised race capable of writing a book, however small." Though written in the first person as the voice of Roberts, the role of this amanuensis is never clarified, and the narrative includes no further details regarding its authorship.

These textual references to the narrative's composition obfuscate rather than clarify the origins of the work. Did Roberts write a manuscript version (which he could have shared with Buchanan, among others), which his amanuensis later revised? Who was this amanuensis? Did the amanuensis create the written voice of Roberts from a series of oral interviews and transcriptions? Or does the entire narrative represent the creation of an unnamed writer seeking to offer a counter to the fantasies of white male solidarity found in the likes of *The Fort Stanwix Captive*?[21]

A more direct approach to these questions might be to simply ask whether James Roberts was a real person. Evidence within the text certainly makes the answer appear doubtful. Some of the most pressing pieces of this evidence, mentioned previously, include Roberts's extraordinarily long life (104 years would be considered impressive even today, but it must be considered doubly so when describing a man born in the mid-eighteenth century under the conditions of chattel slavery); his success in hand-to-hand combat against British soldiers at the age of sixty-one (Roberts claimed to have decapitated six enemies during the fighting); and his multiple encounters with prominent Americans (over the course of the narrative, Roberts argued with Andrew Jackson after the Battle of New Orleans and enjoyed interviews with both Franklin Pierce and James Buchanan). In his foundational study of African American life writing, William Andrews notes that many of Roberts's claims are of "questionable historical authenticity," especially his contention that enslaved men were armed to fight as soldiers in Jackson's army at New Orleans. As Adam Rothman has argued, widespread anxiety over the possibility of a British-sponsored slave revolt in the Deep South would likely have made most slaveholders highly reluctant to have the enslaved supplied with guns and drilled as a military unit in the way Roberts describes.

Although some enslaved men did serve in the American forces during the Revolutionary War, there are no records of a black soldier named James Roberts in the Continental Army. Furthermore, no reference to Roberts's original master, Francis De Shields, can be found in the standard reference work on Revolutionary officers, despite Roberts's statement that De Shields held the rank of colonel. As a commissioned officer, De Shields should have left a clear documentary record—especially in light of Roberts's subsequent claim that De Shields was elected as Washington's vice-president.[22]

While the immediate falsity of this claim further undermines the credibility of the Roberts narrative, it also suggest the possibility of reading the text not as the memoirs of an actual person but rather as a fantastic imitation of both the slave narrative and the veteran narrative, which plays with the facts of history in order to draw a continuous thread through the gaps that have erased African Americans from the national story. In its depiction of an enslaved black man whose life spans the existence of the nation, and whose memory recalls its first two wars, the Roberts narrative posits a competing vision of revolutionary political violence to that found in *The Fort Stanwix Captive,* suggesting that the ideal of the United States as a nation established through the heroic efforts of citizen-soldiers had been a facade to cover the reality of subjugation and exploitation faced by many of those, both black and white, who fought in the Revolution and in 1812.

Roberts argued that his service in both the Revolution and the War of 1812 would be displaced from national history, starting with the treatment he received following the conclusion of the Revolutionary War. Although he had hoped to be given his freedom for his loyal service, Roberts stated that he was sold to a new owner in Louisiana and separated from his wife and children upon the death of De Shields. Following his arrival in Louisiana, his new master confiscated all of Roberts's clothes, including his regimental uniform. This small indignity reflected the larger denial of Roberts's Revolutionary service, as he was stripped of the evidence of his participation in the nation's founding. Roberts referred to these events as "the payment of my wages, for all of my fighting and suffering in the Revolutionary War for the liberty of this ungrateful, illiberal country."[23]

The confiscation of Roberts's regimentals symbolized the effort to erase such involvement and to erase the denial of freedom to those who helped achieve it. Roberts's experiences during the War of 1812 render the most vivid illustration of this effort. Roberts claimed that Andrew Jackson struck a deal with local plantation owners to supply his army with enslaved soldiers and that Jackson came to the fields personally to recruit men by promising them freedom, should there be an American victory. The narrative presents the enslaved soldiers as essential contributors to American success in the battle, but it also states that, once the fighting was over, Jackson ordered them to return to their masters and protested that he had no authority to free them without the consent of their owners. When many of these men, including Roberts, disputed this treatment, Jackson chose to distract them by taking his enslaved regiment to a local tavern and ordering the landlord to ply the men with unlimited liquor. Near the end of this episode, Roberts reports that Jackson gave a speech warning that black men should never again be armed. According to Roberts, Jackson stated, "We have fooled them now, but never trust them again; they will not be fooled again with this example before them."

Roberts's commentary on this speech provides a clear sense of the narrative's efforts to unsettle the history of US political violence as the text challenges the reputation of an American military hero and future president. With regard to Jackson's warning against arming slaves, Roberts asks, "Why was not this speech published in the history of that war? No mention is made of it whatever. Such monstrous deception and villainy could not, of course, be allowed to disgrace the pages of history, and blacken the character of a man who wanted the applause and approbation of his country." Roberts here contrasts the power the victorious Jackson held to shape the history of the battle to the impotence felt by its unacknowledged black participants, whose fighting and suffering had gained them nothing.[24]

While the Roberts narrative proposed a lost example of racist duplicity in its depiction of Jackson at New Orleans, most antislavery discourse of the time looked back to the general's attitude at this moment for a potential recognition of African American equality. Apart from the Roberts narrative, I have found no evidence to support claims that men held in slavery participated in combat on the American side at New Orleans, but the free black residents of Louisiana did in fact join the fight against the British, many serving with distinction. Two battalions of free men of color served in Jackson's army at New Orleans: a unit of around 280 men under the command of Major Pierre LaCoste, and a unit of approximately two hundred men, commanded by Major Louis Daquin, which was almost entirely composed of refugees from Santo Domingo.

Jackson praised the contributions of his African American soldiers in one of the two proclamations he made addressing the free black men of Louisiana; the first called on African American men to serve on the American side, while the second celebrated their efforts. In the later proclamation, Jackson stated that he had high expectations for these African American battalions and that his expectations had been exceeded by their conduct: "*You have done more than I expected.* In addition to the previous qualities I before knew you to possess, I found among you a noble enthusiasm, which leads to the performance of great things" (emphasis in original).

These proclamations would become significant texts within African American historical writing. The earlier address, inviting free black men to join the fight against the British, would gain particular importance because it documented Jackson describing black men as "sons of freedom" who were part of the national American family and who would receive reward equal to that of white soldiers for their service on behalf of that family. John Ernest has called these proclamations "a staple of African American historical writing," which was taken as evidence that African Americans should not have to argue for recognition as citizens and should be included in any sense of national identity.

Ernest also noted that a significant part of the appeal of Jackson's proclamations came from their speaker's reputation as a committed opponent of efforts to end slavery. Indeed, as part of his citation of the proclamations, Martin Delany observed that Jackson respected the manhood of African Americans and simply saw their exploitation as a means to an end. Delany quipped that Jackson "would just as readily have held a white man, had it been the policy of the country, as a black one in slavery." Jackson's proclamations thus positioned the general as a contradictory symbol for African American writers, because the same man who could recognize the valor of black soldiers and imagine them as fellow citizens also stood as an advocate of the institution that prevented such equality. The Roberts narrative dissolved this ambiguity around Jackson as a symbol to emphasize the impulse toward human commodification implied by Delany's comments.[25]

From the perspective of the Roberts narrative, Jackson's proclamations belied the link between fighting for liberty and being included in the body politic as a full citizen. Personal autonomy and popular sovereignty, so often made interchangeable in Revolutionary rhetoric, are revealed as very distinct concepts. The appeal to the recognition of a great man such as Jackson suggests that political inclusion emerges not from collective actions such as political violence but rather from the will of those in power. The Roberts narrative used the Battle of New Orleans less as evidence for black inclusion within the nation than as an illustration of the ways in which an American subjectivity purportedly based in the sovereignty of the people actually depended far more on the prerogatives of political elites who maintained the authority to encourage deference from their less powerful countrymen. Through the figure of the enslaved soldier, the Roberts narrative challenged an ideology that cast commitment to the common weal as the basis of inclusion within the body politic. Unlike the white soldier, the black soldier held as a slave had no property to defend—not even his own person, which belonged to another. The enslaved soldier thus disrupted the circle of substitutions that set white supremacy and an idealized Revolutionary history as ideological compensations for an unequal distribution of landed property and other capital within the nation.

Jackson could offer the right to self-mastery through self-defense, but he could also take that right away. The Roberts narrative implies that, in a society that permits slavery, no one can truly have the right to defend his own liberty as long as that liberty can be commodified and sold to another. The ideal of the republican citizen-soldier served only to obfuscate this reality by giving support to an ideology of whiteness as property.

The Roberts narrative invokes that ideology in its account of the bargain Jackson struck with the slave owners of Louisiana to supply his army with slave labor. Roberts claimed to have heard the discussion between his master, Calvin Smith, and Jackson, in which Smith reiterated the distinctions of value between white and black bodies. Smith asked Jackson to recruit as many slaves as he could so that Smith's sons would not have to join the fight, and he closed this plea with the claim that "if the negroes should get killed, they are paid for; but if my children should go and get killed, they cannot be replaced." For a slave owner like Smith, the enslaved represented the ideal bodies to send to war because their lives had no meaning apart from their economic value, whereas his sons carried an inestimable value to him.

The narrative here captures the sense in which whiteness became valuable property through its exclusivity. White lives became priceless through the contrast with black lives, which could be assigned a specific dollar value. Yet Smith's comments also indicate the degree to which war serves as a leveling process that pays no regard to social differences such as race or class—on the battlefield, his sons were just as likely as his slaves to be killed. Thus, Smith asserted the uniqueness of his sons against the complete fungibility of his slaves.[26]

The Roberts narrative aimed its challenge to national history at the distance between this fungibility and the ideal of the citizen-soldier. The narrative rooted its criticism of Jackson not only in his broken promise of freedom but also in the fact that Jackson realized that this offer had to be made to inspire black service. By offering freedom to the enslaved individuals who fought, Jackson evinced an understanding of black men as more than just armed brutes to be sent to the battlefield, and such recognition indicated that these soldiers could demonstrate the mental self-possession to serve as defenders of the republic, even as they lacked the legal self-possession to truly submit out of liberal obedience. Jackson's offer seemed to grant these enslaved soldiers a temporary measure of autonomy in battle, where they have the freedom to defend themselves from abuse in a way that they lack on the plantation. This invitation to serve stood as a complete ontological transformation. Roberts claimed Jackson asked them, "Had you not as soon go into the battle and fight, as to stay here in the cotton-field, dying and never die?" The phrase Roberts ascribes to Jackson, "dying and never die," defines slavery as an uncanny state between life and death, where the slave lacks the authority to resist his physical exploitation and/or the abusive whims of his master and thus lives through a constant process of suffering he cannot resist.[27]

As noted, for the American citizen-soldier, self-defense represents the defense of his property, but the right to self-defense is denied to the enslaved because they are the property of another. The narrative illustrates this denial through its depictions of individuals who attempt to fight back against their overseers or owners and receive harsh reprisals. Blacks who asserted their right to self-defense were subject to horrific punishments designed to discourage others from following their examples. The narrative demonstrates this through the gruesome story of Ben, an enslaved man who killed an overseer and was subjected to an unspeakably grisly execution. The narrative pairs the example of Ben with that of John, a young black man who was whipped to death for having the insolence to tell a white man he would not like to have him for a master.

Both scenes reiterate slavery's dependence on denying African Americans the power to defend themselves against the whims of white men, though this argument appears most clearly in Roberts's account of a man called Joe. Joe received repeated whippings one day from an overseer named Coonrood, whom he murdered in retaliation that night. When Roberts, as the field leader of Joe's work party, was about to receive punishment for the overseer's disappearance, Joe promptly took credit for the murder, repeatedly justifying the act as self-defense, with the claim "my life is as sweet to me as his was to him." Roberts states that, even as Joe was about to be hung, he refused to apologize for his actions, choosing instead to reassert his basic right to self-defense: "It is no disgrace to me; I die an honorable death. Did not God put these limbs to my body to defend it?" He then advised other African Americans to follow his example: "Let no white man kill you, but you kill him."

The narrative's depiction of Joe's fate implies the arbitrary quality of American rhetoric regarding the defense of personal liberties, as it indicates that the power of self-defense rests not in the individual's capability to defend himself but instead on the legal power of the state.

In its depiction of these African American acts of resistance, the Roberts narrative offered parallels to the political violence on display in its account of the Revolution and the War of 1812, yet it demonstrated that these individual acts stood as illegitimate expressions of rebellion because they could not be considered expressions of the will of a sovereign people. The Roberts narrative indicated that the institution of the nation did not emerge from collective political violence but instead functioned as a means to define when such action was legitimate by defining who counts as the body politic.[28]

The Roberts narrative showed the importance of white supremacy as an ideological cover for the subjugation of ordinary white men. Like men held in slavery, white men too could become agonal subjects in the process of imperial expansion, but discourses of popular sovereignty and white supremacy intersected in ways that obscured this transformation and celebrated their subordination to an ideal of the nation. Roberts claimed that, at one point, Jackson informed his white volunteers from Kentucky that they were a hindrance more than a help and that the march toward New Orleans would have had less trouble with only black troops. This statement positioned white men within the same logic of expendability that the narrative finds ascribed to black men, as Jackson remarked that "it would have been far better for us to have had no whites, for there is not a day or night passes that we do not have to dig a hole and bury five or six of you."

By reversing the standard terms of racial comparison and casting whites as inferior to blacks when it comes to military endurance in the harsh swamps of Louisiana, the narrative sought to illustrate the ease with which distinctions between the races could be made, and the arbitrary quality of such distinctions. Furthermore, the narrative set depictions of the inhumanity of battle, such as rivers turning red with the blood of the slain or incapacitated British soldiers being buried alive by their American adversaries, alongside the sadistic brutality of the plantation, such as the increasingly grisly execution of rebellious slaves. As Laura Doyle has noted, the subjugation of African slaves and Euro-American soldiers are not comparable, but they do work in tandem as expressions of Anglo-Atlantic imperialism. The position of the enslaved soldier collapses the boundary between these subjectivities by depicting a soldier who fights for a freedom from which he is excluded and a slave who fights to secure the state which holds him in thrall. The Roberts narrative thus sought to establish a continuum between war and slavery as practices that degrade individuals into tools of military and/or economic expansion in order to suggest the futility of revolutionary violence. The narrative implies that such violence seems to benefit white men only, through the deliberate erasure of the ways in which it has not benefited black men.[29]

The real story of Isaac Hubbell would support such a claim. While Josiah Priest ended his story with the celebration of a patriotic hero, the actual Hubbell experienced little such recognition. His pension application maintained that the infirmities of his wartime service left him unable to work as frequently as necessary to support his family. As a result of fighting for the nation that would recognize his control over his own labor as the source of his independence, Hubbell in fact lost that capacity and found himself ultimately dependent upon public support.

Read together, *The Fort Stanwix Captive* and the Roberts narrative reveal the central role white supremacy has played in maintaining an ideal of Revolutionary struggle as the source of US liberty. For such struggle to be regarded as a transformative moment that secures individual liberty, those who engage in failed acts of political violence must be cast as independent agents acting in their own interests rather than as representatives of a larger collective. At the same time, those who choose not to actively support the nation must be seen as having undertaken a similar act of selfish disregard for the institution that secures their personal autonomy. These two texts suggest that racist discourse supported nationalist history in the effort to establish a cohesive identity for a country riven by the fault lines of competing interests—fault lines that run from 1783 to 1812 and, ultimately, to 1861.

5

Israel Potter, *Israel Potter*, and the Forgotten Veteran

IN THE WAKE of the disastrous reviews he had received for *Pierre,* Herman Melville described his 1854 novel *Israel Potter: His Fifty Years of Exile* as a turn toward more marketable material. He wrote to his editor at Putnam's, where the novel was first serialized, that there would be "very little reflective writing in it; nothing weighty."[1] Yet *Israel Potter* also can be read as an extension of some of the questions that animate *Pierre,* though wrapped in the accessible package of an adventure story. As in his previous novel, Melville would use *Israel Potter* to question the meaning of the legacy bequeathed to Americans by their Revolutionary forebears.

Adapted from the 1824 *Life and Remarkable Adventures of Israel R. Potter,* the novel incorporates the rhetoric of patriotic service and loyal suffering familiar to readers of the Revolutionary veteran narrative. Through his revisions and additions to Potter's purportedly true story, however, Melville reshapes that story to explore the potential dangers of the veteran's appeal for recognition. Despite the author's claims to be writing pure entertainment, Melville's novel worries over the stability of a culture that encourages every humble soldier to cast himself as an emblematic figure for the nation. *Israel Potter* suggests that the aporia within the figure of the Revolutionary veteran reveals a dangerously antisocial individualism at the heart of national identity.[2]

As in other veteran narratives, Israel Potter's story presents an ordinary American who believed his Revolutionary service had earned him a claim as part of the sovereign people of the United States, yet his status after the war leaves him feeling excluded from the body politic. Like all veteran narratives, the Potter narrative highlights the contrast between the two chronotopes within the text: we see the young Potter serving his country and the old Potter suffering in obscurity. Israel Potter's story adds a spatial dimension to this divide. Potter presents himself as literally excluded from the nation he helped found, during his fifty years in England after the war. His narrative concludes with indignation at the rejection of his federal pension application by a nation "for whose liberties I had fought and bled."[3]

Where the Potter narrative seeks to claim recognition by establishing the merits of its protagonist's suffering, however, Melville's novel focuses less on Israel's years of exile than on his brief moments of glory. Melville heightens the contrast between Potter's wartime service and his peacetime suffering by making his fictional Israel an active participant in many of the Revolutionary War's pivotal moments. Potter's story seeks to inspire a sense of communal responsibility for the aged veteran, but Melville's novel reveals the implicit individualism underlying that story. To the historical Potter's period of service to Benjamin Franklin, Melville adds a stint sailing with John Paul Jones and a brief encounter with Ethan Allen. The novel places Israel alongside characters who, rather than appealing to be acknowledged as members of a collective people, instead assert that "the people" can recognize itself through its heroic actions.

At various points, the narrator describes Franklin, Jones, and Allen as indicative of the American spirit, and as many scholars have noted, Potter's first name alludes to the biblical nation of Israel, implying his own symbolic role as potential national patriarch.[4] These frequent references suggest a process of placing different figures in the void left by the king at the center of American sovereignty. The novel envisions the sly Franklin, the ruthless Jones, the bold Allen, and the unfortunate Potter each at the head of the body politic and insinuates that, in the United States, this space can be filled by anyone who can claim it. In his adaptation of the Potter narrative, Melville imagines the demand for recognition as an assertion of sovereign exceptionalism and implies that the model of the Revolutionary War has defined sovereignty as individual autonomy for future generations of Americans.

Russ Castronovo has argued that Melville seeks, in *Israel Potter*, to recover the perspective of ordinary individuals who have been overshadowed by an approach to history that casts the Founders as monuments of American liberty.[5] I would extend this reading further, however, to suggest that Melville's greater concern is not that ordinary Americans have been overshadowed by the Founders but that the reification of the Founders has provided ordinary Americans with an ultimately self-destructive model to emulate. The novel portrays figures like Franklin and Jones, in particular, as emblematic of a conflation of liberty, autonomy, and sovereignty that fuels social conflict. Writing in the mid-1850s, Melville would have seen the rhetoric of liberty being claimed both by proslavery advocates and abolitionists, by proponents of manifest destiny and by anti-expansionists. *Israel Potter* suggests that such social contests emerge from a view of the Revolutionary past that celebrates the aggressive assertion of individual autonomy.

Donald Pease has described this interpretation of the American Revolution as based on a conception of what he terms "negative liberty"—the belief that liberty primarily consists of freedom from constraint.[6] Melville presents his iconic characters as motivated primarily by a demand for negative liberty, and the novel thus suggests a concern that the nation's Revolutionary history cannot provide a sense of national identity that is not vested in strife and conflict. In this view, the American body politic will be bound not by a shared sense of political community but by an aggressive competition among individuals that will be hardly distinguishable from the state of nature.

Israel Potter argues that conceiving of each individual as vested with sovereignty encourages an understanding of liberty not only as a freedom from coercion or as ownership of the self but as a need for dominance over others that can provide definition through contrast to one's own autonomy. Melville presents Franklin and Jones as driven by a demand for independence that finds expression in their mastery over others. The novel offers these famous figures as a warning to the nation—they model a drive toward a multitude rather than toward a people. In casting Israel Potter as the converse image of men such as Franklin, Jones, and Allen, the novel asks what kind of nation can exist when each individual seeks to embody the whole.

Following the disappointing reception of *Pierre,* and of *Moby-Dick* before it, Melville was likely attuned to the frustrated desire for recognition expressed by a veteran like Israel Potter. Andrew Delbanco has suggested that, in 1854, "this story of a life that starts out gloriously but leads nowhere suited Melville's mood."[7] Though written in the first person, the original Potter narrative, from 1824, was actually the work of an amanuensis, the literary journeyman Henry Trumbull. Trumbull presented Potter's narrative as an attempt to earn a meager subsistence for an aged veteran who has been denied a government pension. The preface promises that the narrative will display the "unprecedented privations and sufferings of which he [Potter] has been the unfortunate subject." We see from this description how Trumbull strove to elevate Potter's story above the many similar stories from other veterans; he writes that "there is not probably another now living who took an equally active part in the Revolutionary war, whose life has been marked with more extraordinary events, and who has drank deeper of the cup of adversity."[8]

Rather unsurprisingly, scholars have found that Trumbull took some artistic license to make this claim for Potter's exceptionality. David Chacko and Alexander Kulcsar have documented the discrepancies between Trumbull's narrative and the documentary evidence on the real Israel Potter, and they assert that Potter either suggested or approved Trumbull's fabrications to create the persona of an ideal patriot.[9] These alterations include Potter's claim to respectable birth, when Rhode Island records indicate that he was the child of an unwed mother and was adopted by the Potter family; his claim to have fought at Bunker Hill, though no regiments from Rhode Island actually faced combat in that battle; and his decision not to mention the onboard mutiny that forced the brigantine *Washington* back to port after only a week at sea during his service in the fledgling US Navy. Any details that might muddy the image of Potter as the quintessential minuteman—a sober, industrious, and respectable New Englander who fought bravely for his country—are scrubbed clean. In the midst of his own turn to historical fiction in pursuit of a fickle audience, Melville no doubt recognized the Potter narrative as a similar attempt to perform for the expectations of a paying readership.

While Melville was likely unaware of the narrative's exaggerations and elisions, it is also likely that he would have been aware of how the narrative cast Potter in a particular patriotic role. In a December 1849 journal entry, Melville recorded acquiring a 1766 map of London as a background resource, should he decide to "serve up the Revolutionary narrative of the beggar."[10]

Such a description might seem a bit unjust to Potter at first. His narrative recounts the many jobs he took to try to support his family, from gardening to brickmaking to mending old chairs. Potter appears to have sought to provide for himself as best he could. Yet Melville's language here neatly encapsulates the narrative's underlying rhetoric. The veteran becomes a beggar—someone engaged in a performance to elicit the charity of an audience. That performance consists, in this case, of a Revolutionary narrative; Potter's wartime experiences become the claim he makes upon the audience's sympathy. In place of the pension he was denied, Potter hopes to monetize his story of suffering.

Melville's revisions and additions to the narrative put this economic appeal under scrutiny. *Israel Potter* the novel emphasizes the performative aspects of the original narrative in order to question the implicit objectification involved in a veteran transforming his own life into a commodity to be sold to an audience that already seems to have neglected him. Many readers of the novel have argued that the ironic tribute to the Bunker Hill Monument in the novel's preface indicates Melville's interest in how the discourses of Revolutionary history and myth have overlooked men like Israel Potter.[11] Reading the novel in relation to the aporia of the veteran narrative as a genre reveals how Melville also might have seen these men as active participants within these discourses and as contributors to their own reification.

Melville's changes to the Potter narrative place greater emphasis on how Potter's economic appeal to his audience merges with his identity as a veteran. This increased emphasis appears prominently in the novel's middle chapters, where Melville adds more action to the story and prolongs the plot before it reaches its conclusion with Potter's exile in the London slums. To better recognize Melville's revisions, we might describe the structure of the original narrative as tripartite: the first section is *potential,* a brief opening section displaying Potter's capacity for independent labor; the second is *service,* a middle section detailing Potter's service at Bunker Hill, his capture and transportation to England, and his escape and service as a courier for Benjamin Franklin; and the third section is *suffering,* an extended conclusion outlining Potter's hardships in London and the neglect he faced upon finally returning to America.

Melville's novel drastically extends the second section of this structure and adds an almost mythic quality to Potter's service. Melville took a story that Chacko and Kulcsar term "a warped enlargement of the truth" and warped it even further by expanding Potter's claim to serve as a secret courier into a series of adventures with Franklin and Jones. He also diminishes the attention to Potter's time in England, covering the bulk of the veteran's years of exile in one chapter (the aptly titled "Forty-Five Years").[12] The effect of these changes makes Potter's service, rather than his suffering, the most compelling evidence of his claim upon the nation. In this way, Melville turns attention to the nature of the claim that veterans like Potter hold upon subsequent generations of Americans. Where the Potter narrative presents the question of obligation as an economic one to be solved through financial support, Melville suggests that the language of debt and pensions fails to account for the larger question of the veteran's relationship to popular sovereignty in the new nation.

Melville rejects the sympathetic appeal of the narrative by turning attention away from the rhetoric of the suffering soldier, in which the debt owed to the veteran can be repaid simply through money. His revisions make Israel Potter a soldier first and a poor old man second. In so doing, the novel puts the question of force that appears in Ethan Allen's demand for Ticonderoga's surrender back at the center of our understanding of the obligation owed to veterans. Melville forces us to see Israel Potter as an agent of violence as much as a forgotten patriot. In this way, the novel asks whether that violence can be a source for national affiliation, especially as it so easily slides into a register of economic assertion.

The structure of the original narrative emphasizes the suffering Potter underwent as a result of his decision to enlist and the earning potential that decision would cost him. The narrative begins with an account of Potter's economic independence before the war in order to emphasize the loss of that independence, which he suffered as a result of his military service. Potter describes the many jobs he worked from the ages of eighteen to twenty, after leaving the home of his parents. He recalls a nearly three-year period of clearing land, hunting game, and other hard labor in the New England frontier, which establishes him as the prototypical American opportunist—like Crèvecoeur's Andrew the Hebridean, Potter sought to earn his independence by the sweat of his brow.[13]

Within the narrative, these brief early scenes form a stark contrast with the longer sections that follow the war and detail the poverty and squalor Potter faced while living in the London slums. Potter recalls struggling to find enough work to support his family in a labor market flooded with soldiers returning from war in the colonies. He recounts his stint in debtors' prison as a result of his unemployment and writes of how his wife and most of his children died from the wretched living conditions they faced for years. Potter states that words ultimately cannot capture his suffering, writing that "pen, ink, and paper would fail, were I to attempt to record the various instances of misery and want that attended me and my poor family."[14] Of course, despite such a claim, recording these instances of misery is clearly Potter's intention with the narrative. Like many veteran writers, he asserts the injustice of his poverty after he has sacrificed his economic potential on behalf of the American cause.

Early national veteran writers such as Lemuel Roberts and Nathaniel Segar share the pattern found in Potter's narrative: youthful examples of vigor are supplanted by scenes of debility in old age as a result of suffering during the war. Roberts closes his 1809 narrative by asserting that because of his "suffering in the public cause," he has "not been able to perform more than half the labor that I might otherwise have done." Segar states, in his 1825 narrative, that the almost three years he spent as a soldier and the sixteen months he spent in Indian captivity led him to be "defeated for several years, in my designs of making provision for future life."[15]

Such examples demonstrate how the genre often depicts the veteran as the disgruntled owner of his person and capabilities. Without a pension or other financial recognition of his suffering, the veteran's service appears to be a bad investment. The argument that the Revolutionary War constrained the economic potential of the veteran rests on the assumption that the veteran's service was, at its most basic level, an economic performance that could have been put to other ends but instead was invested in the war. The Potter narrative, like many veteran narratives, implicitly invokes a logic of possessive individualism by envisioning the veteran as an economic free agent who is equally capable of deciding to join the Revolutionary fight or to pursue his own fortune in the backcountry.

As a young man, the veteran could "sell" his talents to his nation by becoming a soldier; as an older man, he literally sells his story to an audience that he imagines as representing that nation. Both acts invoke an imagined ideal of self-sufficiency in which the veteran exists as an independent individual who gives up some of that independence as a young man and laments that such independence has been lost to him as an older man. Just as the frontier functioned as a pseudo state of nature in which young men like Israel Potter could assert their economic independence, the literary marketplace became a symbolic state of nature in which veterans who felt cut off from an imagined national community could strive to regain that lost independence. Such a notion presumes a presocial liberty that the veteran surrendered in order to fight for an American republic, and it assumes that this liberty remains available to the subject even after the formation of the new nation. Sovereignty as a member of the body politic thus becomes defined primarily as economic autonomy over the self.

Paul Downes has described this vision of sovereignty as autonomous self-sufficiency as "sovereignty's dream of itself."[16] Melville's revisions to the Potter narrative draw the story deeper into this dream of sovereignty to heighten its ultimate unreality. *Israel Potter* traces the spectrum between a poor veteran like Israel, appealing for recognition by selling his story in a book, and a figure like John Paul Jones demanding recognition by torching an English port. Both men imagine themselves as independent actors on the social stage, and both define their political autonomy through their willingness to use force to defend that autonomy.

I do not mean to suggest here that Israel Potter ended up poor in London because of his ruthless self-interest or that his appeal for recognition and support in his old age was an aggressive assertion of that self-interest. Rather, I hope to demonstrate that Melville's novel links the rhetoric of the Potter narrative to the same discourse of self-authorization that produced the Revolutionary War and that could continue to justify political violence in the new nation. Many readers of Melville have noted his attention to the autoimmune self-destructiveness inherent in American popular sovereignty, but few have linked it to *Israel Potter*'s exploration of national origins.

Wai-chee Dimock has explored how authorship in the United States has drawn together the tradition of possessive individualism and a sense of imperial acquisitiveness to imagine what she terms the "imperial" self, "the reproduction of the nation's terms of sovereignty within the self's terms of ownership."[17] Dimock finds evidence of this confluence of individualism and imperialism throughout Melville's novels, but she does not include *Israel Potter* in this review. Similarly, Jonathan Elmer has explored how postmonarchal sovereignty has been largely understood through personification; we apply the language of individual behavior to states and ascribe the autonomy of states to human individuals. He writes of Melville that "sovereignty, for this intense individualist is first and foremost a trait, or difficult achievement of the self."[18] Like Dimock, though, Elmer does not refer to *Israel Potter* within his study, even as he notes that the "problem of the modern sovereign subject emerges for Melville from a matrix in which slave and sovereign, despot and pirate, trade places with confounding frequency"—a description that could apply to Israel Potter perhaps even more aptly than to Elmer's principle examples of Billy Budd and Amasa Delano.

In addition to Franklin, Jones, and Allen, Melville's Israel encounters one other famous historical figure during the course of the novel. While working in the royal gardens at Kew, Israel accidentally bumps into George III as the king strolls through the park. At the start of their meeting, Israel firmly denies the British king's authority over him as a subject and refuses to address the king as *Your Majesty,* preferring instead to use the more republican *sir*. But after George III recognizes Israel as an escaped prisoner of war and promises him protection from arrest, the monarch departs, with Israel blessing him and willingly calling him "your noble majesty." Where once Israel was tempted to regicide by the thought that "the war was imputed more to the self-will of the King than to the willingness of parliament or the nation," by the end of their brief encounter, the monarch's charms have convinced him that "it could not be the warm heart of the king, but the cold heads of his lords in council, that persuaded him so tyrannically to persecute America." The narrator remarks that such a reversal shows "what strange and powerful magic resides in a crown" and wonders whether the king recognized Israel's true status as a prisoner of war through "that swift insight into individual character said to form one of the miraculous qualities transmitted with a crown."[19]

In this scene, Melville imagines sovereignty as a supernatural force that grants its bearer greater persuasive power over others. This meeting also occurs in the original Potter narrative, but the historical Potter makes no reference to sovereignty's magic. Instead, Potter claims to have forthrightly revealed his status and his grievances to the king, who responded with a simple promise of safety from further harassment.[20] Melville's revisions to this scene elevate the British monarch to a level of majesty, whereas the Potter narrative would bring him down to the level of a representative responding to the demand of a constituent. These revisions are indicative of the novel's interest in how the magic of a crown has been transformed in a society where the people share sovereignty.[21] Melville explores how sovereign power can be figured when it is no longer tied to symbols such as a crown but instead is seen as immanent within each individual.[22] If each individual can claim the charismatic "magic" of sovereignty, what power will compel individuals to sacrifice some autonomy for the greater good? Is there a magic to sovereignty at all, or is it merely a justification of force? *Israel Potter* recognizes no special symbol that elevates the individual to the representative status of an immortal royal body, just actual human bodies all demanding to be seen as carrying that sovereign majesty.

The Founders held that the body of the king would be replaced by the body of the people, yet *Israel Potter* displays a skepticism that a multitude can ever fit without conflict into the space once filled by one man. Melville suggests that the discourse of Revolutionary history has become the American replacement for the European divine right of kings; tales of men like Franklin, Jones, and Allen define American sovereignty as an inalienable right to be claimed through struggle.

François Furstenberg has argued that respect for the Founders provided one means for ordinary Americans to imagine themselves as participating within the Revolutionary assertion of sovereignty. Even as individuals transferred to their elected representatives their own claim to act as the sovereign, the idolization of Washington and other Founding Fathers provided cultural compensation for the loss of direct political authority.[23]

Melville, however, asks whether such hero worship might ultimately contribute to an individualistic and predatory society. Israel appears far more overawed in his encounters with Franklin and Jones than in his meeting with George III, and the novel dramatizes how assertive and aggressive men such as Franklin and Jones gain power over people like Israel, who are purportedly their equals. Where once the hereditary monarch stood as an embodiment of divinely ordained sovereignty, each citizen in the United States can become a representative of the body politic. Melville appears to be concerned that such an opportunity has only replaced the mythic basis of royal power with an unstable contest within the public sphere, where each individual must constantly perform his right to represent the people.

Throughout the novel, the examples of Franklin, Jones, and Allen present popular sovereignty as an act of self-assertion—a performative utterance of political authority and a literal performance of the force to underwrite that utterance. Melville's novel questions whether the rhetoric of recognition invoked by veterans like Israel Potter might provide yet another example of such a definition. As we have seen, from Ethan Allen's narrative onward, the veteran narrative posits the violence of war as the ultimate grounds for the veteran's claim to recognition within the body politic. *Israel Potter* suggests that this claim to recognition cannot achieve the equality it demands for the veteran but will inevitably lead back to an assertion of the self.

Alexis de Tocqueville famously described popular sovereignty in the United States as circular. To describe how power was shared in the new nation, he writes, "The people reign in the American political world as the Deity does in the universe. They are the cause and the aim of all things; everything comes from them, and everything is absorbed in them."[24] Like Tocqueville, Jacques Derrida turned to circularity to imagine self-government. In *Rogues,* he writes that freedom can only be shared equitably in a society through such a rotating transfer of power, "the governed becoming in his turn governing, the represented in his turn representing, and vice versa."[25] Yet he also maintains that such sharing, so necessary for a democracy, always exists in tension with the nature of sovereignty as an indivisible power. Derrida describes sovereignty as fundamentally an individual assertion of the self, what he terms "ipseity." Furthering the tautology inherent in Tocqueville's vision of the people as both "the cause and the aim of all things," Derrida suggests that sovereignty turns individuals relentlessly inward upon themselves to claim the center of the body politic and to assert their will as law:

> Before any sovereignty of the state, of the nation-state, of the monarch, or, in democracy, of the people, ipseity names a principle of legitimate sovereignty, the accredited or recognized supremacy of a power or a force, a *kratos* or a *cracy*. That is what is implied . . . in the very self- or autopositioning of *ipseity* itself, everywhere there is some oneself, the first, ultimate, and supreme source of every "reason of the strongest" as the right [*droit*] granted to force or the force granted to law [*droit*].[26]

The historical Potter narrative invokes these grounds in its preface by describing how the aged veteran sought "in common with his countrymen the enjoyment of a few of the blessings produced by American valour, in her memorable conflict with the mother country, and in which he took a distinguished part."[27] Trumbull's phrasing here invokes the circular turn to the self that Derrida ascribes to sovereignty, as Israel Potter becomes a source of the "blessings" from which he claims to be excluded. As Derrida's language would suggest, these blessings are the product of the force marshaled by men like Potter during the Revolutionary War—the source of American sovereignty is the supremacy of American arms.

With its increased attention to Israel's time as a soldier, Melville's novel emphasizes that this link between sovereignty and force remains integral to the way Americans imagine their national origins. The novel depicts Israel as both the agent and the recipient of violence in ways that ponder whether popular sovereignty can find a grounds apart from forceful self-assertion.

Jennifer Greiman has found a more optimistic perspective on popular sovereignty in Melville's work, reading his use of the circle as a figure to represent democracy's capacity for purposeful common action.[28] Her analysis centers on the "Grand Armada" chapter of *Moby-Dick,* in which a pod of whales creates concentric defensive circles in response to the *Pequod*'s predations. *Israel Potter* provides a much less optimistic view of collaborative action, however. In moments such as the covert attack John Paul Jones leads on the British ships at Whitehaven, Melville depicts acts of individual initiative, such as Israel's mad solo dash against the crowd of residents who come out to defend the town:

> Those who had rushed to extinguish what they had deemed but an accidental fire, were now paralyzed into idiotic inaction at the defiance of the incendiary; thinking him some sudden pirate or fiend dropped down from the moon.
>
> While Paul thus stood guarding the incipient conflagration, Israel, without a weapon, dashed crazily towards the mob on the shore. . . .
>
> As he rushed bare-headed, like a madman, towards the crowd, the panic spread. They fled from unarmed Israel, further than they had from the pistol of Paul.[29]

As Israel's crazed confrontation with the mob implies, the novel dramatizes the individual will that provides the centrifugal force that powers a multitude, rather than the shared collective will that inspires a people. Instead of forming a collective, general will as a people, the crowd behaves as a multitude in which each individual seeks self-interest over the commonweal. In this scene, the threat of violence breaks the community's collaborative intentions as each individual seeks self-preservation. Although the people of Whitehaven have come together to extinguish the fire, their collective resolve melts before Israel's more determined will. Israel does not appear as a Revolutionary patriot here so much as an angry man striking out at all sides.

Throughout the novel, Melville questions whether popular sovereignty can be separated from this competitive demand for personal autonomy. More than a lost hero of the Revolution, Israel Potter appears as a man lost in the state of nature. Israel's captivity and flight throughout the novel can be read as the travails of a vulnerable outcast, with the character sometimes forced to adopt false identities to escape persecution and sometimes compelled to fight for self-preservation. The novel abounds with scenes of Israel being reduced to either predator or prey. In the most striking example, Israel becomes accidentally stranded on an English privateer during a failed raid with Jones and must quickly present himself as one of its own crew members in order to avoid imprisonment. Failing to find acceptance among the crew, he is interrogated by the ship's officers, and in the midst of this interrogation, he appears as a man totally outside of social life. Israel responds to the question "Who are you?" with the claim that he is a "poor persecuted fellow" whom "all hands seem to be against."[30]

Melville here alludes to the biblical story of Ishmael (Abraham's first son, by his wife's servant Hagar) by paraphrasing from Genesis 16:12, where God tells Hagar that Ishmael "will be a wild man; his hand will be against every man, and every man's hand against him." As if to fulfill both sides of this biblical verse, this moment of Israel's utter vulnerability on the English ship follows other scenes of the character engaging in brutal violence. While impressed on a British revenue cutter, Israel uses the opportunity provided by Jones's attack on the small ship to attempt an escape. He knocks the captain of the cutter overboard and then takes on the two remaining officers in unarmed combat, which the narrator describes as follows:

> The battle was in the midst of the chaos of blowing canvas. Caught in a rent of the sail, the officer slipped and fell near the sharp iron edge of the hatchway. As he fell, he caught Israel by the most terrible part in which mortality can be grappled. Insane with pain, Israel dashed his adversary's skull against the sharp iron. The officer's hold relaxed; but himself stiffened. Israel made for the helmsman, who as yet knew not the issue of the late tussle. He caught him round the loins, bedding his fingers like grisly claws into his flesh, and hugging him to his heart. The man's ghost, caught like a broken cork in a gurgling bottle's neck, gasped with the embrace. Loosening him suddenly, Israel hurled him from him against the bulwarks.[31]

The helmsman soon dies from his injuries; thus Israel kills three men with his bare hands in order to escape British impressment. The heavily sexual connotations of the scene, with stiff bodies, gurgling bottle's necks, and combatants grabbing each other about the loins, emphasizes the intimacy of the struggle and underscores the contest as one of life and death among the participants. One could even read this scene as suggestive of a rape, with the fighters grappling not just for their own survival but to establish physical mastery over the other.

Melville here reduces the scale of warfare to a struggle between men that reimagines the political violence of the Revolution as a battle for self-preservation and defines self-preservation as an implicit drive to dominance. The novel argues that a nation that defines its politics through the assertion of autonomy will ultimately struggle to rise above such a battle. In one of the novel's best-known lines, the narrator asks, "What separates the enlightened man from the savage? Is civilization a thing distinct, or is it an advanced stage of barbarism?"[32]

Melville imagines American self-government as encouraging an autoimmune drive toward perpetual war, what Downes, in summarizing Thomas Hobbes, has called a "law of self-preservation as self-destruction." Downes argues that, for American revolutionaries such as John Adams and Thomas Jefferson, the Revolution marked a transition from a Hobbesian view of individuals constantly struggling for their survival to a Lockean state of nature in which Reason would teach civilized individuals to avoid doing harm to others. Melville indicates, however, that the distinction between what Locke would call the state of nature and the state of war remains a blurry one. As Downes points out, the Lockean perspective presumed that a clear distinction between the "civilized" and the "uncivilized" could be firmly articulated.[33] While men like Jefferson and Adams may have looked to the Indians on their frontier as proof of the divide between civilization and savagery, *Israel Potter* finds the internecine conflict of the Revolutionary War to be an illustration that the violence born of the demand for autonomy bears no limit such as race or culture. From the Hobbesian perspective that Melville adopts in *Israel Potter*, the will to power that lies at the heart of a Revolutionary history focused on heroic individuals ultimately will produce one of two political situations: either individuals will submit to the security of a powerful sovereign or they will exist in a state of lawlessness.

While they might appear to represent the triumph of popular self-government, Melville suggests that the icons of the American Revolution in fact symbolize that the new nation has not escaped from the state of nature but instead has made the pursuit of self-interest the answer to every political question. The veneration of figures such as Franklin and Jones indicates that the ideal of American popular sovereignty provides an ideological cover for the reality that democracy places each individual in a condition where he must choose how to balance the power and vulnerability he holds as a sovereign subject. The novel's depiction of these figures asserts Melville's concern that such national symbolism cannot provide guidance for the individual responsibility of creating that balance and instead urges each individual to seek to advance his own interests.

Rather than disinterested republicans serving the greater good, Melville depicts Jones and Franklin as men who have responded to the popularization of sovereignty by striving for power. For Melville, these Revolutionary icons signify two poles of a Hobbesian political world. They demonstrate that, in America, every man strives to define himself as exceptional to his peers, and the sovereign and the subject can trade places with ease. The pursuit of power that Melville lays at the heart of his depictions of these characters bodes ill for effective democracy, and both Franklin and Jones will, at various points in the novel, symbolize the commanding authority of an all-powerful sovereign and the anarchic demand for individual autonomy.

Although this tension between tyranny and anarchy can be seen in the behavior of both Franklin and Jones within the novel, each character tends to linger more clearly on one side of this binary than the other. Franklin appears as a controlling sovereign, a monarch in republican drag, while Jones symbolizes a roguish figure engaged in a continuous *bellum omnium contra omnes.* These primary symbolic associations make the sequence of Israel's encounters with famous Americans an allegorical account of the potential negative consequences of revolution. The ideal of popular sovereignty might descend into either demagoguery or perpetual strife. But the novel ultimately illustrates that both outcomes emerge from the same ideology, which imagines sovereignty as an assertion of the individual will. A close reading of the presentation of both Franklin and Jones demonstrates this argument and illustrates Melville's critique that the Revolutionary past is a corrupt guide for the nation.

The narrator repeatedly comments on Franklin through analogies that imply a cunning and domineering quality to the famous man. As part of an extended commentary on Franklin's character, the narrator establishes the biblical patriarch Jacob, along with Thomas Hobbes, as historical precedents for the genius of Franklin. The narrator describes these three figures as men who were "at once politicians and philosophers; keen observers of the main chance; prudent courtiers, practical magians in linsey-woolsey." The connection to Jacob appears particularly significant, as the narrator comments on how this figure blends the "diplomatist and the shepherd . . . the apostolic serpent and the dove" and further describes Jacob as a "tanned Machiavelli in tents."[34]

These metaphors adduce a sense of the benevolent and the manipulative to Franklin's character and emphasize an ethos that adapts to changing contexts in order to achieve its own ends. As the allusion to Machiavelli indicates, the narrator imagines Jacob as, above all, a master strategist focused on obtaining and maintaining power, and while Jacob symbolizes the founder of a nation, his character also carries the association of his shrewd manipulation of his brother, Esau, and his deception of his nearly blind father, Isaac, in order to claim his brother's birthright. The novel insinuates that, much as Jacob covered himself in goatskins to pose as his brother, Franklin might be playing the character of the simple and practical man in order to achieve a particular end.

Throughout their meetings, Franklin plays the part of Poor Richard to Israel, constantly proffering homespun aphorisms to the younger man and encouraging him to adopt a style of virtuous simplicity. Franklin even supplies Israel with a copy of "The Way to Wealth" at the conclusion of their first encounter. Yet the novel also implies that an ulterior motive lurks beneath this performance, and that Franklin seeks less to encourage Israel on the path to virtue than to control his behavior. Over the course of their encounters, Franklin advises Israel against drinking spirits, confiscates the luxury items from his hotel room, and warns him against socializing with a French chambermaid, leading the younger man to eventually protest that "every time he comes in he robs me . . . with an air all the time, too, as if he were making me presents. If he thinks me such a very sensible young man, why not let me take care of myself?"[35]

This telling question points to the novel's positioning of Franklin as a savvy political agent who seeks his own interest and his own authority over others, behind a shield of self-denial and republican sacrifice. Franklin presents himself as seeking to support Israel's own natural virtue, even as his actions tend to leave the younger man little room for individual decision-making. When Franklin removes the liquor from Israel's hotel room, he presents this action as made in benevolence, but the novel insinuates that Franklin's true motivations are less than magnanimous, with the narrator remarking that "not till the first impression of the venerable envoy's suavity had left him, did Israel begin to surmise the mild superiority of successful strategy which lurked beneath this highly ingratiating air."[36] Whether the novel implies that Franklin has hypocritically barred Israel from luxuries he himself enjoys or simply that he seeks to prevent his courier from getting distracted, its central claim of Franklin is clear: the older man's constant offers of wisdom and his maintenance of a simple style form part of a carefully wrought social performance designed to keep Israel in a position that best meets Franklin's purpose.[37] Melville's depiction of Franklin asks whether a stable ground for identity exists underneath such performances or each individual simply puts on the best face to achieve his own interests.

In place of the tradition of a hereditary monarch, whose bloodline holds its claim to power through divine fiat, the novel imagines a society in which individuals perpetually negotiate the claim to sovereignty in relationship to their present social context. The claim to power thus becomes a social drama with no script. The narrator directly comments on Franklin's improvisational sense of identity, in an extended reflection on the character of the famous man. The narrator remarks that "having carefully weighed the world, Franklin could act any part in it" and goes on to list the many different pursuits that Franklin had undertaken, before concluding that Franklin proved "Jack of all trades, master of each and mastered by none—the type and genius of his land."[38]

The key to the novel's depiction of Franklin as a symbol of the challenges of sovereignty in the new nation comes in this description of him as "master of each and mastered by none." On the surface, this phrase asserts Franklin's equality to any other individual practitioner in his numerous professions, suggesting that he is no mere dilettante but an expert in each of these walks of life, yet this phrase also hints at a condition of radical autonomy that the novel presents as part of the dangerous underside of American liberty. "Mastered by none" will come to describe a condition of total self-possession wherein the individual observes no enduring social obligations beyond his own will.

The effort by each individual to lay claim to the power of sovereignty, and the instability of identity that Melville suggests accompanies this effort, implies that the United States exists as a society in which the social contract has been signed with false names. Each individual remains in pursuit of his own self-preservation, as in the state of nature, yet instead of an open struggle against his fellow men, the war of all against all will now be carried out through subterfuge. Franklin lays claim to the authority of the sovereign by creating a persona that gives him power over Israel. Through the example of the clever and strategic Franklin, the novel suggests that such a political arrangement creates opportunity for potential demagogues to gain authority over others by offering a replacement for the organizing figure of the hereditary monarch. The novel also suggests the chaotic and competitive context that emerges as a field of purportedly equal republican citizens all strive to establish themselves within the hierarchy of social authority, and the resultant lack of a stable sense of identity that emerges from this competition.

Many critics have noted the novel's emphasis on masquerade, with both Franklin and Israel himself suggesting Melville's commentary on the slipperiness of American identity.[39] What remains unstated in these accounts is Melville's concern in the novel that such instability might make the American democratic project untenable. The novel imagines a society in which citizenship becomes a contest to fill the vacuum left by the hereditary monarch—a space that cunning men like Franklin will be happy to inhabit.

This potential for demagoguery would be problem enough, but in drawing a line between Franklin's performance and the many false identities that Israel must assume, the novel suggests the larger chaos created by each man believing that he holds an equal claim to the autonomy of the sovereign. In contrast to Franklin, Israel appears "mastered by all" as he repeatedly adopts subservient roles, culminating in the narrator comparing him to a slave, during his stint as a brickmaker in the suburbs of London. But with its emphasis on how both men present an undefined and flexible sense of identity, the novel suggests a parallel between Franklin and Israel that belies their opposing social positions and indicates the possibility that such roles could be inverted at any moment.

The figuration of Franklin as Jacob highlights this parallel, given that the biblical patriarch was, of course, renamed Israel. As Israel observes in the midst of his brickmaking: "Kings as clowns are codgers—who ain't a nobody."[40] The novel depicts this sentiment not as a recognition of human equality but rather as an initiation into a brutal society in which the state of nature has become the rule of law. Such a connection implies the absence of any stable boundary to divide sovereign from subject, ruler from ruled, powerful from powerless in American democracy.

The novel captures the sense in which popular sovereignty creates the potential for both anarchy and tyranny, and it emphasizes Franklin's role as a symbol of both possibilities. Similarly, the novel offers John Paul Jones as a converse image of this symbol; where Franklin appears as a figure of order containing (or obscuring) chaos, Jones stands as a chaotic principle striving to lay claim to sovereign power. Melville draws attention to Jones as a figure who embodies the continuing possibility of the state of nature and the struggle for self-preservation that remains within the heart of democratic society.

The novel frequently portrays Jones as a liminal figure on the cusp between civilization and savagery, in order to suggest the irresolvable nature of this line in American democracy. Jones blurs national and racial distinctions—a man born in Scotland fighting for American independence while embodying the airs and attitudes of Native American and Pacific societies.[41] In part, this mix of cultures supports his claim to be a "citizen and sailor of the universe."[42] Yet, when combined with the frequent references to Jones's fundamental quality of solitary individualism, the opposite interpretation of these analogies comes into play as well, so that Jones's status as universal citizen also suggests that he stands as a citizen of nowhere in particular. Jones appears less the enlightened cosmopolitan than an antisocial and rootless brigand, a figure outside of any sense of social order save his own. In a variation on the notes sounded by Franklin's appearance as a jack-of-all-trades, Jones appears as a man who embodies multiple cultures yet belongs to none.

Much as in its depiction of Franklin, the novel portrays Jones as deeply self-interested, but while this interest seems submerged behind a mask of virtue in the case of Franklin, Jones openly and aggressively asserts his own goals as his chief priority. Jones symbolizes an individualism based in negative liberty that proves itself largely incapable of empathy as a result of its ruthless pursuit of its own interests. Such individualism becomes a major obstruction to the pursuit of common social goals that is necessary in a democratic society. Jones pledges that any efforts he takes as part of the American war effort must be made on his own terms, vowing that "whatever Paul Jones does for the cause of America, it must be done through unlimited orders: a separate, supreme command; no leader and no counselor but himself."[43] In this statement, we find a variation on the narrator's description of Franklin being "mastered by none."

Likewise, Jones expresses his frustration with the cautious approach of the Continental Congress toward the war with the exclamation, "Why was I not born a Czar!" And when he is told that Israel is an escaped prisoner of war, he immediately thinks of his own reputation: "'Ah, captured in a ship?' asked Paul eagerly;—'what ship? None of mine! Paul Jones never was captured.'"[44] Jones wishes for the unfettered power of a despot, and he shows himself well prepared for the absolutism of such a role through his inability to think of Israel's experiences without referencing his own.

Like Franklin, Jones symbolizes Melville's fear that popular sovereignty reveals political life to be a constant struggle among individuals seeking to establish their own claim to autonomy. Whereas the account of Franklin implies a manipulation of others to achieve this end, however, the novel's vision of Jones imagines this drive to power as an open contest of force. Ultimately, though, both characters serve to demonstrate the foreboding potential of popular sovereignty and the individualism it inspires.

Jones and Franklin stand as inverted images of each other—Franklin as the sovereign whose polished demeanor covers his will to dominate, Jones as the rogue whose seemingly lawless violence strives to claim sovereign authority. But the novel also emphasizes the parallel each character offers to its protagonist in order to emphasize the degree to which this will to power represents the legacy of the American Revolution for all citizens.[45] As we have seen, Israel shares Franklin's unstable sense of identity, but the novel draws even more compelling similarities between the main character and Jones through its depiction of their shared propensity to extremes of violence. These similarities reflect Melville's sense that, in a nation where all citizens are both sovereign and subject, there likely will be far more individuals caught in the ruthless pursuit of power typified by Jones than in the cunning use of power symbolized by Franklin. Nonetheless, the similarities among all three figures point to Melville's larger question: If these are the symbols that define the nation for future generations, what kind of future of must await the United States?

Israel Potter imagines a United States in which the sovereignty once held within the king's two bodies has been unleashed into a multiheaded body politic. In America, the royal body of the monarch has become the law, and the physical body of the king has multiplied into an infinite number of citizens, each imagining himself emblematic of the nation. Melville imagines the American Revolution as having brought this sense of the individual as nation to its fulfillment. In figures like Benjamin Franklin and John Paul Jones, we find men proudly carrying themselves as lords of all they see, nations unto themselves. And in Israel Potter, Melville offers an ordinary member of the multitude, formed as every individual seeks to follow this model.

In some of the novel's most widely read passages, Melville probes the moral crisis that emerges when sovereignty becomes an expression of personal autonomy rather than an act of shared responsibility. The ultimate problem this belief inspires is the loss of any collective identification with one's neighbors. If each individual is akin to an independent nation, then internal and external conflict become indistinguishable. Melville's account of the famous sea battle between the American *Bonhomme Richard* and the British *Serapis* demonstrates the perpetual and self-destructive violence that such a condition cannot help but produce:

> There would seem to be something singularly indicatory in this engagement. It may involve at once a type, a parallel, and a prophecy. Sharing the same blood with England, and yet her proved foe in two wars; not wholly inclined at bottom to forget an old grudge: intrepid, unprincipled, reckless, predatory, with boundless ambition, civilized in externals but a savage at heart, America is, or may yet be, the Paul Jones of nations.[46]

The narrator here summarizes the specific qualities of Jones's antisocial behavior and reiterates the idea of Jones as a savage in genteel dress. But we should pay closest attention to the rhetorical arrangement of this analogy. John Paul Jones does not represent the United States. He does not act on behalf of the body politic and he is not a synecdoche for the will of the people. Rather, Jones serves as an allegory for the nation. The character of a ruthless and rootless individual provides the means to describe the complexity and diversity of an entire polity. And such rhetoric casts the nation as an individual in a global state of nature, where self-preservation and the defense of autonomy become the ultimate rule.

This context of global opposition was described by one of the novel's contemporary reviewers, who circled the "Paul Jones of nations" passage for particular emphasis. An anonymous reviewer in the *Albion* of New York quoted this passage as a contrast to the national self-image portrayed in the Ostend Manifesto, the 1854 statement written by the US ambassadors to Spain, Great Britain, and France, in which they argue for immediate annexation of Cuba to prevent its falling subject to a slave insurrection and threaten war with Spain should diplomacy fail to achieve that goal. The manifesto asserts an international rule of self-preservation as justification for such action, stating that "self-preservation is the first law of nature, with States as well as with individuals."[47]

Many readers of the manifesto rejected such a justification, however, viewing it as a blatant excuse to acquire new territory for the expansion of slavery. The manifesto was well publicized in Europe, and it drew condemnation from the European press as well as from American abolitionists and opponents of slavery's expansion. An 1856 political cartoon, "The Ostend Doctrine," summarized the spirit of much of this condemnation; it depicts President Buchanan (who, as ambassador to Great Britain, had been an author of the manifesto) being robbed on the street by men who justify the attack by using quotes from the manifesto, which hangs on a wall over the forlorn president's shoulder.

The *Albion* reviewer asserts that, like this cartoon, Melville's novel reveals the Ostend Manifesto as the self-rationalization of an outlaw. To this writer, "Mr. Melville comes to the point" by casting John Paul Jones as the embodiment of a rapacious and self-interested America, as opposed to the "set of fine phrases about 'conscious rectitude' and 'approbation of the world'" with which the authors of the Ostend Manifesto attempt to conceal "a scheme of spoliation."[48] The reviewer rejects the niceties of the manifesto as a mere dressing over its aggressive intent and cites *Israel Potter* as a far more honest account of the character of the United States on the international stage.

In the "Paul Jones of nations" passage, we also find a warning about

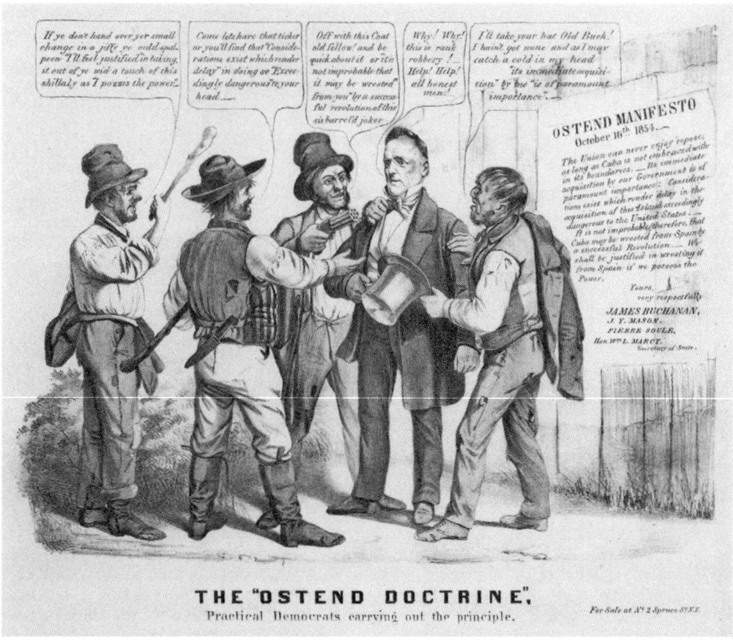

"The Ostend Doctrine," by Nathaniel Currier, 1856. *Library of Congress, Prints and Photographs Division.*

what havoc this ideology might wreak when applied as national character. The reference to the United States "sharing the same blood with England" brings to mind both domestic and foreign strife and stands as a microcosm of the way in which sovereign exceptionality characterizes individual citizenship within the United States. The nation came to being through violent self-assertion against a people with whom it was bound by consanguinity—a people that had to be defined as outsiders in order for an American nation to come into being.

Melville questions the moral legitimacy of such distinctions through a vision of the battle that renders all difference between the two sides meaningless. The narrator surveys the scene of the battle and instead of two ships sees only "a lurid cloud, incessantly torn in shreds of lighting." He describes the yardarms of the two ships becoming tangled, bringing the enemies "cheek by jowl." At this point, the analogies suggest an even stronger connection, with the narrator first comparing the two ships to "the Siamese twins, oblivious of their fraternal bond, [raging] in unnatural fight" and later describing them as "a co-partnership and joint-stock combustion company." The more the two ships fight, the more united their fates become, leading to the narrator's observation, near the end of the battle, that "mutual obliteration from the face of the waters seemed the only natural sequel to hostilities like these." The results of the battle only further emphasize the shared fate of the warring ships, since the "loss of life in the two ships was about equal."[49]

The clash between the two ships appears to be a zero-sum game in which neither side gains any advantage in the end. Edgar Dryden has argued that Melville's extended account of the battle, with its rushing stream of allusions to other literary works and national cultures, mixes symbols in a deliberate disruption of the imagined stability of national boundaries.[50] Melville intimates that the nationalism represented by John Paul Jones is a threat to domestic and foreign peace precisely because it destabilizes any sense of belonging to a community whose interests outweigh those of the self. In describing the battle as a type and a prophecy, Melville positions this moment as both a reflection on the ideology encouraged by the Revolutionary War and a presentiment of future wars that this ideology will bring forth.[51]

While Franklin and Jones appear as dangerous parallels to Israel Potter and serve as foreboding omens for the American republic, the final famous figure of the Revolution in the novel presents a contrast to these negative portrayals. Melville's Ethan Allen appears in the text without the suggestions of ruthless individualism that characterize Franklin and Jones and lurk as latent potential within the figure of Israel. Instead, Allen seems to present the ideal balance of liberal self-regard and egalitarian respect.[52] However, this ideal comes loaded with qualifications that make it clear Melville considers it either exceptional or imaginary.

The narrator describes Allen as "a curious combination of a Hercules, a Joe Miller, a Bayard, and a Tom Hyer; had a person like the

Belgian giants; mountain music in him like a Swiss; a heart as plump as Coeur de Lion's."[53] In order, these analogies compare Allen to a mythical warrior who was half man, half god; an English actor; a famous French soldier; an American prizefighter; a seven-foot-tall Belgian who toured US cities as an attraction; and a celebrated English king. Based on these references, Allen would seem either to border on myth or to be a consummate performer—or perhaps to be a mix of both. And this characterization invests the values he represents with a similar degree of unreality.

Melville compresses many scenes and details from Allen's 1778 narrative into a single scene of the captive Vermonter meeting the crowd gathered to see him at Pendennis Castle; as a result, the fictional Allen's behavior stands as a potent distillation of the historical Allen's literary self-representation. We find Allen haranguing an English crowd to "respect a gentleman and a Christian, though he be in rags and smell of bilge-water" while displaying the "marred aspect . . . of some wild beast; but of a royal sort, and unsubdued by the cage."[54] As in the 1778 narrative, Allen demands from his captors social recognition as an officer and sees himself as a representative of an American nation who cannot bow to disrespect from the British. At the same time, Allen appears fair-minded toward those who show him this respect. Melville invents a brief moment when Allen chivalrously flirts with an English lady, and he revises Allen's account of how a spectator offered Allen a bowl of punch, which Allen insisted the man give him by his own hand, as a sign of equality. At the end of this exchange, Melville's Allen pledges his service to the giver, observing that "one gentleman never knows when it may be his turn to be helped of another."[55]

The phrase "his turn" draws us back to Derrida's account of the circularity necessary for freedom to be shared. In this brief scene of gentlemanly reciprocity, Allen appears as a symbol of the Revolution that emphasizes the sharing of power rather than its accumulation or its loss. Despite his physical imprisonment, Allen maintains his social authority through his bold performance, which by turns charms and intimidates the British crowd. Allen appears neither completely abject (like Israel) nor completely autonomous (like Franklin and Jones). In addition, despite the national difference between Allen and the giver of the bowl, they are able to reach a plane of mutual respect based on an acknowledgment of the ever-changing conditions of social life. Unlike Jones and Franklin, then, Allen appears as a figure with a limit on his drive toward self-assertion. He seeks fair treatment but does not measure his social status through the accumulation of power over others. Rather, Melville's Allen subscribes to a pragmatic vision of equality based on reciprocal recognition among individuals.

Unlike Ethan Allen's self-presentation in his own narrative, Melville's character employs a mode of political authority that has not been underwritten by force. This Allen's claim to represent the nation comes from his acknowledgment of human vulnerability and his commitment to supporting others in times of need. When Allen asserts his power here, he defends his claim to recognition as a human, not his demand for recognition of his sovereign authority. Melville's Allen models a different response to vulnerability than the fear that inspires the multitude. Rather than banding with others in pursuit of greater strength, the character suggests an acceptance that vulnerability defines social existence. Instead of finding the answer to vulnerability in the strength of the collective military body, it suggests we might find that answer in admitting to our own weakness as individuals. We might put aside the will to defend our own autonomy rather than declaring that will to be our claim to sovereignty.

Allen's appearance in the novel precedes another key moment of hopeful possibility. In one of the novel's many coincidences, Israel is recognized and hailed by another American prisoner at Pendennis Castle, who turns out to be a former romantic rival whom "Israel had all but detested" after this man married Potter's youthful sweetheart. In response, Israel must deny his country of birth and claim to be a loyal English subject to avoid arrest by the suspicious guards. Singles, the American prisoner, realizes the danger in which he has inadvertently placed Israel and pretends to have made a mistake. Echoing the language of unity from the battle between the *Serapis* and the *Bonhomme Richard,* Melville describes this scene as an act of connection between Singles and Israel. The narrator states that, while the men might have once hated each other, "now, as if the Atlantic rolled, not between two continents, but two worlds—this, and the next—these alien souls, oblivious to hate, melted down into one."[56] Israel and Singles come to a moment of fellowship not through a political recognition of their shared nationality but through acknowledgment of their mutual vulnerability.

In these brief scenes, the novel implies that the magic of sovereignty might reside not in dominance but in communion. Melville suggests that we have to become more attentive to vulnerability in narrating Revolutionary history. The stories of men like Israel Potter become a discourse of individualism and competition when we fail to recognize the human frailty behind claims of obligation, debt, and violence.

The need for such recognition was likely not lost on Melville. It's worth remembering that he wrote this novel as the phrase "popular sovereignty" gained a uniquely American connotation, one that would lead to severe domestic turmoil. In early 1854, Senator Stephen Douglas introduced the Kansas–Nebraska Act, which repealed the geographic ban on slavery created by the 1820 Missouri Compromise and allowed the legality of slavery to be decided by popular vote among a state's residents. The ensuing flood of pro- and antislavery forces into Kansas to gain control of this vote sparked the beginning of the bloodiest era of the nation's history. From the perspective of *Israel Potter,* the violence that erupted in Kansas appears as a further expression of the sort of violence that brought the nation into being—violence that would stretch from Yorktown, across the decades, to places like Springfield and Pittsburgh, Fallen Timbers and Tippecanoe, Plattsburgh and New Orleans, Buena Vista and Chapultepec, all the way to Pottawatomie and beyond.

Coda

The "Best Illustration" of Patriotism

JAMES FENIMORE COOPER describes patriotism as the theme of his second novel, *The Spy: A Tale of the Neutral Ground.* In the introduction he prepared for the book's 1849 edition, Cooper relates how the novel was inspired by a conversation with John Jay about an unnamed individual who served as a secret agent under Jay during the Revolutionary War. Cooper writes of how he was impressed by this individual's selfless commitment to the American cause, because the spy refused any offer of compensation until "his country was entirely in a condition to bestow it." *The Spy* adapts this anonymous man into its main character, Harvey Birch, whose heroism during the Revolution remains unknown until his death during the War of 1812, in the novel's final chapter. Despite this direct line of inspiration, however, Cooper dismissed attempts to find the factual analogue to his fictional character. The author admits in the introduction that he never knew the identity of Jay's spy, and he states that the man has faded among the numerous other "secret emissaries" used by both sides during the war.[1]

This dismissal would not stop readers from speculating on the identity of Jay's anonymous spy, of course. One well-known attempt came in 1828, when the Connecticut engineer and author H. L. Barnum published *The Spy Unmasked,* which presents the memoirs of Enoch Crosby, the man Barnum claimed as the model for Harvey Birch. Barnum held that he had learned this information from an unnamed friend of Cooper, a "gentleman of good standing and respectability," who assured Barnum that Crosby was the original that Cooper had in mind.[2] From this tip, Barnum interviewed Crosby and produced a narrative of his experiences in the war.

Yet, like many heavily mediated veteran narratives, *The Spy Unmasked* includes fictional elements, and in this case those elements undermine Barnum's argument for Crosby as Birch. Crosby gave testimony to claim a veteran's pension in 1832, and as was the case with Isaac Hubbell and *The Fort Stanwix Captive,* that account of his service does not totally align with the commercially sold version. Tremaine McDowell noted, in one of the earliest issues of the journal *American Literature,* that any detail in *The Spy Unmasked* that could not be found in Crosby's pension testimony could be found in Cooper's novel, suggesting that Barnum collated Cooper's plot alongside Crosby's memories to create a resemblance to Harvey Birch that would not exist otherwise.[3]

Cooper's dismissal of works like *The Spy Unmasked* might be read as resentment at efforts to capitalize on his success, but I want to explore a different possibility. What if Cooper dismissed these attempts specifically because he did not want to know the spy's identity? Cooper calls Jay's unknown spy "the best illustration" of his subject of patriotism.[4] As readers, we should pause on the fact that Cooper's creation Harvey Birch is an imperfect, fictional attempt to represent this perfect example of patriotism. Where Harvey Birch illustrates an ideal of sacrifice, Jay's spy actually experienced it. Unlike Cooper's character, Jay's spy appears completely disinterested because his identity as a private citizen remains forever unknown. This unnamed man represents a symbol of patriotism precisely because his individual identity has been erased. His value as a symbol of the body politic depends on asserting, then sacrificing, the value of his individual human body.

The inspiration Cooper found in this unnamed spy reveals a larger truth about military service in the United States: popular sovereignty needs the veteran to be forgotten. More precisely, popular sovereignty as a discourse needs the figure of the veteran as an ideal, but it does not need any one veteran specifically as an individual. Jay's spy is a perfect symbol within this discourse because he was a real but unknown person. He embodies the sacrifices of the Revolutionary army that brought the nation into being, but he requires no actual recognition as an individual. He demonstrates how power emanates from the people but makes no demands of that power once it has been established. Since readers are required to acknowledge that man in his civilian capacity, but not to recognize him as an individual, he resolves the tautology within popular sovereignty in which subjects and sovereigns are indistinguishable. Jay's spy can exist as a pure sovereign, thanks to his service, and as a pure subject, thanks to his anonymity.

Cooper's praise of the spy offers a synecdoche of the larger pattern in the Revolutionary War veteran narrative. As I noted in the introduction, many of the most prominent examples of this genre frequently blur the line between fact and fiction. Although the subjects of veteran narratives obviously eschewed the anonymity of Jay's spy, the ways in which their stories border on fiction stand as a similar means of dividing the sovereign military body from the subject civilian body. This tendency implies a cultural need for stories of veterans that feel true while also elevating the soldier to the level of myth. Popular sovereignty demands a real sacrifice, but it remains easier to acknowledge soldiers in their symbolic role than in their human fullness. The veteran narrative, like Jay's spy (or like the surprise public reunion in our own time), gives audiences the reality of the veteran experience at a mediated remove.

Jay's spy, as the extreme end point of this tendency, might also offer ways to rethink how we remember and represent soldiers and veterans in the United States. Cooper's treatment of the spy indicates a distinction between two concepts that might seem synonymous at first. Cooper *acknowledges* the spy, but he does not *recognize* him. These words are so closely related that they are often used to define each other. A review of the two terms in the Oxford English Dictionary finds many overlapping definitions, such as "*acknowledge*: to recognize or confess (someone or something) to be the thing specified," and "*recognize*: to acknowledge, consider, or accept (a person or thing) *as* or *to be* something."

Both terms describe the perception of a fact, typically one connected to a claim of identity or authority. But *recognize* offers one key distinction from *acknowledge,* in this definition: "to identify from knowledge of appearance or character, esp. by means of some distinctive feature." Recognition carries a denotation of individuality that is absent in acknowledgment. Representations of individual veterans appeal for recognition, yet they have often been met with acknowledgment. We acknowledge the sacrifices made by veterans in their military bodies while failing to recognize the civilian bodies that give those sacrifices meaning. Revising this tendency will require thoughtful consideration of soldiers as both a collective, heroic body and a distinctive, human body.

NOTES

INTRODUCTION

1. The surprise public reunion became popular enough at the start of the 2010s that two cable television networks sought to make it the premise of an ongoing series. Lifetime produced twenty-five episodes of *Coming Home* between 2011 and 2012, while TLC offered seven episodes of the aptly titled *Surprise Homecoming,* in 2011. Neither series achieved long-term success (despite *Surprise Homecoming* being hosted by country singer and actor Billy Ray Cyrus). Yet their creation suggests that an audience existed for these reunions, and that audience doesn't seem to have disappeared along with these programs. As of this writing, news outlets like the cable channel Fox News and the syndicated news program *Inside Edition* continue to offer collections of the "best" reunions from a given year, and talk show host Ellen DeGeneres has featured reunions as part of her program more than once. The surprise military reunion, like the war in Afghanistan itself, has become an ongoing part of contemporary American culture.

2. Frank Newport, "Americans' Confidence in Institutions Edges Up," Gallup, June 26, 2017, http://news.gallup.com/poll/212840/americans-confidence-institutions-edges.aspx?g_source=link_NEWSV9&g_medium=tile_7&g_campaign=item_1597&g_content=Americans%27%2520Confidence%2520in%2520Institutions%2520Edges%2520Up.

3. These events are not without their critics. In 2009, the *New York Times* talked to several military families, some of whom enjoyed the surprise reunions and some of whom preferred a more private approach. Jan Hoffman, "War's Other Enduring Videos," *New York Times,* November 27, 2009, https://www.nytimes.com/2009/11/29/fashion/29video.html. In 2011, the *Washington Post* interviewed several mental health experts who advised that the surprise reunion could be an additional stressor for military children. Many of these children report anxiety over their parents' deployment, and studies found that this anxiety typically did not decline after a reunion. Stephen Xenakis, a child psychiatrist and retired army brigadier general, warned that the "tears of joy" viewers saw from young children might actually be signs of emotional distress. Tara Swords, "Surprise Family Reunions May Not Be Good for Soldiers' Children, Mental Health Experts Say," *Washington Post,* September 2, 2011, https://www.washingtonpost.com/entertainment/television/surprise-family-reunions-may-not-be-good-for-soldiers

-children-mental-health-experts-say/2011/08/22/gIQAM7wVxJ_story.html?utm_term =.f668c8121137. In 2015, the irreverent sports website *Deadspin* criticized the practice after the Saint Louis Rams surprised a cheerleader with her Marine husband—and both wife and husband just happened to be scions of wealthy and well-connected families. The cheerleader's mother was in fact running for the state legislature at the time of the reunion. Tom Ley, "Surprise Military Reunions at NFL Games Reach Peak Bullshit," *Deadspin,* September 2, 2015, https://deadspin.com/surprise-military-reunions-at-nfl-games-reach-peak-bull-1727940877. Also in 2015, Arizona senators John McCain and Jeff Flake released a report criticizing the broader trend of military tributes at professional sporting events, as their research found that many of these tributes were funded not by the sports teams or leagues but by the Department of Defense, at taxpayers' expense. John McCain and Jeff Flake, *Tackling Paid Patriotism: A Joint Oversight Report,* November 4, 2015.

4. David Waldstreicher, *In the Midst of Perpetual Fetes: The Making of American Nationalism, 1776–1820* (Chapel Hill: University of North Carolina Press, 1997); Sarah J. Purcell, *Sealed with Blood: War, Sacrifice, and Memory in Revolutionary America* (Philadelphia: University of Pennsylvania Press, 2002).

5. John C. Dann provides a brief introduction to these two pension acts, while Emily J. Teipe offers a full-length study of the topic. Dann, ed., *The Revolution Remembered: Eyewitness Accounts of the War for Independence* (Chicago: University of Chicago Press, 1980); Teipe, *America's First Veterans and the Revolutionary War Pensions* (Lewiston, NY: Edwin Mellen, 2002).

6. Teipe, *America's First Veterans,* 24.

7. Dann, *Revolution Remembered,* 8–9.

8. Joseph Plumb Martin, *Private Yankee Doodle: Being a Narrative of Some of the Adventures, Dangers, and Sufferings of a Revolutionary Soldier,* edited by George Scheer (New York: Little, Brown, 1962), 186.

9. Scott E. Casper, *Constructing American Lives: Biography & Culture in Nineteenth-Century America* (Chapel Hill: University of North Carolina Press, 1999), 156. For examples of narratives in a more biographical style, see Alexander Graydon, who devotes much of his text to his failed political career as a staunch Federalist in Jeffersonian Pennsylvania, or John Robert Shaw, who recalls how he eventually overcame the drunkenness that characterized his life after the army, through a religious conversion. Graydon, *Memoirs of a Life, Chiefly Passed in Pennsylvania, Within the Last Sixty Years; with Occasional Remarks upon the General Occurrences, Character and Spirit of that Eventful Period* (Harrisburg, PA: John Wyeth, 1811); John Robert Shaw, *The Life and Travels of John Robert Shaw: A Narrative of the Life and Travels of the Well-Digger, Now Resident of Lexington, Kentucky, Written by Himself* (Lexington, KY: Daniel Bradford, 1806).

10. Ann Fabian has cataloged the various classes of personal narrative published by such writers in the nineteenth century. Fabian, *The Unvarnished Truth: Personal Narratives in Nineteenth-Century America* (Berkeley: University of California Press, 2000).

11. For example, Christopher Hawkins defines his audience, in the preface to his

narrative, as his "children, grandchildren, and their descendants," and his manuscript remained unpublished during his lifetime. Hawkins, *The Adventures of Christopher Hawkins, Containing Details of his Captivity, a First and Second Time on the High Seas, in the Revolutionary War, by the British, and His Consequent Sufferings, and Escape from the Jersey Prison Ship, Then Lying in the Harbor of New York, by Swimming* (New York: Charles I. Bushnell, 1864), x.

12. Carl Schmitt, *Political Theology: Four Chapters on the Concept of Sovereignty,* translated by George Schwab, foreword by Tracy B. Strong (Chicago: University of Chicago Press, 2005), 12.

13. David Perry, *Recollections of an Old Soldier. The Life of Captain David Perry, a Soldier of the French and Revolutionary Wars* (Windsor, VT: Republican and Yeoman, 1822), 67.

14. Robert G. Parkinson argues that the outbreak of actual violence during the American Revolution produced a need for union among what had been a more fractious patriot movement. Parkinson, "War and the Imperative of Union," *William and Mary Quarterly* 68, no. 4 (2011): 634.

15. See David C. Williams, *The Mythic Meanings of the Second Amendment: Taming Political Violence in a Constitutional Republic* (New Haven, CT: Yale University Press, 2003), introduction and first chapter.

16. Alexis de Tocqueville, *Democracy in America,* translated by Henry Reed (1899), chapter 4. Available from the American Studies Program of the University of Virginia, http://xroads.virginia.edu/~HYPER/DETOC/1_ch04.htm.

17. Schmitt, *Political Theology,* 49.

18. Jennifer Greiman, *Democracy's Spectacle: Sovereignty and Public Life in Antebellum American Writing* (New York: Fordham University Press, 2010), 9.

19. Schmitt, *Political Theology,* 49.

20. The landmark study of this concept remains Ernst Kantorowicz, *The King's Two Bodies: A Study in Medieval Political Theology* (Princeton, NJ: Princeton University Press, 1957).

21. Michael Rogin, "The King's Two Bodies: Lincoln, Wilson, Nixon, and Presidential Self-Sacrifice," in *Ronald Reagan, the Movie: And Other Episodes in Political Demonology* (Berkeley: University of California Press, 1987), 84.

22. Elizabeth D. Samet, *Willing Obedience: Citizens, Soldiers, and the Progress of Consent in America, 1776–1898* (Stanford, CA: Stanford University Press, 2004), 3.

23. John Joseph Henry, *An Accurate and Interesting Account of the Hardships and Sufferings of That Band of Heroes, Who Traversed the Wilderness in the Campaign Against Quebec in 1775* (Lancaster, PA: William Greer, 1812), 143, 189.

24. Nathaniel Segar, *A Brief Narrative of the Captivity and Sufferings of Lt. Nathaniel Segar, Who Was Taken Prisoner by the Indians and Carried to Canada, During the Revolutionary War* (Paris, ME: The Observer Office, 1825), 30.

25. Graydon, *Memoirs of a Life,* 308.

26. William B. Wallace, *To the Honorable, the Members, of Both Houses of Congress, This Condensed Sketch of the Service, and Some of the Privations and Sufferings of Wil-*

liam B. Wallace, A Lieutenant of Artillery of the U. States in the Revolutionary War, Chiefly Relating to His Captivity, Is Humbly Submitted (Frankfort: Jacob H. Holeman, 1826), 9.

27. Segar, *A Brief Narrative*; Lemuel Roberts, *Memoirs of Captain Lemuel Roberts* (Bennington, VT: 1809).

1. ETHAN ALLEN, DANIEL SHAYS, AND THE INVENTION OF A REVOLUTIONARY HERO

1. This approach to Ethan Allen's narrative can be seen in works such as John McWilliams, "The Faces of Ethan Allen: 1760–1860," *New England Quarterly* 49 (1976): 257–282; and Daniel E. Williams, "Zealous in the Cause of Liberty: Self-Creation and Redemption in the Narrative of Ethan Allen," *Studies in Eighteenth-Century Culture* 19 (1989): 325–347. Biographical approaches to Allen can be found in Michael A. Bellesiles, *Revolutionary Outlaws: Ethan Allen and the Struggle for Independence on the Early American Frontier* (Charlottesville: University Press of Virginia, 1993); and Robert E. Shalhope, *Bennington and the Green Mountain Boys: The Emergence of Liberalism in Vermont, 1763–1850* (Baltimore: Johns Hopkins University Press, 1996).

2. Ethan Allen, *A Narrative of Colonel Ethan Allen's Captivity,* edited by Stephen Carl Arch (Acton, MA: Copley, 2000), 7.

3. Jacques Derrida, "Force of Law: The 'Mystical Foundation of Authority,'" *Cardozo Law Review* 11, 5–6 (July/August 1990), 927.

4. Allen met with Luke Day and Eli Parsons, co-commanders, along with Daniel Shays, of the populist militia that attempted to capture the arsenal at Springfield. In March 1787, Allen publicly repudiated the protesters in a Boston newspaper, stating that he "heartily despised both them and their cause." The primary account of this meeting comes from Ira Allen's "History of Vermont," in *Records of the Council of Safety and Governor and Council of the State of Vermont,* edited by E. P. Walton (Montpelier, VT: 1873), 3:375–380. Also see the accounts in Stewart H. Holbrook, *Ethan Allen* (New York: Macmillan, 1940), 241–243; and Bellesiles, *Revolutionary Outlaws,* 251–253.

5. For a concise overview of the changes in Shays's reputation over the course of US history, see Robert A. Gross, ed., "The Uninvited Guest: Daniel Shays and the Constitution," in *In Debt to Shays: The Bicentennial of an Agrarian Rebellion,* 1–46 (Charlottesville: University Press of Virginia, 1993). The most widely cited history of Shays's Rebellion is David Szatmary, *Shays's Rebellion: The Making of an Agrarian Insurrection* (Amherst: University of Massachusetts Press, 1980). Leonard L. Richards has focused on the economic and social connections that precipitated the event. Richards, *Shays's Rebellion: The American Revolution's Final Battle* (Philadelphia: University of Pennsylvania Press, 2002).

6. See, for example, the interview between Shays and Rufus Putnam, included in Charles O. Parmenter, *History of Pelham, Massachusetts, from 1738–1848* (Amherst, MA: Carpenter and Morehouse, 1898), 395–398.

7. A representative example can be found in *Massachusetts Centinel,* December 6, 1786.

8. See the *Pennsylvania Gazette*, July 22, 1776.

9. Peter Force, *American Archives*, series 4 (Washington, DC, 1835–1857), 2:858.

10. On patterns of leadership among backcountry rebellions, see Richard Maxwell Brown, "Back Country Rebellions and the Homestead Ethic in America, 1740–1799," in *Tradition, Conflict, and Modernization: Perspectives on the American Revolution*, edited by Richard Maxwell Brown and Don E. Fehrenbacher (New York: Academic Press, 1977), 85–91.

11. Stephen Carl Arch, *After Franklin: The Emergence of Autobiography in Post-Revolutionary America, 1780–1830* (Hanover, NH: University Press of New England, 2001), 94–96.

12. Reducing the populist protests in Massachusetts to primarily a response to the debt crisis, however, appears to be based more on the rhetoric of the pro-government side than on historical fact. Richards has argued that little evidence exists to make a fear of debt suits the central cause of the court closings, as his review of state court records uncovers no correlation between towns that participated in these protests and a large number of individuals involved in litigation over outstanding debt. Rather than debt, Richards argues, the primary motivation for the movement was the perception that the state government sought to enrich the few at the expense of the many through its hierarchal constitution and aggressive tax policy. Richards, *Shays's Rebellion*, 60–63.

13. Ronald Formisano has argued that the construct "Shays's Rebellion" has oversimplified a diverse populist movement in western Massachusetts and other rural regions during the mid-1780s. See Formisano, "Teaching Shays/The Regulation," *Uncommon Sense* 106 (1998): 24–35; and Formisano, *For the People: American Populist Movements from the Revolution to the 1850s* (Chapel Hill: University of North Carolina Press, 2008), 24–34. Terry Bouton notes that the tendency to describe backcountry protests as rebellions casts protesters as a radical fringe rather than as citizens seeking a greater voice in their governance. Bouton, *Taming Democracy: "The People," the Founders, and the Troubled Ending of the American Revolution* (New York: Oxford University Press, 2007), 216–219.

14. William Pencak has argued against this idea, as he suggests that most participants in the court closings and protests were likely young men with little to no actual experience fighting in the Revolutionary War. He holds that more veterans of this conflict actually served on the pro-government side. Pencak, "'The Fine Theoretic Government of Massachusetts Is Prostrated to the Earth': The Response to Shays's Rebellion Reconsidered," in Gross, *In Debt to Shays*, 128–130.

15. Richards bases this argument on a careful reading of the lists of participants in the uprising, which demonstrates the solidarity found among families and extended kinship networks in supporting the protests. Richards, *Shays's Rebellion*, 89–116.

16. Formisano, "Teaching Shays/The Regulation," 31 (emphasis in original).

17. Jay Fliegelman, *Declaring Independence: Jefferson, Natural Language, and the Culture of Performance* (Stanford, CA: Stanford University Press, 1993), 149.

18. Misty G. Anderson, "Zombie Sovereignty," *Restoration: Studies in English Literary Culture, 1660–1700* 40, no. 2 (2016): 105–114.

19. Paul Downes, *Democracy, Revolution, and Monarchism in Early American Literature* (Cambridge: Cambridge University Press, 2002); Jonathan Elmer, *On Lingering and Being Last: Race and Sovereignty in the New World* (New York: Fordham University Press, 2008).

20. Downes, *Democracy, Revolution, and Monarchism,* 51.

21. Ed White, *The Backcountry and the City: Colonization and Conflict in Early America* (Minneapolis: University of Minnesota Press, 2005), 5–13.

22. Allen, *A Narrative of Colonel Ethan Allen's Captivity,* 3.

23. Ibid., 5.

24. Ibid., 6.

25. Ibid., 6.

26. Williams, "Zealous in the Cause of Liberty," 327.

27. Allen French, *The Taking of Ticonderoga in 1775: The British Story* (Cambridge, MA: Harvard University Press, 1928), 44.

28. Force, *American Archives,* series 4, 2:557.

29. Ibid.

30. Michael Warner, *The Letters of the Republic: Publication and the Public Sphere in Eighteenth-Century America* (Cambridge, MA: Harvard University Press, 1990).

31. See, for example, Jacques Derrida's assertion regarding the relationship between the reader and the monarch created in histories of kingship: "The narrative or the representation here don't come *after* the event, to report, recount, depict, or represent the providential power of the sovereign, but . . . the narrative and this representation are a structural part of this sovereignty, its constitutive structure, its dynamic or energetic essence, its force, its *dynamis,* or even its dynasty." Derrida, *The Beast and the Sovereign,* translated by Geoffrey Bennington (Chicago: University of Chicago Press, 2009), 1:289 (emphasis in original).

32. Ibid., 1:217.

33. Trish Loughran, *The Republic in Print: Print Culture in the Age of U.S. Nation Building, 1770–1870* (New York: Columbia University Press, 2007).

34. Jason Frank, *Constituent Moments: Enacting the People in Postrevolutionary America* (Duke University Press, 2010), 2–6.

35. Allen, *A Narrative of Colonel Ethan Allen's Captivity,* 3.

36. Ibid., 72.

37. Ibid., 26.

38. Ibid., 56–57.

39. Alexander Hamilton, James Madison, and John Jay, *The Federalist Papers,* edited by Ian Shapiro (New Haven, CT: Yale University Press, 2009), 52–53.

40. Eric Slauter, *The State as a Work of Art: The Cultural Origins of the Constitution* (Chicago: University of Chicago Press, 2009), 127, 164.

41. Suzette Hemberger, "A Government Based on Representations," *Studies in American Political Development* 10 (1996): 302.

42. See George Washington's letters to Philip Schuyler and James Clinton, from

November 6, 1780, in John C. Fitzpatrick, ed., *The Writings of George Washington* (Washington, DC: US Government Printing Office, 1939), 20:304–306. For an account of Allen's ambiguous negotiations with the British, see Bellesiles, *Revolutionary Outlaws,* 194–206.

43. See, for example, the appeal that Allen makes at the end of his 1779 pamphlet *A Vindication of the Opposition of the Inhabitants of Vermont to the Government of New York, and of Their Right to Form an Independent State.* Allen argues that the addition of the people of Vermont to the American confederation is an overwhelming boon to national character: "What a nursery of hardy soldiers may in future be nourished and supported in this fertile country . . . stimulated with the spirit of liberty, having a perfect detestation and abhorrence of arbitrary power, from the exertion of which they have suffered so much evil; will instill the principles of liberty and social virtue in their children, which will be perpetuated to future generations . . . and be a valuable support to the rising empire of the new world."

44. "Anecdotes of Daniel Shaise, Leader of the Insurgents," *Massachusetts Centinel,* December 6, 1786.

45. Henry Lee to George Washington, November 11, 1786, in "Letters of Delegates to Congress, vol. 24, November 6, 1786–February 29, 1788," Library of Congress, *A Century of Lawmaking for a New Nation: U.S. Congressional Documents and Debates, 1774–1875,* https://memory.loc.gov/ammem/amlaw.

46. Fitzpatrick, *The Writings of George Washington,* 24:169.

47. Ibid., 24:52.

48. Parmenter, *History of Pelham, Massachusetts from 1738–1848,* 400.

49. "A Speech, Delivered by a Minister to his People in the Town of ******, in the State of Massachusetts, on the 4th of January, 1787, Previous to Reading the Address of the General Court, of That State, at a Lecture Held for That Purpose," *American Museum,* May 1788.

50. Carl J. Richard and Eran Shalev have analyzed the significance Caesar and Catiline held for early American elites. See Richard, *Greeks and Romans Bearing Gifts: How the Ancients Inspired the Founding Fathers* (Lanham, MD: Rowman and Littlefield, 2008); and Shalev, *Rome Reborn on Western Shores: Historical Imagination and the Creation of the American Republic* (Charlottesville: University of Virginia Press, 2009).

51. Shalev, *Rome Reborn,* 198.

52. Hamilton, Madison, and Jay, *Federalist Papers,* 104.

53. Francis Samuel Drake, ed., *Life and Correspondence of Henry Knox, Major-General in the American Revolutionary Army* (Boston, 1873), 92.

54. William M. E. Rachal, ed., *The Papers of James Madison* (Chicago: University of Chicago Press, 1975), 9:154.

55. George Richards Minot, *The History of the Insurrections in Massachusetts,* 2nd ed. (Boston: James W. Burdett, 1810), 95.

56. Alan Taylor, *Liberty Men and Great Proprietors: The Revolutionary Settlement on the Maine Frontier, 1760–1820* (Chapel Hill: University of North Carolina Press, 1990), 6–7.

57. Minot's references to these letters in his history suggest that these peaceful intentions were not credited by Shays's detractors and were read as the appeals of a party that has suddenly recognized its own weakness. Minot, *History of the Insurrections in Massachusetts,* 109–110.

58. Formisano, *For the People,* 35.

2. HUGH HENRY BRACKENRIDGE, THE CRAWFORD EXPEDITION, AND AN IDEAL NATIONAL ARMY

1. Hugh Henry Brackenridge would first publish the narratives of Dr. John Knight and John Slover in April 1783, when he submitted the text to the *Freeman's Journal.* The narratives were published serially from April 30 to May 28, and Francis Bailey would reprint them, along with Brackenridge's commentary, later that year, as a pamphlet titled *Narratives of a Late Expedition Against the Indians, with an Account of the Barbarous Execution of Col. Crawford; and The Wonderful Escape of Dr. Knight and John Slover from Captivity, in 1782.*

2. Parker Brown discusses this issue at length in Brown, "The Historical Accuracy of the Captivity Narrative of Doctor John Knight," *Western Pennsylvania Historical Magazine* 70 (1987): 53–67.

3. Brackenridge, *Narratives of a Late Expedition,* 38.

4. Christopher Looby, *Voicing America: Language, Literary Form, and the Origins of the United States* (Chicago: University of Chicago Press, 1996), 263; Lynn Haims, "Of Indians and Irishmen: A Note on Brackenridge's Use of Sources for Satire in *Modern Chivalry,*" *Early American Literature* 10 (1975): 89.

5. Hugh Henry Brackenridge, *The Battle of Bunker's Hill* (Philadelphia: Robert Bell, 1776); Brackenridge, *The Death of General Montgomery in Storming the City of Quebec* (Norwich, CT: J. Trumbull, 1777).

6. Brackenridge, *Narratives of a Late Expedition,* 10, 12, 21.

7. Ibid., 36.

8. Daniel Marder, ed., *A Hugh Henry Brackenridge Reader, 1770–1815* (Pittsburgh, PA: University of Pittsburgh Press, 1970), 23.

9. Brackenridge, *Narratives of a Late Expedition,* 37.

10. Ibid., 31.

11. Ibid., 3.

12. John Heckewelder, *A Narrative of the Mission of the United Brethren Among the Delaware and the Mohegan Indians* (Philadelphia: McCarty and Davis, 1820), 314–324; George Henry Loskiel, *History of the Mission of the United Brethren Among the Indians in North America,* translated by Christian Ignatius LaTrobe (London: Brethren's Society for the Furtherance of the Gospel, 1794), 175–189; David Zeisberger, *Diary of David Zeisberger: A Moravian Missionary Among the Indians of Ohio,* translated by Eugene F. Bliss (Cincinnati, OH: Robert Clarke, 1885), 79–82.

13. See Heckewelder, *A Narrative*, 320; Loskiel, *History of the Mission of the United Brethren*, 180.

14. White, *The Backcountry and the City*, 111–113.

15. Leonard Sadosky, "Rethinking the Gnadenhutten Massacre: The Contest for Power in the Public World of the Revolutionary Pennsylvania Frontier," in *The Sixty Years' War for the Great Lakes, 1754–1814*, edited by David Curtis Skaggs and Larry L. Nelson (East Lansing: Michigan State University Press, 2001), 193–196. The Delaware Nation had signed the first treaty between the independent United States and an Indian tribe, the 1778 Treaty of Fort Pitt, which promised that the United States would provide material assistance and protection to the tribe in exchange for intelligence regarding the movements of British-allied Indian groups. See Charles J. Kappler, ed., "Treaty with the Delawares, 1778," *Indian Affairs: Laws and Treaties* (Washington, DC: Government Printing Office, 1904), 2:3–5. http://dc.library.okstate.edu/digital/collection/kapplers/id/25855.

16. Rob Harper, "Looking the Other Way: The Gnadenhutten Massacre and the Contextual Interpretation of Violence," *William and Mary Quarterly* 64, no. 3 (2007): 641–642. In 1841, Ohio resident John Struthers gave testimony to claim a veteran's pension and described his experience as a member of the militia at Gnadenhutten. Struthers claimed that he declined to participate in the killing and that this choice came "at the risk of my popularity as a soldier." Dann, *Revolution Remembered*, 236.

17. William Irvine to George Washington, April 20, 1782, in C. W. Butterfield, ed., *Washington–Irvine Correspondence: The Official Letters* (Madison, WI: David Atwood, 1882), 99.

18. William Irvine to Ann Irvine, April 12, 1782, in Butterfield, *Washington–Irvine Correspondence*, 344 (brackets in original).

19. Irvine presented this request to his wife as follows: "Whatever your private opinion of these matters may be, I conjure you by all the ties of affection and as you value my reputation, that you will keep your mind to yourself, and that you will not express any sentiment for or against these deeds;—as it may be alleged, the sentiments you express may come from me or be mine. No man knows whether I approve or disapprove of killing the Moravians."

20. Irvine to Washington, February 7, 1782, in Butterfield, *Washington–Irvine Correspondence*, 83–94.

21. Irvine to Washington, April 20, 1782, in Butterfield, *Washington–Irvine Correspondence*, 104.

22. William Irvine to William Moore, May 9, 1782, in Butterfield, *Washington–Irvine Correspondence*, 241–245.

23. Mark Rifkin, "Indigenizing Agamben: Rethinking Sovereignty in Light of the 'Peculiar' Status of Native Peoples," *Cultural Critique* 73 (2009): 88–124; Jayan Nayar, "On the Elusive Subject of Sovereignty," *Alternatives: Global, Local, Political* 32, no. 2 (2014): 124–147.

24. Irvine to Moore, May 9, 1782, in Butterfield, *Washington–Irvine Correspondence*, 244.

25. Irvine to Washington, May 21, 1782, in Butterfield, *Washington–Irvine Correspondence,* 113–114; 118–119, note 1.

26. John Rose, "Journal of a Volunteer Expedition to Sandusky, from May 24 to June 13, 1782 (continued)," *Pennsylvania Magazine of History and Biography* 18, no. 3 (1894): 294, 364.

27. Heckewelder writes that William Crawford served as David Williamson's scapegoat in execution: "His [Crawford] being however, taken in company with the very man who led the party on, and who was at the committing of that cruel act, was so much against him, that no one would even listen to an apology." Heckewelder, *A Narrative,* 341. Irvine also writes, in a July 10, 1782, letter to Washington, that both Slover and Knight reported that their captors informed them that their executions were planned in retaliation for the Gnadenhutten massacre. Butterfield, *Washington–Irvine Correspondence,* 126–127.

28. Patrick Griffin, *American Leviathan: Empire, Nation, and Revolutionary Frontier* (New York: Hill and Wang, 2008), 166.

29. Charles Royster, *A Revolutionary People at War: The Continental Army and American Character, 1775–1783* (Chapel Hill: University of North Carolina Press, 1979), 22–23.

30. Brackenridge, *Narratives of a Late Expedition,* 12, 25.

31. See Brown, "Historical Accuracy," 58–59.

32. For a biography of Simon Girty, albeit one that was written with a popular rather than an academic audience in mind, see Edward Butts, *Simon Girty: Wilderness Warrior* (Toronto: Dundurn, 2011).

33. Brackenridge, *Narratives of a Late Expedition,* 23–24.

34. Ibid., 23.

35. Ibid., 26.

36. J. Hector St. Jean Crèvecoeur, *Letters from an American Farmer* (New York: Fox, Duffield, 1904), 67–69. http://xroads.virginia.edu/~hyper/crev/home.html.

37. Brackenridge, *Narratives of a Late Expedition,* 35.

38. Ibid., 14.

39. Ibid., 16.

40. Ibid., 6–7.

41. Brown, "Historical Accuracy," 66.

42. Parker B. Brown, "The Battle of Sandusky: June 4–6, 1782," *Western Pennsylvania Historical Magazine* 65 (1982): 144, note 78.

43. Brackenridge, *Narratives of a Late Expedition,* 17.

44. See John Rose to Irvine, June 13, 1782, in Butterfield, *Washington–Irvine Correspondence,* 372–373.

45. Rose, "Journal of a Volunteer Expedition," 308.

46. Ibid., 294. See 294–295 for Rose's assessments of the other officers commanding the expedition; 296–297 for his frustrations with the mounted troops during the mission.

47. Ibid., 304.

48. Dann, *Revolution Remembered,* 314.

49. Jason Shaffer, "Making 'an Excellent Die': Death, Mourning, and Patriotism in the Propaganda Plays of the American Revolution," *Early American Literature* 41 (2006), 13–20; Purcell, *Sealed with Blood*, 48.

50. Hugh Henry Brackenridge, *Modern Chivalry,* edited by Claude Newlin (New York: American Book Company, 1937), 225.

51. Hugh Henry Brackenridge, "Thoughts on the Present Indian War," *National Gazette,* February 2, 1792: 1; Brackenridge, "Further and Concluding Thoughts on the Indian War," *National Gazette,* February 4, 1792: 2.

52. Jeremy Engels, *Enemyship: Democracy and Counter-Revolution in the Early Republic* (East Lansing: Michigan State University Press, 2010), 133–134.

53. Christian G. Fritz, *American Sovereigns: The People and America's Constitutional Tradition Before the Civil War* (New York: Cambridge University Press, 2008), 4–8.

54. Christopher Castiglia, *Interior States: Institutional Consciousness and the Inner Life of Democracy in the Antebellum United States* (Durham: Duke University Press, 2008), 18.

55. Elizabeth Maddock Dillon, "Aesthetic Aesthesis: Books and *Sensus Communis* in the New World," *Early American Literature* 51, no. 2 (2016): 367; Paul Gilmore, "Republican Machines and Brackenridge's Caves: Aesthetics and Models of Machinery in the Early Republic," *Early American Literature* 39 (2004): 311; Dana D. Nelson, "'Indications of the Public Will': *Modern Chivalry*'s Theory of Democratic Representation," *ANQ* 15 (2002): 27.

56. Hugh Henry Brackenridge, *Incidents of the Insurrection in the Western Parts of Pennsylvania, in the Year 1794* (Philadelphia: John McCullough, 1795), 1:5, 1:113.

57. Paolo Virno, *A Grammar of the Multitude,* translated by Isabella Bertoletti, James Cascaito, and Andrea Casson (New York: Semiotext(e), 2004), 42.

58. Brackenridge, *Incidents of the Insurrection,* 1:79.

59. Ibid.

60. Ibid., 2:9.

61. Ibid., 1:123.

62. Ibid., 1:104–105.

63. Ibid., 2:45, 2:51, 3:131.

64. Ibid., 2:52.

65. William Warner, *Protocols of Liberty: Communication Innovation and the American Revolution* (Chicago: University of Chicago Press, 2013), 19–20.

66. Brackenridge, *Incidents of the Insurrection,* 2:53.

67. Ibid., 3:19.

3. JOSEPH PLUMB MARTIN, DEBORAH SAMPSON, AND THE SOLDIER'S TWO BODIES

1. As was a convention of the time, Martin's narrative was originally published anonymously.

2. This reading of Martin as a critic of early national accounts of the Revolution finds support in Catherine Kaplan, "Theft and Counter-Theft: Joseph Plumb Martin's Revolutionary War," *Early American Literature* 41, no. 3 (2006): 515–534; William Hunting Howell, "Starving Memory: Joseph Plumb Martin Un-tells the Story of the American Revolution," *Common-Place* 10, no. 2 (January 2010), http://www.common-place-archives.org/vol-10/no-02/howell; Philip Mead, "'Adventures, Dangers, Sufferings': The Betrayals of Private Joseph Plumb Martin, Continental Soldier," in *Revolutionary Founders: Rebels, Radicals, and Reformers in the Making of the Nation,* edited by Alfred F. Young, Gary B. Nash, and Ray Raphael (New York: Vintage, 2012), 117–134.

3. See Robert Middlekauff and David McCullough as examples of modern histories that present an enraged Washington at Kip's Bay. Middlekauff, *The Glorious Cause: The American Revolution, 1763–1789,* revised and expanded edition (Oxford: Oxford University Press, 2005), 355; McCullough, *1776* (New York: Simon and Schuster, 2005), 214–215. Closer to the event, General George Weedon wrote, in a letter dated five days after the battle, that Washington "was so exasperated that he struck several officers in their flight, three times dashed his hatt [*sic*] on the ground, and at last exclaimed, 'Good God, have I got such troops as those!.'" Henry Steele Commager and Richard B. Morris, eds., *The Spirit of Seventy-Six: The Story of the American Revolution as Told by Participants* (New York: Bobbs-Merrill Company, 1958), 467. In his 1798 memoirs, General William Heath claims that Washington threw his hat to the ground "and exclaimed, 'Are these the men with which I am to defend America?'." William Heath, *Heath's Memoirs of the American War,* edited by Rufus Rockwell Wilson (New York: A. Wessels Company, 1904), 70.

4. Martin, *Private Yankee Doodle*, 41.

5. Alfred F. Young, *Masquerade: The Life and Times of Deborah Sampson* (New York: Alfred A. Knopf, 2004) 163.

6. I will refer to Sampson Gannett by her maiden name throughout this chapter, for the sake of clarity and because I will be largely discussing the literary persona created for her by Herman Mann.

7. Judith Hiltner has meticulously traced the different literary strands that Mann used to create the fictional Sampson, such as the story of Hannah Snell, the British woman who served as a marine in the 1750s, and frontier narratives of men such as Daniel Boone. See Hiltner "'She Bled in Secret': Deborah Sampson, Herman Mann, and *The Female Review,*" *Early American Literature* 34, no. 2 (1999): 190–220.

8. Many scholars have made note of the performative aspects of Sampson Gannett's cross-dressing, especially in light of the public speaking tour she undertook in 1802, where she gave a speech written for her by Mann and performed military drill dressed in her Continental uniform. See, for instance, Robert Alan Brookey, "Keeping a Good Wo/Man Down: Normalizing Deborah Sampson Gannett," *Communication Studies* 49, no. 1 (1998): 73–85; Sandra Gustafson, "The Genders of Nationalism: Patriotic Violence, Patriotic Sentiment in the Performances of Deborah Sampson Gannett," in *Possible Pasts: Becoming Colonial in Early America,* edited by Robert Blair St. George (Ithaca, NY: Cornell University Press, 2000), 380–400; and Judith Hiltner, "'Like a Bewildered Star':

Deborah Sampson, Herman Mann, and 'Address, Delivered with Applause,'" *Rhetoric Society Quarterly* 29, no. 2 (1999): 5–24.

9. Samet, *Willing Obedience*, 3.

10. A brief sampling: medical history (Ranlet), military history (Lapp), social history (Mead), and sports history (Ledbetter). Philip Ranlet, "The British, Slaves, and Smallpox in Revolutionary Virginia," *Journal of Negro History* 84, no. 3 (1999): 217–226; Derrick E. Lapp, "Did They Really 'Take None But Gentlemen'? Henry Hardman, the Maryland Line, and a Reconsideration of the Socioeconomic Composition of the Continental Officer Corps," *Journal of Military History* 78, no. 4 (2014): 1239–1261; Mead, "'Adventures, Dangers, Sufferings'"; Bonnie S. Ledbetter, "Sports and Games of the American Revolution," *Journal of Sport History* 6, no. 3 (1979): 29–40.

11. *New York Gazette,* January 10, 1784. Sampson has been the subject of *Soldier's Secret* (2009), a novel for young adult readers by Sheila Solomon Klass, and *Revolutionary* (2014), a novel for mature readers, whose marketing strategy emphasized that its author, Alex Myers, was a transgender man and activist.

12. Young, *Masquerade,* 10–11.

13. Karen A. Weyler, "An Actor in the Drama of Revolution: Deborah Sampson, Print, and Performance in the Creation of Celebrity," in *Feminist Interventions in Early American Studies,* edited by Mary C. Carruth (Tuscaloosa: University of Alabama Press, 2006), 186–187.

14. Judith Hiltner, "'The Example of Our Heroine': Deborah Sampson and the Legacy of Herman Mann's *The Female Review,*" *American Studies* 41, no. 1 (2000): 93.

15. Charles Patrick Neimeyer, *America Goes to War: A Social History of the Continental Army* (New York: New York University Press, 1996), 160.

16. Mercy Otis Warren, *History of the Rise, Progress and Termination of the American Revolution* (Boston: E. Larkin, 1805), 3:268–269; Salma Hale, *History of the United States, from their First Settlements as Colonies, to the Close War with Great Britain in 1815* (New York: Collins and Hannay, 1827), 175–176; George Bancroft, *History of the United States of America, from the Discovery of the Continent* (Boston: Little, Brown, 1879), 6:40–46.

17. Ray Raphael, *Founding Myths: Stories That Hide Our Patriotic Past* (New York: New Press, 2004), 160–165.

18. M. M. Bakhtin, *The Dialogic Imagination: Four Essays by M. M. Bakhtin,* translated by Caryl Emerson and Michael Holquist (Austin: University of Texas Press, 1981), 84–85.

19. John Resch, *Suffering Soldiers: Revolutionary War Veterans, Moral Sentiment, and Political Culture in the Early Republic* (Amherst: University of Massachusetts Press, 1999), 5.

20. Andrew Sherburne, *Memoirs of Andrew Sherburne: A Pensioner of the Navy of the Revolution. Written by Himself,* 2nd ed. (Providence, RI: H. H. Brown, 1831), 266–267.

21. Benjamin Tallmadge, *Memoir of Col. Benjamin Tallmadge, Prepared by Himself, at the Request of his Children* (New York: Thomas Holman, 1858); Francis T. Brooke, *Narrative of My Life; for My Family* (Richmond: MacFarlane and Ferguson, 1849), 56–60.

22. Martin, *Private Yankee Doodle,* 287–288.

23. Roberts, *Memoirs of Captain Lemuel Roberts,* 57–58.

24. Examples of narratives that depict extended captivity aboard the *Jersey* include Sherburne, *Memoirs of Andrew Sherburne;* Thomas Andros, *The Old Jersey Captive: or a Narrative of the Captivity of Thomas Andros (Now Pastor of the Church in Berkley), on Board the Old Jersey Prison Ship at New York, 1781. In a Series of Letters to a Friend, Suited to Inspire Faith and Confidence in a Particular Divine Providence* (Boston: William Peirce, 1833); Albert G. Greene, *Recollections of the Jersey Prison-Ship; Taken and Prepared for Publication from the Original Manuscript of the Late Captain Thomas Dring, of Providence, RI* (Providence, RI: H. H. Brown, 1829); Ebenezer Fox, *The Adventures of Ebenezer Fox, in the Revolutionary War* (Boston: Charles Fox, 1838); and Christopher Hawkins, *The Adventures of Christopher Hawkins, Containing Details of his Captivity, a First and Second Time on the High Seas, in the Revolutionary War, by the British, and his Consequent Sufferings, and Escape from the Jersey Prison Ship, then Lying in the Harbor of New York, by Swimming. Now First Printed from the Original Manuscript. Written by Himself. With an Introduction and Notes by Charles I. Bushnell* (New York: Charles I. Bushnell, 1864).

25. François Debrix and Alexander D. Barder, *Beyond Biopolitics: Theory, Violence, and Horror in World Politics* (New York: Routledge, 2012), 20–21.

26. Martin, *Private Yankee Doodle,* 172.

27. For a detailed account of the Battle of Fort Mifflin, see Jeffrey M. Dorwart, *Fort Mifflin of Philadelphia: An Illustrated History* (Philadelphia: University of Pennsylvania Press, 1998), 45–56.

28. Martin, *Private Yankee Doodle,* 91–92.

29. Ibid., 92.

30. John Frost, *History of the United States of North America* (London: Charles Tilt, 1838), 201; Hale, *History of the United States,* 175; Hugh Henry Brackenridge, ed., "Materials for an Account of the Taking of Fort Mifflin—from the 28th of September to the 16th of November, 1778," *United States Magazine,* May 1779; reprinted as "The Siege of Fort Mifflin," *Pennsylvania Magazine of History and Biography* 11 (1887): 82–88.

31. Debrix and Barder, *Beyond Biopolitics,* 21–22.

32. Giorgio Agamben, *Homo Sacer: Sovereign Power and Bare Life,* translated by Daniel Heller-Roazen (Stanford, CA: Stanford University Press, 1998).

33. Debrix and Barder, *Beyond Biopolitics,* 33.

34. Martin, *Private Yankee Doodle,* 134–135.

35. Rodney Atwood asserts that Hessian soldiers were technically auxiliaries, not mercenaries. He notes that *mercenaries* were foreigners who enlisted in a country's army in exchange for pay, while *auxiliaries* were troops sent by one sovereign to aid another in exchange for subsidies. As Atwood has shown, this distinction meant little to the Patriot side in the Revolutionary conflict, since the involvement of non-British troops was taken by many as a sign that reconciliation between Britain and the colonies would be impossible. Atwood, *The Hessians: Mercenaries from Hessen-Kassel in the American Revolution* (Cambridge: Cambridge University Press, 1980), 1, 31.

36. Adriana Cavarero, *Horrorism: Naming Contemporary Violence,* translated by William McCuaig (New York: Columbia University Press, 2011), 17.

37. Ibid., 285.

38. Hiltner, "'She Bled in Secret,'" 209; Fabian, *Unvarnished Truth,* 4.

39. Mann, *Female Review,* 109–110. All quotes from *The Female Review* come from William Abbatt's 1916 reprint of John Adams Vinton's annotated 1833 edition.

40. See Hiltner, "'She Bled in Secret,'" 192, 214 note 10; David Ramsay, *The History of the American Revolution,* edited by Lester H. Cohen (Indianapolis, IN: Liberty Classics, 1990), 2:269–270; William Gordon, *The History of the Rise, Progress, and Establishment of the Independence of the United States of America,* vol. 4 (London: 1788), 193–192.

41. Mann, *Female Review,* 131–132.

42. Ibid., 132.

43. Young, *Masquerade,* 152–153.

44. Hiltner comments that Mann depicts Sampson in these sections as indistinguishable from Daniel Boone or any other example of the frontier scout, and Young draws a comparison between this section and the 1787 Panther Captivity narrative, a highly fictionalized text, attributed to "Abraham Panther," that features a young woman lost in the wilderness and living in a cave after killing her (possibly supernatural) captor. Hiltner, "'She Bled in Secret,'" 209; Young, *Masquerade,* 153.

45. Mann, *Female Review,* 146–152.

46. Elizabeth F. Ellet, *The Women of the American Revolution* (New York: Baker and Scribner, 1848), 2:126.

47. Young suggests that Sampson could have read and been inspired by Snell's narrative or by reprinted excerpts from it. Young, *Masquerade,* 88.

48. Sandra Gustafson, "Genders of Nationalism," 391.

49. Mann, *Female Review,* 89.

50. Ibid., 154.

51. Greta L. LaFleur, "Precipitous Sensations: Herman Mann's *The Female Review* (1797), Botanical Sexuality, and the Challenge of Queer Historiography," *Early American Literature* 48, no. 1 (2013): 99–102.

52. Mann, *Female Review,* 161–162.

53. Debrix and Barder, *Beyond Biopolitics,* 42–43.

54. Ellet, *Women of the American Revolution,* 2:126.

55. Martin, *Private Yankee Doodle,* 114–115, 246.

4. ISAAC HUBBELL, JAMES ROBERTS, AND THE FANTASY OF A WHITE ARMY

1. Jonathan Burnham, *The Life of Col. Jonathan Burnham, Now Living in Salisbury, Mass.; Being a Narrative of his Long and Useful Life* (Portsmouth, NH: Whidden's Printing Office, 1814), 7–8.

2. John Smith Hanna, *A History of the Life and Services of Captain Samuel Dewees, a Native of Pennsylvania, and Soldier of the Revolutionary and Last Wars. Also Reminiscences of the Revolutionary Struggle (Indian War, Western Expedition, Liberty Insurrection in Northampton County, Pa.) and Late War with Great Britain. In All of Which He was Patriotically Engaged. The Whole Written (in Part from Manuscript in the Hand Writing of Captain Dewees), and Compiled by John Smith Hanna* (Baltimore: Robert Neilson, 1844); Perry, *Recollections of an Old Soldier.*

3. Josiah Priest, *The Fort Stanwix Captive, or New England Volunteer, Being the Extraordinary Life and Adventures of Isaac Hubbell Among the Indians of Canada and the West, in the War of the Revolution, and the Story of His Marriage with the Indian Princess, Now First Published, From the Lips of the Hero Himself* (Albany, NY: 1841); James Roberts, *The Narrative of James Roberts, a Soldier Under Gen. Washington in the Revolutionary War, and Under Gen. Jackson at the Battle of New Orleans, in the War of 1812: "A Battle Which Cost Me a Limb, Some Blood, and Almost My Life"* (Chicago: 1858). http://docsouth.unc.edu/neh/roberts/menu.html.

4. Recent studies of the social bonds within the Continental Army include Caroline Cox, *A Proper Sense of Honor: Service and Sacrifice in George Washington's Army* (Chapel Hill: University of North Carolina Press, 2004); Sarah Knott, *Sensibility and the American Revolution* (Chapel Hill, NC: University of North Carolina Press, 2009); and Gregory Knouff, *The Soldier's Revolution: Pennsylvanians in Arms and the Forging of Early American Identity* (University Park: Pennsylvania State University Press, 2004).

5. Josiah Priest's writings have received limited scholarly attention. The most through study of his work comes from Winthrop Hillyer Duncan's bibliographic essay. Duncan, "Josiah Priest, Historian of the American Frontier, A Study and Bibliography," *Proceedings of the American Antiquarian Society* 44 (1935): 45–102. A more recent study, focused on one of Priest's historical romances, can be found in De Villo Sloan, "*The Crimsoned Hills of Onondaga:* Josiah Priest's Hallucinatory Epic," *Journal of Popular Culture* 36 (2002): 86–104. The Roberts narrative is discussed briefly in Russ Castronovo, *Fathering the Nation: American Genealogies of Slavery and Freedom* (Berkeley: University of California Press, 1995), 203–206.

6. The literature on nineteenth-century white supremacist discourse is vast, but a good overview can be found in George M. Fredrickson, *The Black Image in the White Mind: The Debate on Afro-American Character and Destiny, 1817–1914* (New York: Harper and Row, 1971); and Reginald Horsman, *Race and Manifest Destiny: The Origins of American Racial Anglo-Saxonism* (Cambridge, MA: Harvard University Press, 1981). On the unifying effect of white supremacy among white men of different economic classes, see Edmund S. Morgan, *American Slavery, American Freedom: The Ordeal of Colonial Virginia* (New York: W. W. Norton, 1975), 380–381; David R. Roediger, *The Wages of Whiteness: Race and the Making of the American Working Class,* rev. ed. (New York: Verso, 1999), 33–36; and Dana D. Nelson, *National Manhood: Capitalist Citizenship and the Imagined Fraternity of White Men* (Durham, NC: Duke University Press, 1998), 29–60.

7. Priest, *Fort Stanwix Captive,* 64.

8. Resch, *Suffering Soldiers*, 1–10; Samet, *Willing Obedience*, 6–7.

9. Priest, *Fort Stanwix Captive*, 5, 16–17. Affidavit of Isaac Hubbell, S. 36601, *Case Files of Pension and Bounty-Land Warrant Applications Based on Revolutionary War Service, compiled ca. 1800–ca. 1912, documenting the period ca. 1775–ca. 1900*, National Archives and Record Administration microfilm publication M804, digital images courtesy "Revolutionary War Pension and Bounty-Land Warrant Application Files," Fold3, accessed October 1, 2012, http://fold3.com.

10. Priest, *Fort Stanwix Captive*, 43.

11. Affidavit of Isaac Hubbell; Walter Hubbell, *History of the Hubbell Family, Containing a Genealogical Record, by Walter Hubbell* (New York: 1881), 90–92. Priest, *Fort Stanwix Captive*, 43.

12. Lucy Maddox, *Removals: Nineteenth-Century American Literature and the Politics of Indian Affairs* (New York: Oxford University Press, 1991), 8–9. Examples of the historical romance might include James Fenimore Cooper's *The Spy: A Tale of the Neutral Ground* (1821) and his series of Leatherstocking novels; Lydia Marie Child's *Hobomok: A Tale of Early Times* (1824) and *The Rebels, or Boston Before the Revolution* (1825); and William Gilmore Simms's *The Partisan: A Romance of the Revolution* (1835).

13. Knouff, *The Soldier's Revolution*, xv. On the potential western land held for Revolutionary soldiers, see John Shy, *A People Numerous and Armed: Reflections on the Military Struggle for American Independence* (Ann Arbor: University of Michigan Press, 1990), 252, 258. J. G. A. Pocock, *The Machiavellian Moment: Florentine Political Thought and the Atlantic Republican Tradition*, 2nd ed. (Princeton, NJ: Princeton University Press, 2003), 201.

14. Cheryl Harris has described whiteness as "a shield from slavery"—a form of property that consists of free access to one's legal rights and protects the individual from the legal commodification possible under slavery. See Cheryl Harris, "Whiteness as Property," in *Critical Race Theory: The Key Writings that Formed the Movement*, edited by Kimberle Crenshaw et al. (New York: New Press): 276–291.

15. Priest, *Fort Stanwix Captive*, 64. Laura Doyle describes moments such as Hubbell's loss of his Indian family as the "swoon," a trope she identifies across Anglo-Atlantic writing, which presents a protagonist being overwhelmed and losing consciousness (and self-control) before awakening to a new state of (racial) identity. Doyle, *Freedom's Empire: Race and the Rise of the Novel in Atlantic Modernity, 1640–1940* (Durham, NC: Duke University Press, 2008), 2–3.

16. Josiah Priest, *Slavery, as it Relates to the Negro, or African Race, Examined in the Light of Circumstances, History and the Holy Scriptures; with an Account of the Black Man's Color, Causes of His State of Servitude and Traces of His Character as Well as in Ancient as in Modern Times: With Strictures on Abolitionism* (Albany, NY: 1843), 295–309, 288.

17. The standard history of black service in the Revolutionary War remains Benjamin Quarles, *The Negro in the American Revolution* (Chapel Hill, NC: University of North Carolina Press, 1961). Profiles of many individual African Americans who chose to fight for the American cause during the Revolution can be found in Gary Nash, *The Forgotten*

Fifth: African Americans in the Age of Revolution (Cambridge, MA: Harvard University Press, 2006), 1–67. See also Sidney Kaplan and Emma Nogrady Kaplan, *The Black Presence in the Era of the American Revolution* (Amherst: University of Massachusetts Press, 1989).

18. François Furstenberg, *In the Name of the Father: Washington's Legacy, Slavery, and the Making of a Nation* (New York: Penguin, 2006), 192–193.

19. David Walker, *David Walker's Appeal to the Coloured Citizens of the World,* edited by Peter P. Hinks (University Park: Pennsylvania State University Press, 2000), 78–79.

20. William C. Nell, *The Colored Patriots of the American Revolution* (Boston: Robert F. Wallcut, 1855); William Lloyd Garrison, *The Loyalty and Devotion of Colored Americans in the Revolution and War of 1812* (Boston: R. F. Wallcut, 1861). For an account of the first of the Boston Massacre commemorations, see "The Boston Massacre, March 5, 1770: Commemorative Festival in Faneuil Hall," *Liberator,* March 12, 1858. Martin Delany gives a full account of the story of the cotton bale ramparts. Delany, *The Condition, Elevation, Emigration, and Destiny of the Colored People of the United States, Politically Considered* (Philadelphia: 1852), 80–82. Robin Reilly notes that the widespread notion of ramparts made of cotton bales was likely a distortion of the facts, as he points out that such ramparts would have easily caught fire from the hot British shot. He asserts that cotton bales covered in heavy mud were used to provide sturdy embrasures for the American artillery but did not form the actual ramparts of the US fortifications. Reilly, *The British at the Gates: The New Orleans Campaign in the War of 1812* (New York: G. P. Putnam's Sons, 1974), 279–280.

21. Roberts, *Narrative of James Roberts,* 30, iii.

22. William L. Andrews, *To Tell a Free Story: The First Century of Afro-American Autobiography, 1760–1865* (Urbana: University of Illinois Press, 1986), 184–185, 318 note 33; Adam Rothman, *Slave Country: American Expansion and the Origins of the Deep South* (Cambridge, MA: Harvard University Press, 2005), 144–151. In a review of *Slavery and the Making of America,* Rothman also notes the unreliability of the Roberts narrative as a source; see Adam Rothman, "This Guilty Land," review of *Slavery and the Making of America* by James Oliver Horton and Lois E. Horton, *Reviews in American History* 33 (2005): 301–308. The Maryland General Assembly approved the enlistment of slaves as soldiers in October 1780, yet no listing of a James Roberts has yet been found among the names of those who served. See Eric Grundset, ed., *Forgotten Patriots: African American and American Indian Patriots in the Revolutionary War: A Guide to Service, Sources, and Studies* (Washington, DC: National Society Daughters of the American Revolution, 2008), 454. If Francis De Shields was a Continental Army officer, he should have been listed in Francis Bernard Heitman, *Historical Register of Officers of the Continental Army during the War of the Revolution, April 1775, to December, 1783* (Washington, DC: Rare Book Shop Publishing Company, 1914). Given its relative obscurity, little scholarship has been devoted to establishing the conditions of authorship for the Roberts narrative. This situation has been compounded, however, by the tendency among some scholars to accept the narrative uncritically as a factual account. For example, Jon Latimer uses the Roberts narrative as the basis for his claim that enslaved men served in combat in the

US Army at the Battle of New Orleans. Latimer, *1812: War with America* (Cambridge, MA: Belknap Press of Harvard University Press, 2007), 387. James Oliver Horton and Lois E. Horton also rely on the Roberts narrative to provide nearly their entire description of the African American experience at this battle. Horton and Horton, *Slavery and the Making of America* (Oxford: Oxford University Press, 2005), 82–83. Karin L. Stanford uses the Roberts narrative to support the claim that Jackson recruited soldiers from local plantations and that he promised his enslaved African American soldiers pay equal to that of whites, and their freedom after service. Stanford, ed., *If We Must Die: African American Voices on War and Peace* (Lanham, MD: Rowman and Littlefield, 2008), 32. William E. Alt and Betty L. Alt also use the Roberts narrative as their primary example of a black soldier's experience of this battle, though they do note that Roberts's account cannot be supported by most historical records and might be questionable. Alt and Alt, *Black Soldiers, White Wars: Black Warriors from Antiquity to the Present* (Westport, CT: Praeger, 2002), 28–29. In all of these examples, the Roberts narrative serves as a "reliable" source that is considered to require little or no corroboration, despite its many dubious elements.

23. Roberts, *Narrative of James Roberts,* 10.

24. Ibid., 17–18.

25. Gerard T. Altoff, *Amongst My Best Men: African Americans and the War of 1812* (Put-in-Bay, OH: Perry Group, 1996), 149; Roland C. McConnell, *Negro Troops of Antebellum Louisiana: A History of The Battalion of Free Men of Color* (Baton Rouge: Louisiana State University Press, 1968), 84–85; Rothman, *Slave Country,* 144–146; Kai Wright, *Soldiers of Freedom: An Illustrated History of African Americans in the Armed Forces* (New York: Black Dog and Leventhal, 2002), 45–50; John Ernest, *Liberation Historiography: African American Writers and the Challenge of History, 1794–1861* (Chapel Hill, NC: University of North Carolina Press, 2004), 84; Delany, *Condition, Elevation, Emigration, and Destiny,* 82. Jackson's proclamations can be found in Nell, *Colored Patriots,* 286–288.

26. Roberts, *Narrative of James Roberts,* 13.

27. Samet traces the arguments surrounding African American military service during the Civil War, particularly the claim that blacks must have a preexisting conception of freedom in order to fight for it. See Samet, *Willing Obedience,* 140–152; Roberts, *Narrative of James Roberts,* 13.

28. Roberts, *Narrative of James Roberts,* 23–25.

29. Ibid., 14; Doyle, *Freedom's Empire,* 8.

5. ISRAEL POTTER, *Israel Potter*, AND THE FORGOTTEN VETERAN

1. Herman Melville, *Correspondence,* edited by Lynn Horth (Evanston, IL: Northwestern University Press, 1989), 265.

2. Ideological criticism of the novel has frequently viewed Melville's project here as a critique of conventional narratives of US history. For example, Peter J. Bellis argues

that the novel demonstrates how the absorption of individual lives into national historic narratives involves a fictionalization of the reality of those lives. Bellis, "*Israel Potter:* Autobiography as History as Fiction," *American Literary History* 2 (1990): 607–626. Brian Rosenberg describes the text as a "wry rebellion" against the conventions of Victorian British historical fiction. Rosenberg, "*Israel Potter:* Melville's Anti-history," *Studies in American Fiction* 15 (1987): 175–186. John Samson sees Melville challenging the vision of the Revolutionary past offered by American historians such as George Bancroft and Jared Sparks. Samson, *White Lies: Melville's Narratives of Facts* (Ithaca, NY: Cornell University Press, 1989), 173–177. Russell Reising asserts that Melville works in the novel both to recover alternative visions of history and to clarify the discursive economy that limits the inclusion of such accounts. Reising, *Loose Ends: Closure and Crisis in the American Social Text* (Durham, NC: Duke University Press, 1996), 163.

3. Israel R. Potter, *The Life and Remarkable Adventures of Israel R. Potter* (Providence, RI: Henry Trumbull, 1824), 104–105.

4. For examples, see Judith Hiltner, "'A Parallel and a Prophecy': Arrest, Superimposition, and Metamorphosis in Melville's *Israel Potter,*" *ATQ* 2 (1988): 41–55; Daniel Reagan, "Melville's *Israel Potter* and the Nature of Biography," *ATQ* 3 (1989): 257–276; and Rosenberg, "*Israel Potter,*" 181.

5. Castronovo, *Fathering the Nation*, 146.

6. Donald E. Pease, *Visionary Compacts: American Renaissance Writings in Cultural Context* (Madison: University of Wisconsin Press, 1987), 6.

7. Andrew Delbanco, *Melville: His Life and Work* (New York: Alfred A. Knopf, 2005), 226.

8. Potter, *Life and Remarkable Adventures,* 3–4.

9. David Chacko and Alexander Kulcsar, "Israel Potter: Genesis of a Legend," *William and Mary Quarterly* 41, no. 3 (1984): 365–389.

10. Herman Melville, *Journals,* edited by Howard C. Horsford and Lynn Horth (Evanston, IL: Northwestern University Press, 1989), 43. Reising reverses the standard reading of this line to suggest that, rather than a story about a Revolutionary soldier turned beggar, Melville might have intended to write a narrative about a beggar that would be revolutionary in its critique of popular American history. Reising, *Loose Ends,* 126.

11. For example, Russ Castronovo sees the novel as an attack on a "monumental culture" that attempts to represent the nation's history through a discourse that reifies certain figures and symbols as monuments to the past at the expense of political and biographical specificity. Castronovo, *Fathering the Nation,* 146–151. William V. Spanos describes Melville's use of the character of Israel Potter to subvert an ideology of national heroic history that supports American exceptionalism. Spanos, *Herman Melville and the American Calling: The Fiction After Moby-Dick, 1851–1857* (Albany: State University of New York Press, 2008), 58–68. Edgar Dryden calls *Israel Potter* "Melville's counterversion of the dominant national narrative of the American Revolution," and he argues that Melville gestures to this dominant narrative through allusion to Daniel Webster's

famous speech dedicating the Bunker Hill Monument, in 1843. Dryden, *Monumental Melville: The Formation of a Literary Career* (Stanford, CA: Stanford University Press, 2004), 34.

12. Chacko and Kulcsar, "Israel Potter," 386.

13. Potter, *Life and Remarkable Adventures,* 6–10.

14. Ibid., 65, 70, 85.

15. Lemuel Roberts, *Memoirs of Captain Lemuel Roberts*, 96; Segar, *A Brief Narrative*, 30.

16. Paul Downes, *Hobbes, Sovereignty, and Early American Literature* (Cambridge: Cambridge University Press, 2015), 41.

17. Wai-chee Dimock, *Empire for Liberty: Melville and the Poetics of Individualism* (Princeton, NJ: Princeton University Press, 1989), 47.

18. Elmer, *On Lingering and Being Last*, 80.

19. Herman Melville, *Israel Potter: His Fifty Years of Exile* (New York: Penguin, 2008), 34–35. All page numbers from the novel come from the recent Penguin Classics edition, which follows the Northwestern-Newberry edition edited by Harrison Hayford, Hershel Parker, and G. Thomas Tanselle.

20. Potter, *Life and Remarkable Adventures,* 44–45.

21. Paul Downes has written extensively of the "functional absence" that the loss of a hereditary king created within the American political system. Downes, *Democracy, Revolution, and Monarchism,* 64–66.

22. Samson notes that while Israel denies the authority of George III, he is easily overawed in his encounters with Benjamin Franklin, John Paul Jones, and Ethan Allen. From these scenes, Samson concludes that Melville "indicates that in America's hero worship grow the seeds of the very monarchism that the heroes fought against." Samson, *White Lies,* 189.

23. Furstenberg, *In the Name of the Father*, 20–22. Michael Paul Rogin reads the novel as a direct challenge to such veneration of the Founders. Rogin, *Subversive Genealogy: The Politics and Art of Herman Melville* (Berkeley: University of California Press, 1985), 224.

24. Alexis de Tocqueville, *Democracy in America*, chapter 4.

25. Jacques Derrida, *Rogues: Two Essays on Reason,* translated by Pascale-Anne Brault and Michael Naas (Stanford, CA: Stanford University Press, 2005), 24.

26. Ibid., 12.

27. Potter, *Life and Remarkable Adventures,* 3–4.

28. Jennifer Greiman, "Circles upon Circles: Tautology, Form, and the Shape of Democracy in Tocqueville and Melville," *J19: The Journal of Nineteenth-Century Americanists* 1, no. 1 (2013): 121–146.

29. Melville, *Israel Potter,* 117–118.

30. Ibid., 157.

31. Ibid., 100.

32. Ibid., 148.

33. Paul Downes, "Does the Declaration of Independence Declare a State of Emergency?," *Canadian Review of American Studies* 42 (2012): 14–17.

34. Melville, *Israel Potter,* 51.

35. Ibid., 50, 60.

36. Ibid., 58.

37. Hiltner aptly describes Melville's Franklin as "absorbed with appropriating the primal energies of others." Hiltner, "'A Parallel and a Prophecy,'" 51.

38. Melville, *Israel Potter,* 53.

39. For examples, see Alexander Keyssar, *Melville's* Israel Potter*: Reflections on the American Dream* (Cambridge, MA: Harvard University Press, 1969), 19; Samson, *White Lies,* 199; and Gale Temple, "Fluid Identity in *Israel Potter* and *The Confidence Man,*" in *A Companion to Herman Melville,* edited by Wyn Kelley (Malden, MA: Blackwell, 2006): 451–466.

40. Melville, *Israel Potter,* 178.

41. Melville repeatedly chooses analogies that connect Jones to indigenous people, while also emphasizing these analogies as a reflection of a powerful demand for political dignity. Jones appears as "a disinherited Indian chief in European clothes" (ibid., 63). He sits "erect upon his chair, like an Iroquois" (64). He questions Israel "with a look as of a parading Sioux demanding homage to his gew-gaws" (65). Jones's forearm is wrapped in "a sort of tattooing such as is seen only on thorough-bred savages—deep blue, elaborate, labyrinthine, cabalistic" (69–70). Jones possesses a "grim and Fejee air," and terms himself "a bloody cannibal" (102–103).

42. Ibid., 64.

43. Ibid.

44. Ibid., 65.

45. The domineering quality in the characters of Franklin and Jones has been remarked by multiple readers. Castronovo calls Franklin "a pervasive and prohibitive patriarch who insists upon dependence at each turn." Castronovo, *Fathering the Nation,* 153. Hennig Cohen notes that while Israel serves under Jones, the narrator switches from third-person singular to third-person plural, implying the subordination of the protagonist to the famed sea captain. Cohen, "*Israel Potter:* Common Man as Hero," in *A Companion to Melville Studies,* edited by John Bryant (New York: Greenwood, 1986), 279–313. Robert Zaller suggests that the two men not only seek to dominate Israel but also use each other toward their individual aims, and he finds in this portrayal Melville's concern that "sovereign anarchy" lies at the heart of power. Zaller, "Melville and the Myth of Revolution," *Studies in Romanticism* 15 (1976): 607–622.

46. Melville, *Israel Potter,* 136.

47. James Buchanan, John Y. Mason, and Pierre Soulé, "The Ostend Manifesto," in *History Leaflets: Colonial and Constitutional No. 2,* American Studies at the University of Virginia, http://xroads.virginia.edu/~hyper/hns/ostend/ostend.html. For more on the manifesto, see Robert E. May, *The Southern Dream of a Caribbean Empire, 1854–1861,* 2nd ed. (Gainesville: University Press of Florida, 2002), 69–76; and David M. Potter, *The Impending Crisis, 1848–1861* (New York: Harper and Row, 1976), 190–193.

48. "New Books," *The Albion: A Journal of News, Politics and Literature,* March 17, 1855, 129.

49. Melville, *Israel Potter,* 141–143, 147–148.

50. Dryden, *Monumental Melville,* 52.

51. Carolyn L. Karcher also notes the sea battle as a presentiment of the Civil War. Karcher, *Shadow over the Promised Land: Slavery, Race, and Violence in Melville's America* (Baton Rouge: Louisiana State University Press, 1980), 105–107. Similarly, Arnold Rampersad reads Jones's ruthless drive for self-fulfillment as indicative of the spirit that will lead the United States to civil war. Rampersad, *Melville's Israel Potter: A Pilgrimage and a Progress* (Bowling Green, KY: Bowling Green University Press, 1969), 100–102.

52. For other accounts of Allen as the positive ideal of American character within the novel, see Joyce Sparer Adler, *War in Melville's Imagination* (New York: New York University Press, 1981), 83; and Rampersad, *Melville's Israel Potter,* 62.

53. Melville, *Israel Potter,* 170.

54. Ibid., 163–164.

55. Ibid., 169. The scene of Allen taking the bowl may be found in Allen, *A Narrative of Colonel Ethan Allen's Captivity,* 27. However, this scene does not include Allen's musings on the reciprocal obligations gentlemen should feel toward each other. Melville draws this sentiment from a later scene in the narrative, in which Allen is emotionally overcome by the kind treatment given him by a Captain Smith, commander of the man-of-war on which Allen is transported from Canada to New York City (42).

56. Melville, *Israel Potter,* 173.

CODA: THE "BEST ILLUSTRATION" OF PATRIOTISM

1. James Fenimore Cooper, *The Spy: A Tale of the Neutral Ground* (New York: P. F. Collier and Son, 1891), 8–9.

2. H. L. Barnum, *The Spy Unmasked; or, Memoirs of Enoch Crosby, alias Harvey Birch* (New York: J. & J. Harper, 1828), ix. For an alternative theory of Birch's inspiration, see James S. Diemer, "A Model for Harvey Birch," *American Literature* 26 (1954): 242–247. Diemer argues that Birch was modeled after John Champe, whose story Cooper encountered in Henry Lee's *Memoirs of the War in the Southern Department of the United States.*

3. Tremaine McDowell, "The Identity of Harvey Birch," *American Literature* 2 (1930): 111–120. Crosby's pension testimony can be found in Dann, *Revolution Remembered,* 339–347.

4. Cooper, *The Spy,* 8.

INDEX

Index